BEYOND SEDUCTION

A RETURN TO BIBLICAL CHRISTIANITY

DAVE HUNT

HARVEST HOUSE PUBLISHERS
Eugene, Oregon 97402

Scripture quotations are taken from the King James Version of the Bible.

BEYOND SEDUCTION

Copyright © 1987 by Harvest House Publishers
Eugene, Oregon 97402

Library of Congress Catalog Card Number 86-080987
ISBN 0-89081-558-5 (trade paper)
ISBN 0-89081-562-3 (cloth)

Printed in the United States of America.

This book is dedicated to the many friends
around the world who have been concerned
enough to take the time and effort to supply me
with vital information, without which my research
would be inadequate and books such as this
would be an almost-impossible task.

I owe a very special debt of gratitude to Bill
and Eileen of Harvest House, whose devotion to
our Lord and dedication to His service have been
a great inspiration, and whose contributions
to this book were invaluable.

Contents

Back to the Source

IN AUGUST 1985 *The Seduction of Christianity*, a book which I had coauthored, was published. Its reception was overwhelming. Some reviewers declared it to be the most important Christian book in decades. Others who were equally sincere termed it the most destructive. While many pastors across America were enthusiastically preaching sermons based upon *The Seduction of Christianity*, it was at the same time being denounced from other pulpits and on radio and TV. Many were the solemn warnings not to read it. Yet few readers were able to ignore its message or to remain neutral when faced with its alarming implications. Almost all agreed that, through the publication of *Seduction*, serious issues which had troubled concerned Christians for years had finally been brought out of the closet of private conversation and into the arena of earnest and open discussion.

Such strong reactions caught me by surprise. It was awesome and humbling to see that a sudden and unexpected revolution had apparently begun. Some hailed the book's advent as the start of a much-needed purification of the church, while others charged that it would lead to a major schism in Christendom. One of several books written to express the latter view declared that *The Seduction of Christianity* was "doing more to divide the Body of Christ than any other single event of modern history."[1] The charge grieved me, for as D. Martyn Lloyd-Jones has observed, "We must all regard schism as a grievous sin."[2] He added this word of caution, however:

> But having said that, one must also point out that there is obviously great confusion, and much disagreement, as to what constitutes unity, as to what is the nature of unity, and as to how unity is to be obtained and preserved.[3]

From the vast majority of readers, the reaction to *Seduction* has been overwhelmingly favorable. Thousands of letters continue to pour in expressing gratitude for deliverance from false doctrines and practices. Many confess to having turned their backs on God through disillusionment with prominent teachings and teachers, and having been restored to the joy of the Lord. Among the small number of critical letters received, however, some have been almost vitriolic in their denunciations, as have some reviews.

What made this particular book so controversial? A major factor seemed to be its claim that many highly respected and well-intentioned church leaders, some of whom it quoted, were promoting teachings and practices that were drawing Christians away from biblical faith. *Seduction*, moreover, linked many of these questionable beliefs and methods with ancient shamanism (witchcraft or sorcery). The disturbing charge was made that basic Hindu/Buddhist occultism had invaded not only modern secular society but Christianity as well, where it was being accepted under the umbrella of psychological terminology and alleged charismatic experiences. Documenting Charles Colson's indictment that "we have embraced the world rather than exposed its folly,"[4] we attempted in *Seduction* to identify the worldly "folly" being embraced by today's church not merely as immorality but as an even more seductive and destructive form of worldliness: the cultivation of occult powers attributable to human potential and its concomitant evil—the idolatrous deification of self.

The problem of pagan and occult influences and subversive infiltration has plagued the church from its very beginnings. My intention in *The Seduction of Christianity*, however, was to provide extensive documentation to support the charge that the shamanization of Christianity was accelerating explosively in apparent fulfillment of the prophecy by Christ and His apostles that the last days prior to His second coming would be characterized by the greatest religious deception and apostasy in history. Other observers have made similar charges. Colson repeats theologian Donald Bloesch's warning that for the church in the U.S. today "the primary danger is not persecution by the culture but seduction."[5]

The "New Age" shamanism that secular society has embraced

(especially its Hindu and Buddhist forms) is also powerfully seducing the church. A number of examples of this phenomenon were given in *Seduction*, and it was pointed out that the merger of pseudo-Christianity with shamanism is essential to the formation of Antichrist's coming world religion. This is only possible when, as is the growing tendency today, sound biblical doctrine is set aside in favor of whatever "works," and experience and "new revelation" take the place of the Bible. One of my major intentions in writing *The Seduction of Christianity* was to document in a thorough and unassailable manner the evidence that this merger is already in process through the growing acceptance, promotion, and practice of the basic shamanic techniques described by anthropologists: visualization, psychotherapy, hypnotherapy, Positive Thinking, and Positive Confession.[6] Not only is this merger taking place in liberal churches, but also among those of evangelical/fundamentalist, Pentecostal, and charismatic persuasion.[7]

Since the publication of *The Seduction of Christianity,* the apostasy which the book warned about and the popular delusions sweeping the church have not abated. Far from repenting, those promoting questionable doctrines have, with few exceptions, hardened their position. Critics have repeatedly voiced the charge that *Seduction*'s quotes have been largely "taken out of context."[8] Yet examples are seldom offered. The nearly 450 footnotes in *Seduction* were included so that each reader, if he so desired, could check the context for himself, and the nearly 600 notes in the following pages are given for the same reason.

The attempt that *Seduction* made to correct or even question the doctrinal accuracy of certain teachings has been labeled "divisive" by some. But why should it be considered "divisive" to test popular teachings against the Bible? In apparent response to *Seduction*, there is a new push for "unity" based not upon sound doctrine but upon the pledge not to question the biblical accuracy of one another's teaching. Biblical unity, however, is not something we establish through ecumenical discussion and compromise and an agreement not to disagree with each other. We are to *keep* the unity that has already been established by

God the Holy Spirit (Ephesians 4:3), of whom Christ said, "When he, the Spirit of truth, is come, he will guide you into all truth" (John 16:13). Christians are united in Christ not by some joint effort they put forth but by the Holy Spirit, who indwells each member of His body, and by the truth that each member has embraced. Such unity is not *maintained* but *broken* by compromise. Moreover, this "unity of the faith" (Ephesians 4:13) can only be maintained by "earnestly contend[ing] for the faith which was once delivered unto the saints" (Jude 3); and this unity is denied by those who consider contending for the faith unnecessary or divisive.

We must each be certain that what we believe, teach, and live is firmly based upon God's unchanging Word. The only real remedy for apostasy is to return to a solidly biblical foundation for Christian living. It has become more urgent than ever not only to recognize what is false in the world around us and has even crept into the church, but to know and love the truth. We need to heed Christ's exhortation to those who "believed on him":

> If ye continue in my word, then are ye my disciples indeed; and ye shall know the truth, and the truth shall make you free (John 8:31,32).

It is with the earnest desire to encourage the many who genuinely long for revival, and to further the spiritual health and welfare of the body of Christ, that the following pages are offered as an antidote to the popular delusions sweeping the church. The goal that Scripture holds out before us and that must be the united purpose of every Christian was clearly declared by the apostle Paul:

> Till we all come in the unity of the faith, and of the knowledge of the Son of God, unto a perfect man, unto the measure of the stature of the fulness of Christ: that we henceforth be no more children, tossed to and fro, and carried about with every wind of doctrine, by the sleight of men and cunning craftiness, whereby they lie in wait to deceive; but speaking the truth in love, may grow up into him in all things, which is the head, even Christ (Ephesians 4:13-15).

The clear issue is *maturity and stability in the faith, soundness of doctrine,* and *proclamation of the truth*, all of which must be communicated in love. There are, of course, some peripheral beliefs upon which Christians have always differed and will continue to do so. But there are other issues of such importance and clarity that we are required to guard and defend them against all opposition or compromise. At the very heart of all of this is God Himself, who will not be known in vague or false suppositions, but can be known only for who He is and on His terms. Jesus said:

> This is life eternal, that they might know thee, the only true God, and Jesus Christ, whom thou has sent (John 17:3).

What it all comes down to in the final analysis is a matter of one's personal relationship with God through Jesus Christ. Whether we really *know* God or not makes the difference between eternal life and eternal death. Beyond that, what matters most is how much more we desire to know Him. This desire seems to be largely lacking in the contemporary church. As a consequence, there is a defective knowledge of God. As one well-known Christian leader has written:

> Why is the church weak? Why are individual Christians weak? It is because they have allowed their minds to become conformed to the "spirit of this age".... They have forgotten what God is like....
>
> Ask an average Christian to talk about God. After getting past the expected answers, you will find that his god is a little god of vacillating sentiments.[9]

God makes Himself known not to casual intellectual curiosity, but to passionate thirst. "Ye shall seek me and find me when ye shall search for me with all your heart" (Jeremiah 29:13) is His promise. He is always eager to satisfy our thirst for Him. It is tragic beyond description that in spite of the thousands of sincere souls who are grieved at the current situation, such a large part of the church today seems to be falling into the two primary sins with which God indicted Israel:

> My people have committed two evils: they have forsaken

me, the fountain of living waters, and hewed them out cisterns, broken cisterns that can hold no water (Jeremiah 2:13).

The Seduction of Christianity identified many of the broken cisterns and warned of the pollution that seeps in through the cracks and the death that breeds in these brackish waters. The purpose of this book as the sequel to *Seduction* is to call for a return to biblical Christianity and to encourage the many who share this hope by pointing the way beyond seduction back to "the fountain of living waters"—to the One who is the only true source of life and satisfaction for the deepest longings of the heart. Jesus said:

> If any man thirst, let him come unto me and drink. He that believeth on me, as the Scripture hath said, out of his belly [innermost being] shall flow rivers of living water (John 7:37,38).
> Whosoever drinketh of the water that I shall give him shall never thirst; but the water that I shall give him shall be in him a well of water springing up into everlasting life (John 4:14,15).

While we want to use as little space as possible upon further developments of current errors that were covered in *Seduction*, identifying the disease is a necessary part of effecting a cure. Whenever necessary documentation requires naming individuals, it should be remembered that every person cannot be quoted. Moreover, it should be clearly understood that hearts, motives, and ministries are not being judged but doctrines only, and that there are varying degrees of error. The Bible must be presented not in a vacuum but as the antidote both to the seductions of secular society and to related false doctrines that come into the church. Much of the Bible was written for this purpose. Therefore, to be true to God's Word some exposure of error is essential, though it will be kept to a minimum. Our focus will always be upon a return to biblical Christianity.

I want to express my very deep appreciation for the many thousands of letters—both critical and supportive—that have been received in response to *Seduction*. I have learned a great deal from them, and the insights they have given me have been very important in writing this book. It is offered with much fear and trembling and the earnest prayer that God has guided in it and will use it to His glory.

1
A Return to Biblical Christianity

> No prophecy of the Scripture is of any private interpretation. For the prophecy came not in old time by the will of man, but holy men of God spoke as they were moved by the Holy Ghost (2 Peter 1:20,21).
> He humbled thee and suffered thee to hunger...that he might make thee know that man doth not live by bread only, but by every word that proceedeth out of the mouth of the Lord doth man live (Deuteronomy 8:3).

TO SPEAK OF "knowing God" or "thirsting for God" immediately raises several important questions: What does it mean to *know* God, how does one get to *know* Him in contrast to merely knowing *about* Him, and how is this universal thirst to be quenched? It is becoming increasingly popular today, not only in the East but now also in the West, to seek for God in mystical experiences. Unfortunately, this growing trend in the secular world has influenced the thinking of some Christian leaders, and, through their teaching, is impacting the church. Before seeking for *experiences* of God or communion with God through the practice of certain guaranteed techniques, however, we ought to give our attention first of all to the written Word of God that He has gone to such lengths to provide for all of mankind. Jeremiah's attitude toward God's Word should be our own:

> Thy words were found, and I did eat them; and thy word was unto me the joy and rejoicing of mine heart (Jeremiah 15:16).

For anyone setting out on a spiritual quest to seek and know

God, the most logical place to start is with His Word, the Bible. Although it continues year after year to be the world's number one best-seller, the Bible is, to many of its perusers, not an easy book to read, and it ends up largely neglected on their shelves. Far from being surprising, such reader reaction as this is exactly what one would logically expect if the Bible is in fact what it claims to be: the Word of God, sent not only to guide but to *correct* God's often-rebellious creatures. When was reproof ever popular or easy to take?

Man's reaction to Scripture, however, raises an interesting question: If the all-wise Creator really inspired the writers of the Bible, why does it contain so much of a seemingly "negative" nature? Why didn't God take into account the "psychological harm" that such an approach would cause to fragile psyches and self-images? In *Foundations of the Christian Faith*, James Montgomery Boice writes:

> If Madison Avenue executives were trying to attract people to the Christian life, they would stress its positive and fulfilling aspects. . . .
> Unfortunately, we who live in the West are so conditioned to this very thinking (and to precisely this type of Christian evangelism or salesmanship) that we are almost shocked when we learn that the first great principle of Christianity is negative.
> It is not, as some say, "Come to Christ, and all your troubles will melt away." It is as the Lord himself declared, "If any man would come after me, let him deny himself and take up his cross and follow me."[1]

No wonder the Bible is losing its appeal and is being subjected to so complete a reinterpretation, now that self-affirmation and a positive mental attitude are accepted by so many people as the universal panacea. On the other hand, there has always been strong opposition to the Bible. Could it be that current psychological theories are only providing a more sophisticated rationale to justify a long-standing attitude of rebellion?

Facing the Evidence

That its claims of inspiration, infallibility, and doctrinal purity are not simply dismissed as absurd but have been vigorously attacked down through the centuries attests to the convicting power with which the Bible speaks. It is in fact its claim to be *the* Word of God to man (and its blunt condemnation in the most "negative" terms of all other religions and their scriptures and their gods) that arouses such strong resentment and angry opposition. Rare indeed is the person, whether atheist or religious zealot, who finds it easy to admit he has been wrong, particularly on that most controversial and emotional of all subjects, religion.

Harvard University Professor Simon Greenleaf, who together with Supreme Court Justice Joseph Story was credited with "the rise of the Harvard Law School to its eminent position,"[2] abandoned his agnosticism only after months of careful study and heart-searching. Recognized as America's greatest authority on legal evidence, Greenleaf found himself logically forced to conclude, after lengthy and critical examination, that the literal and historical death, burial, and resurrection of Christ as the Son of God in payment of our sins was established by undeniable and overwhelming evidence. In full agreement, Professor Thomas Arnold, who held the chair of Modern History at Oxford, wrote:

> I have been used for many years to study the histories of other times, and to examine and weigh the evidence of those who have written about them, and I know of no one fact in the history of mankind which is proved by better and fuller evidence of every sort, to the understanding of a fair inquirer, than the great sign which God hath given us that Christ died and rose again from the dead.[3]

Many other eminent authorities have come to the same conclusion, among them Lord Lyndhurst, recognized as one of the greatest legal minds in British history. He wrote: "I know pretty well what evidence is; and I tell you, such evidence as that for the Resurrection has never broken down yet."[4] In *A Lawyer Examines The Bible*, Irwin H. Linton argues that because they are trained "in sifting and weighing evidence about disputed matters," a higher percentage of his profession than any other submits to the claims of Christ when they take the time to honestly face the facts.[5] For the majority of mankind, however (and that includes lawyers), what the evidence proves to the head is not readily accepted by the heart because the Bible seems to contain so much that is "negative." Writing to his colleagues, Professor Greenleaf minced no words:

> The religion of Jesus Christ aims at nothing less than the utter overthrow of all other systems of religion of the world; denouncing them as inadequate to the wants of man, false in their foundations and dangerous in their tendency....
>
> These are no ordinary claims; and it seems hardly possible for a rational being to...treat them with mere indifference or contempt.[6]

Confronting Self-Deception

Unfortunately, the more convincing the evidence the more opposition it arouses in those who refuse to accept its implications. It is therefore not surprising that no book in history has ever been so viciously and persistently attacked as the Bible. Such attacks have only proved the Bible's claims. As Tim Stafford, editor of *Campus Life* magazine, has written: "...we cannot knock the real gospel down with a few clumsy questions. Only our illusions will crumble so that truth stands out more clearly."[7]

The reaction of the overwhelming majority of humanity has always been to reject the Bible's message. That rejection manifests itself in two ways: Some people openly admit their refusal to submit at all to God's correction; many others, however, cloak their rejection of God's Word in the pious pretense of religious zeal and devotion. As though deceived by their own hypocrisy, they protest their innocence: "But, Lord, we did it all in your name!" They have selfishly contrived to "interpret" the Bible as saying what they want it to say rather than what God intended it to say. That is a common tendency which anyone who studies the Bible must guard against.

Never have so many given so much honor to a book they apparently have so little genuine intention of heeding. Until we have been set free from our innate self-centeredness, our natural interest is really in ourselves, no matter how loudly we protest our concern for God's kingdom. After citing some best-selling titles such as *Looking Out for Number One, Crisis Investing,* and

How to Prosper in the Coming Bad Times, Charles Colson
suggests that even those Christians who consider themselves to
be most spiritual need to take another look at their real motives.
He writes:

> But while millions of Americans, myself included, pray fer-
> vently for revival, we must ask ourselves whether we are asking
> God to save our society, ourselves, or our souls. . . .
>
> The real trouble is that we Christians are not willing to accept
> the gospel for what it is. It doesn't tell us how to save anything
> but our souls.[8]

Prayer, even for revival, all too often becomes a religious
technique for getting God to bless one's own plans. We decide
what we want and spend the "sweet hour of prayer" trying to
persuade God to work it out for us. And if someone offers a
guaranteed technique for getting prayers answered through
visualization or thinking or speaking "positively," many Christians are only too eager to buy the package, forgetting that it
effectively turns God into a magic genie at their service when they
"rub the lamp" the right way.

So great is the human capacity for self-deception that we can
be blind even to our own insincerity. In the process of investigating
the presumption that often passes for faith, Charles Farah
concluded: "The power of the human mind to deceive itself seems
infinite."[9] David's recognition of the duplicity of his own heart
caused him to voice what must become the anguished cry of every
sincere seeker after God and truth:

> Search me, O God, and know my heart; try me, and know
> my thoughts; and see if there be any wicked way in me, and
> lead me in the way everlasting (Psalm 139:23,24).

Unless this same cry becomes the passion of one's heart, there
can be no deliverance from the self-delusion that is the universal
blindness of mankind. Jay Adams points out that when two
doctors studied more than 200 criminals, "they discovered that
of the lot there was not a single criminal 'who believed he was
evil. Each criminal thought of himself as a basically good
person. . . even when planning a crime.' "[10] This and other studies

with similar results contradict the scores of books by Christian psychologists and innumerable sermons preached by earnest pastors and evangelists from pulpit, radio, and television that promote the unbiblical but popular theory that today's primary need is to combat a raging epidemic of "the disease of poor self-image."[11]

We are even being warned that this "terrible disease"[12] will affect in adult life "over 90 percent of our children growing up today."[13] Nothing could be better calculated to silence the God-given voice of conscience than the selfist humanistic theories now sweeping society and the church. One of the Bible's major purposes is to correct man's high view of himself, yet it is now interpreted by Christian leaders to intend just the opposite. How can creatures whose besetting sin is thinking too highly of themselves be convinced that their problem is in fact low self-esteem? Jeremiah answered that question 2600 years ago:

> The heart is deceitful above all things, and desperately wicked: who can know it? I the Lord search the heart (Jeremiah 17:9,10).

Interpreting the Bible

Another classic excuse for avoiding the "negative" aspects of God's Word that one does not wish to believe or obey is the often-heard specious complaint, "Well, you can interpret the Bible to say anything you want!" The implication is that the Bible is written in such a clever and devious way that any one of a thousand different meanings fits as well as any other. We are therefore absolved of any responsibility to understand and obey what God has said in His Word. If true, that alone would make the Bible a miraculous book. To put words together in sentences so that innumerable conflicting ideas could be drawn equally from them would be an impossible feat. Moreover, the fact that so many readers don't like a great deal of what the Bible says is proof enough that it can't be made to support each man's opinion. To attempt to do so is patently dishonest.

Of course there can be honest difficulties in interpreting the Scriptures. Because the Bible is intended to teach us what we could not otherwise know, there could be a legitimate lack of *understanding*. If, as the Bible declares, we are rebels who are blinded by pride and sin, deceived by our own selfish lusts and ambitions, and conditioned by years of living in a world that has exalted man and forgotten God, then it will not be easy to throw off our old ways of thinking and begin to see through new eyes and from God's perspective. The Bible doesn't cater to our self-deception; it seeks to *correct* it.

We must be *willing* to let God change us completely from what we were to what He wants us to be. Boice reminds us, "We must not assume that we will be able fully to understand any passage of Scripture unless we are willing to be changed by it."[14] To bring about this supernatural change (transformation/correction) is a major purpose of our Creator's instruction manual. And until we are willing to *obey* what God has said in His Word, even the most devout practice of what seems to be Christianity will merely be an attempt in one form or another to avoid God's truth in our lives while honoring Him with our lips. To the religious leaders in His day Christ administered this stern rebuke:

> Ye hypocrites, well did Esaias [Isaiah] prophesy of you, saying, This people draweth nigh unto me with their mouth, and honoreth me with their lips, but their heart is far from me (Matthew 15:7,8).

Biblical Christianity

The spiritual transformation that mankind so desperately needs is both impossible for man to effect on his own and exactly what God offers in His grace and love. Biblical Christianity is not a list of moral requirements that one must live up to in order to get to heaven. To attempt to force sinners under threat of hell to act like saints, when they really have neither the heart nor power to do so, can only produce hypocrites.

The real Christian has a new heart, a new mind. His outlook on life has changed completely. He loves God and righteousness and hates sin. His whole delight is in pleasing God and doing His will. By faith in Him, Christ has become his very life. As Andrew Murray said, "This is the root of the true Christian life: to be nothing before God and men; to wait on God alone; to delight in, to imitate, to learn of Christ, the meek and lowly

One."[15] At the same time, however, the true Christian despairs of being able to fulfill his new desires, because he has gotten at last, under the searchlight of the Holy Spirit, a horrifying glimpse of the evil person that he is. Like Paul he cries:

> I know that in me (that is, in my flesh) dwelleth no good thing; for to will is present with me, but how to perform that which is good I find not. For the good that I would, I do not; but the evil which I would not, that I do.
> O wretched man that I am! Who shall deliver me from the body of this death? (Romans 7:18,19,24).

Until a man has seen himself as a hopeless slave of sin and self, it is not possible either to understand or experience what Paul said next: "I thank God through Jesus Christ our Lord!" (Romans 7:25a). Why would Paul not only thank God for deliverance from sin through Jesus Christ but also for the revelation of his hopeless condition? Because it is only at this point that a repentant man finally realizes that he cannot possibly "imitate" Christ, and he ceases completely his proud attempts to live the Christian life in his own strength. This truth had transformed John Wesley's life, and to share this joy with others he wrote:

> If thou knowest He hath taken away thy sins, so much the more abase thyself before Him in a continual sense of thy total dependence on Him for every good thought and word and work, and of thy utter inability to all good unless He "water thee every moment."[16]

To confess this truth is to admit at last the painful but liberating fact that the Christian life is impossible for any mere man to live—no one but Christ Himself ever has or ever could do so. The person who sees this fact is well on his way to learning that the secret of abundant life and inexpressible joy is simply by faith to allow Christ to live this supernatural life through him. And it all begins with admitting what Charles Spurgeon expressed so well:

> Jesus did not die for our righteousness, but He died for our sins. He did not come to save us because we were worth saving,

but because we were utterly worthless, ruined, and undone.
He did not come to earth out of any reason that was in us, but
solely and only because of reasons which He took from the depths
of His own divine love. In due time He died for those whom He
describes not as godly but as *ungodly*, applying to them as hopeless
an adjective as He could have selected.[17]

This is the gospel, God's "good news" to man. It is not
calculated to build up man's self-esteem, which some Christian leaders are telling us "is the greatest single need facing
the human race today."[18] Nor is it intended to restore man's
"loss of pride as a human being."[19] The purpose of the Bible
is not to glorify man, but God; not to delude us with lies
about our self-importance, but to tell us the humbling yet
burden-lifting truth. "Own thyself guilty of eternal death,"
said John Wesley, "and renounce all hope of ever being able to
save thyself. Be it all thy hope to be washed in His blood and
purified by His Spirit, 'who Himself bore all thy sins in His own
body upon the tree.' "[20] As A. W. Tozer said:

> True faith requires that we believe everything God has said
> about Himself, but also that we believe everything He has said
> about *us*.
> Until we believe that we are as bad as God says we are, we can
> never believe that He will do for us what He says He will do.
> Right here is where popular religion breaks down.[21]

Christ said, "I came not to call the righteous, but *sinners* to
repentance" (Luke 5:32). However, there are many people who
call Jesus their Savior but do not yet understand that He saves
not only from hell but from *self*. Unfortunately, this biblical
salvation seems to appeal to very few people who call themselves
Christians, because Christian books, radio, television, and
sermons are bombarding the church with the new religion of
selfism: self-acceptance, self-esteem, self-image, self-talk, self-
love, self-confidence. "Pride is the cause of all our trouble
and...it is not surprising," writes D. Martyn Lloyd-Jones.
"Everything is telling us to believe in ourselves, pandering to our
pride, building us up and inflating us."[22] "There is nothing more
acceptable to the human mind than flattery," said John Calvin.[23]

Showing the full agreement of men of God from the past and present, and the contrast between what the church has always believed and today's increasingly popular psychologized gospel, Andrew Murray wrote in his classic book *Absolute Surrender*:

> Self is our greatest curse. But, praise God, Christ came to redeem us from self.
> And there you have the reason why many people pray for the power of the Holy Ghost, and they get something, but oh, so little! because they prayed for power for work, and power for blessing, but they have not prayed for power for full deliverance from self.[24]

It takes a simple but firm decision *based upon the facts* to exchange the self-life for the Christ-life. Knowing the awful truth about self and the wonderful truth about Christ, who would not eagerly make that exchange when offered the opportunity to do so! That carefully considered and intelligent commitment marks the beginning of miraculous living. This decision, however, must be reaffirmed continually. Faith in Christ to be all we need and to live His resurrection life through us must be renewed moment by moment. Biblical Christianity is nothing less than miraculous. There is much emphasis upon miracles today and the pursuit of "signs and wonders," but by far the greatest and most needed miracle is the inner transformation from self-will to absolute and joyful surrender. Of such a biblical Christian Tozer said:

> His interests have shifted from self to Christ. What he is or is not no longer concerns him. . . .
> Christ is now where the man's ego was formerly. The man is now Christ-centered instead of self-centered, and he forgets himself in his delighted preoccupation with Christ.[25]

The Cross and Self

How does the biblical Christian reach this point? It is gloriously simple. Believing that God's love for him is infinite and personal, and that God is also infinitely wise and therefore able to plot the best course for his life, he surrenders himself completely into God's hands. It is not a reluctant sacrifice but a joyous privilege and an eternal commitment from which he will never turn back, for only a fool would refuse to let infinite love and infinite wisdom guide and guard his life and destiny.

Yes, there can be deep pain and perhaps even momentary fear as for the first time one faces the full implications of the cross of Christ. The death of one's own self through His death becomes an awesome reality. But the fear and pain turn to indescribable joy at the discovery that one has been at last unshackled from self. Such exquisite freedom! C. S. Lewis described it as the "feeling of infinite relief of having for once got rid of all the silly nonsense about your own dignity which has made you restless and unhappy all your life."[26]

Nothing can describe the great sense of relief or take away the heavenly joy that comes when all that one is or ever hoped to be has been nailed to the cross with Christ, and Christ has become one's very life through the power of His resurrection. This deep satisfaction is not to be mistaken for the frothy and shallow enthusiasm of "Christian show biz," which is often so painfully visible on television. Today's popularized brand of Christianity appeals to the world and generates false disciples: Instead of self-denial it offers self-acceptance, self-love, self-esteem, a high sense of self-worth, and a positive self-image. The cross is no longer an instrument of death but somehow has been made to "sanctify the ego trip."[27] Tozer explained it poignantly:

> If I see aright, the cross of popular evangelicalism is not the cross of the New Testament. It is rather a new bright ornament upon the bosom of a self-assured and carnal Christianity....
>
> The old cross slew men; the new cross entertains them. The old cross condemned; the new cross amuses. The old cross destroyed confidence in the flesh; the new cross encourages it....
>
> The flesh, smiling and confident, preaches and sings about the cross; before that cross it bows and toward that cross it points with carefully staged histrionics—but upon that cross it will not die, and the reproach of the cross it stubbornly refuses to bear.[28]

What is it above all that stands in the way of new life in Christ? It is the fear of the death of self, of giving up life as one would live it in exchange for the life that Christ offers. Biblical Christianity is not *religion*; it is a *relationship* to God through Jesus Christ that begins at the cross, where through accepting Christ's death in my place for my sins I admit that I deserved to die, and in that admission I give up life as I would have lived it in order to experience Christ's resurrection life as my very own. My will has been surrendered once-and-for-all to His will.

Jesus said, "He that loveth his life shall lose it, and he that hateth his life in this world shall keep it unto life eternal" (John 12:25). He is telling us that if we clutch at life selfishly, we have at best a few short years to live as we please; but if we surrender self to Him, the far more abundant life we receive in exchange will never end. Jim Elliot, one of the young missionaries martyred by the Aucas in Ecuador, put it like this: "He is no fool who gives up that which he cannot keep to gain that which he cannot lose."

The fear of *death* that keeps us in bondage (Hebrews 2:14,15) is the fear of losing everything that life involves—all the ambitions and pleasures that revolve around self. This includes the fear of losing the approval of contemporaries at school, work, or even church, fear of losing that promotion, of missing out on some pleasure or ambition if we stand true to our Lord and to His Word. But those who have been crucified with Christ are no longer bound by such fears. Sin has lost its hold. Dead men don't become angry or anxious or covetous.

When we have accepted Christ's death as our very own, since He died in our place, then we are set free from the fear of losing our life, and Satan's hold is broken. This is a major theme of the New Testament, the very heart of the solution offered in the gospel. Consider the following verses:

> Knowing this, that our old man is crucified with him, that the body of sin might be destroyed, that henceforth we should not serve sin. For he that is dead is freed from sin. Now if we be dead with Christ, we believe that we shall also live with him....
> Likewise reckon ye also yourselves to be dead indeed unto sin, but alive unto God through Jesus Christ our Lord. Let not sin therefore reign in your mortal body, that ye should obey it in the lusts thereof (Romans 6:6-8,11,12).

The Only Real Barrier

Here we confront the only real barrier to understanding the Bible. The big problem is not *intellectual* but *moral*. It is not that we *cannot* understand, but in fact that we *do* understand that the Bible is intended to correct us—but we are not willing to accept the consequences of letting God have His way in our lives. Let the reader not imagine that this indictment applies only to others. No one is immune from self-centeredness. Our hearts are all the same (Proverbs 27:19); yet we can each allow God to effect in us that transformation to which Paul testified:

> I am crucified with Christ; nevertheless I live, yet not I, but Christ liveth in me; and the life which I now live in the flesh I live by the faith of the Son of God, who loved me and gave himself for me (Galatians 2:20).

When we approach the Bible, we must be very careful to do so with an honest and submissive heart and a teachable spirit, eager and willing to have our thinking and desires changed into conformity with God's will. We must beware of imposing our preconceived ideas upon the Bible—of trying to use it to justify our prejudices, of searching for verses here and there that can be made to support our own peculiar views. And we must beware of interpretations of Scripture that depend upon a knowledge of customs peculiar to certain cultures or the prevailing opinions during a certain era, especially our own.

We must also take care not to fall into modernism in our sincere desire to communicate the gospel to modern man. As Oswald Chambers pointed out, "We must never confuse our desire for people to accept the gospel with creating a gospel that is acceptable to people." But modernism does exactly that—it takes the latest ideas from the world, dresses them up in biblical language, and passes them off as gospel truth. Much that masquerades today as Christianity on radio, on television, in many evangelical books, and in large, "successful" churches is in this category. There are popular teachings and practices widely accepted in the church that did not originate as insights into God's unchanging truth gained by men and women of God studying the Bible on their knees. Instead, the latest self-centered theories from psychology, sociology, or success/motivation training have been accepted and a proof-text found here and there to make it seem that this was what Holy Writ had always taught. In a talk to church leaders in 1945 Lewis warned:

> Our business is to put what is timeless (the same yesterday, today and tomorrow—Hebrews 13:8) in the particular language of our own age.
> The bad preacher does exactly the opposite: he takes the ideas of our own age and tricks them out in the traditional language of Christianity.[29]

God Has Spoken

If God, as the Bible claims, has actually spoken to man, *that is awesome!* If this is a fact, as the evidence indicates, then it demands an earnest and honest and *individual* response. And the response that is made will determine for each person his eternal destiny. We ought to tremble at God's Word, as did men of old. But that reverent sense of holy awe is little known today. Nor is it the efforts of the atheists that have been most successful in dragging God down to the level of mankind, but those who claim to love and worship Him and even to speak as His oracles.

One watches in amazement and even horror as a popular television preacher or healer pauses dramatically in his sermon, cocks an ear toward heaven, carries on a "conversation," holds up a hand to let God know He's talked long enough, then confides to his eager audience what God has supposedly just said—or else announces, with an air of mystery, that it can't be "revealed" now, but perhaps God will allow him to let them in on it later. Such performances are usually carried on with an almost flippant camaraderie, as though God existed solely to perform on command.

How vastly different the biblical scenes of God's mighty encounters with prophets and apostles of old! Consider Moses on the Mount at the giving of the law, or Isaiah crying, "Woe is me!" or John the apostle falling as dead at the feet of the resurrected Christ, whose voice was as the sound of many waters and His eyes as a flame of fire. How very appropriate today is Tozer's earnest rebuke:

The Christian conception of God current in these middle years of the twentieth century is so decadent as to be utterly beneath the dignity of the Most High God and actually constitutes for professed believers something amounting to a moral calamity.

With our loss of the sense of majesty has come the further loss of religious awe and consciousness of the divine Presence.[30]

Observing in dismay those Christian television personalities who claim to have a special hotline to God, one often has the distinct impression that one is watching *entertainers.* Jacques Ellul decries the tendency of mass media "to distract and entertain rather than to stimulate reflection."[31] It would not require much reflection to recognize that beneath the bluster and superlatives and shameless exhibitionism of Christian celebrities something is radically wrong. With great concern Charles Colson writes:

> ...to me, the miracle is that He has not already brought judgment on us *all* for the apostasy of our times.
>
> ...we live in an age when Christians glibly toss around cliches like "God told me" this or that. Some preachers, especially a few I've seen on television, sound like they've just hung up from a private phone session with Him....
>
> Our biblical forebears had no such casual view of God's holy voice. When the children of Israel received the Ten Commandments, they fell on their faces....
>
> It is no frivolous matter to hear the voice of God; and certainly it is an awesome trust to deign to speak for Him. Luther said that preaching made his knees knock. Spurgeon, the brilliant British preacher, said he "trembled" lest he should misinterpret the Word.[32]

That sense of awe—the fear of misinterpreting, disobeying, or adding to or taking from what God has said—was lost in the shuffle when the Bible somehow became God's psychological counseling manual designed to make us feel better about ourselves, to increase our sense of self-worth, and to inspire us to achieve personal success. As one of television's leading pastors has put it, *"The Bible is God's Book of Success...*the greatest success book you could ever read."[33] Like so many other Positive Confession or Faith movement leaders, he puts heavy emphasis upon *financial* success. After all, as the wife of another leader in this movement writes, "The Body of Christ is going to end up with all the money" because *God's will is prosperity.*[34] How strange, then, that so many of the heroes of the faith immortalized in that great faith chapter, Hebrews 11, "were stoned, they were sawn asunder, were tempted, were slain with the sword; they wandered about in sheepskins and goatskins, being destitute, afflicted, tormented" (Hebrews 11:37). Exchanging persecution for the promised prosperity may seem a great bargain from earth's point of view, but when seen from eternity's perspective it will be recognized at last as trading a heavenly inheritance for Esau's "mess of pottage."

This is not to say that God cannot grant financial success where it is part of His plan—but it also carries a heavy responsibility. Christians ought to do their best on the job. We are not to be "slothful in business." However, we are to be "fervent in spirit, serving the Lord" (Romans 12:11). God may for His purpose allow one young Christian to rise to the presidency of a large corporation, while another Christian, equally talented and diligent, may be passed over again and again for promotions that he would have had except for the hostility to his clear testimony for Christ. He is not to be pitied, for his reward is in heaven— and so is the real reward of the one who rose to the top, if he truly did all for God and not from covetousness or a desire to receive the plaudits of men.

Whatever Happened to the Fear of God?

Jesus warned His disciples, "Beware when all men shall speak well of you" (Luke 6:26). Those who seek such popularity today by presenting what people want to hear will be judged accordingly by God, and those supporting them will also be held accountable. The psalmist said of the ungodly in his day, "There is no fear of God before his eyes" (36:1). That same indictment applies to many who call themselves Christians in our day. It is no longer in style to "fear God and keep his commandments" (Ecclesiastes 12:13). Much of the blame rests with Christian television programs that make merchandise and entertainment out of the gospel and portray God, as Tozer lamented, as "our servant to wait on our will. 'The Lord is *my shepherd,*' we say, instead of '*The Lord* is my shepherd,' and the difference is as wide as the world."[35] Joyce Main Hanks, translator of Ellul's *The Humiliation of the Word*, makes a similar indictment of Christian media in the preface to that valuable book:

> ...the Church indulges our desire to "feel good" instead of responding to our need to be spiritually challenged and fed through solid exposition of the Scriptures.
> The electronic Church in particular panders to our appetite for entertainment rather than authentic discipleship and maturity.[36]

In this age of "positive thinking," fear is considered to be "negative" and thus to be avoided. Yet we are told that Noah "by faith" was "*moved with fear*" when he was "warned of God," and as a result he and his family were saved from the flood (Hebrews 11:7). The fear of God that is "the beginning of knowledge" (Proverbs 1:7), and brings true reverence and worship, seems conspicuously absent in so many churches today. This is all too evident in the careless way His Word is so often handled. Tragically, not only the secular world but also much of the church seems far out of step with the spirit of reverent fear that runs through the entire Bible and is so pleasing to God: "But to this man will I look, even to him that is poor and of a contrite spirit, and trembleth at my word" (Isaiah 66:2).

Why is there so little indication of this trembling at God's Word today? We are more afraid of men, of offending one another, than we are of offending Almighty God; of losing the rewards that men pass around—financial gifts, plaudits, influence, favors—than of losing the eternal reward that God alone can bestow. A passion for success is more seductive than a thirst for pleasure, for the latter is easily recognized as wrong, while the former may even seem to be admirable.

The fear of the Lord is "clean, enduring forever" (Psalm 19:9). It brings God's protection and deliverance (Psalm 34:7) as well as His salvation (Psalm 85:9), mercy (Psalm 103:11), and blessing (Psalm 115:13). It is our "strong confidence" and "fountain of life" (Proverbs 14:26,27). The scarcity of this fear betrays a serious deficiency in today's popular Christianity.

Facing the Truth

If there is to be a return to biblical Christianity, it will be necessary first of all to admit that something is wrong with "Christianity" as it is now generally taught and practiced. In an attempt to awaken the church to what he considers to be the unpleasant truth, Charles Colson calls attention to the shocking contradiction of growing biblical illiteracy along with declining morals in the United States at the same time that the influence of Christianity has been on the rise. He cites polls that revealed the following: "81 percent considered themselves Christians, but only 42 percent knew Jesus delivered the Sermon on the Mount... between 1963 and 1982 the percentage of Americans who believed the Bible infallible dropped from 65 percent to 37 percent.... When 1382 people were asked what book had most influenced their lives, fifteen cited the Bible—barely more than 1 percent!"[37]

Such stunning statistics ought to cause a serious reevaluation of the personal life of every Christian and of the gospel we preach and the manner in which we present it. Something essential seems to have fallen out of Christianity in the process of turning the gospel into a "message that can appeal to the secular world."[38] What Herbert Schlossberg has said of evangelical colleges seems to be true of vast numbers of Christians: Instead of challenging the world with the godliness and purity of their lives, they seem "to have a vision, rather, for assimilating what they think is the best of the world into the Christian life."[39]

McCandlish Phillips points out, "You can have religion... without knowing God. Satan does not hate religion; he has invented most of it."[40] Too often the *gifts* seem to be valued above the *fruit* of the Spirit, and the pursuit of "miracles" and "new revelations" leaves little time to know the Giver and what He has already said in His Word. Christianity can become just another *religion* which, like the rest, is practiced for the selfish benefits of healing and prosperity. J. I. Packer gives us a more scriptural perspective:

> There are many of us for whom the role model is Joni Eareckson rather than John Wimber. We see the powers of the kingdom operating, but mainly in regeneration, sanctification, the Spirit

as a comforter, the transformation of the inner life, rather than in physical miracles which just by happening prevent much of that other kingdom activity whereby people learn to live with their difficulties and glorify God.[41]

In a sobering appraisal, A. W. Tozer suggested that an angel who was accustomed to "the bliss of intimate communion with God" would find it difficult to "understand the casual, easily satisfied spirit which characterizes most evangelicals today." And if he had known "such blazing souls as Moses, David, Isaiah, Paul . . . he might logically conclude that 20th century Christians had misunderstood some vital doctrine of the faith . . . and had stopped short of a true acquaintance with God."[42]

In spite of much evidence to the contrary—and that ought to put us on our faces in reverent fear before God—many of today's most influential church leaders seem to be sincerely convinced that we are in the midst of "the greatest revival in Church history."[43] In this "new move of the Spirit,"[44] as it is called, all around the world, "the Spirit of the Lord is falling . . . miracles are happening."[45]

Others are convinced of just the opposite. A flier promoting the 1984 Congress On The Christian World View that was attended in Denver by many evangelical leaders carried this headline: "Do you agree that the Evangelical Church is sick, frightened, confused, unholy, and in need of revival, renewal, and reformation?"[46] Boice writes, "We do not have a strong church today, nor do we have many strong Christians."[47] There does seem to be strong disagreement on this important issue.

A Revival of Today's Christianity

There are those who liken the church today to Israel bringing down the walls of Jericho and marching into the promised land in the flush of victory. However, the situation after the defeat at Ai seems more applicable. Joshua was on his face crying to God when the Lord told him to get up because prayer was useless. There was sin in the camp, and it had to be exposed and repented of before Israel could have God's blessing again (Joshua 7). We must not fault the desire for revival; but perhaps there is too little concern about the quality of the "Christianity" we would thereby be multiplying. These sobering words from Tozer seem timely:

> So strongly is the breeze blowing for revival that scarcely anyone appears to have the discernment or the courage to turn around and lean into the wind. . . .
>
> I believe that the imperative need of the day is not simply revival, but a radical reformation that will go to the root of our moral and spiritual maladies and deal with causes rather than with consequences, with the disease rather than with symptoms.
>
> It is my considered opinion that under the present circumstances we do not want revival at all. A widespread revival of the kind of Christianity we know today in America might prove to be a moral tragedy from which we would not recover in a hundred years.[48]

Though such a view sounds depressing, it is actually liberating. The desperately ill man who thinks he is healthy will never consult a physician. We must admit that something is wrong before we will seek a cure. Tozer was not referring to *biblical* Christianity but to its modern counterfeit. There is nothing wrong with the manufacturer's Handbook—only with its application.

If something vital is lacking, at least we know where we must turn for the answers. If we are to return to *biblical Christianity*, then surely the Bible itself must be our guide. It is absolutely essential that we have a passion to know God and immerse ourselves in and meditate upon His Word. There is a victory over sin and self that God has made available in Christ, but that is often not given the prominence that it ought to have today. Perhaps the following words of nineteenth-century pastor Charles Spurgeon will inspire us to find in Christ alone the full remedy we seek:

> If, however, you are troubled about the power of sin and about the tendencies of your nature, as you well may be, here is a promise for you. . . . God, who cannot lie, has said in Ezekiel 36:26, "A new heart also will I give you, and a new spirit will I put within you. . . ."
>
> What a wonderful promise! . . . Let us lay hold of it, accept it as true, and appropriate it to ourselves. Then shall it be fulfilled in us, and we shall have, in after days and years, to sing of that

wondrous change which the sovereign grace of God has made in us.

He who made the promise has the responsibility of keeping the promise, and He is equal to the occasion. God, who promises this marvelous change, will assuredly carry it out in all who receive Jesus, for to all of them He gives power to become the sons of God.[49]

2

The Church's Most Desperate Need

Happy is the man whom God correcteth; therefore despise not thou the chastening of the Almighty (Job 5:17).

Whom the Lord loveth he correcteth, even as a father the son in whom he delighteth (Proverbs 3:12).

Preach the word...reprove, rebuke, exhort with all longsuffering and doctrine (2 Timothy 4:2).

ALTHOUGH THE EARLIER STATEMENT by A. W. Tozer putting the need for reformation ahead of revival was made about 30 years ago, it is no less true today. In fact, the situation is all the more desperate now because of the dominance over Christian media achieved by the teachers of Positive/Possibility Thinking and Positive Confession. As a consequence, millions of Christians will never take the opportunity to consider prayerfully and honestly whether the appraisals of men such as Boice, Colson, Stafford, Tozer, and others are true or false. They have been convinced that merely entertaining a "negative" thought will cause an adverse influence in one's life and can even make the thought come true, especially if it is spoken aloud. Not only the extremists in the Positive Confession movement, but to some extent nearly all Christians, have been influenced by the "positive mental attitude" syndrome. It pervades today's success-oriented society.

A Growing Popular Delusion

One of the most seductive and popular fads from the secular world ever to be dressed in Christian terminology and to be widely accepted in the church as Bible truth is the belief that positive is necessarily good and negative is conversely bad. In keeping with this delusion, the major message from the pulpits of some of America's largest churches and from many Christian television programs is to emphasize only what is "positive" from Scripture—something "comforting" or "uplifting"—and to avoid anything "negative." The pastor of the world's largest church writes, "Fill your mind with success and you will become successful.... I ask my people never to allow negative thoughts to dwell in their minds but to think positive things."[1] To exercise so flagrant a discrimination is a far cry from biblical Christianity.

This subtle and very appealing delusion provides the ideal rationale for avoiding the correction that God's Word is intended to bring into our lives, and it does so in the name of Christ and sound Bible teaching. It takes little reflection to realize, however, that "negative" and "positive" can be completely amoral, humanistic terms if used in the wrong context. "A *positive* approach" or "a *positive* attitude" are popular phrases in the secular world but are nowhere found in the Bible and should never be substituted for faith in God or used as an escape from reality.

Positive and *negative* have a definite meaning in electricity or mathematics or physics, but such terms have nothing whatever to do with truth, righteousness, holiness, obedience to God and His Word, the gospel of Jesus Christ, or the power of the Holy Spirit in living the Christian life. When used in such a context, these terms cause great confusion.

It is often said, in all sincerity, "I don't see what could be wrong with anything Pastor Jones teaches; he's always so positive!" It is astonishing how many Christians seem to equate *positive* with *true*. Philippians 4:8 is a favorite verse for those who insist that the Bible teaches "positive thinking": "Finally, brethren, whatsoever things are true...honest...just...pure... lovely...of good report; if there be any virtue and if there be any praise, think on these things." This is a perfect illustration of the confusion that has been generated.

Somehow, "positive" is not only erroneously equated with *true*, but it is also seen as the equivalent of *honest, just, pure, lovely,* etc. It is not difficult to realize that rather than being honest, it would in some cases be very *dishonest* to be "positive." Moreover, we could hardly call a judge *just* who failed to convict and sentence criminals because he desired to be "positive." Some people take a very "positive" view of free sex, but that can hardly be called *pure*. Nor could we say that anything else mentioned in Philippians 4:8 is the equivalent of "positive." To declare instead that this verse is advocating "positive thinking" is to destroy the specific moral, ethical, and spiritual values of that which it tells us we are to meditate upon. And it is a denial of God's holy character to call Him, in the words of a leader in the Positive Confession movement, "the greatest Positive Thinker who ever was."[2]

Most often what is meant by "positive" is simply favorable or pleasing, and whatever is unpleasant is called "negative." This relativistic and self-oriented attitude reflects today's secular mentality and is destructive of morals and spiritual values. What actually matters is not whether something is "positive" but whether something is true or false, biblical or not biblical. In that context, then, the terms "positive" or "negative" are not only irrelevant but a smoke screen that obscures real issues. Applying such terms to biblical truth is an insult to the God whose Word is filled with "negative" corrections and warnings of judgment.

Let us state clearly that we are not questioning the charitable and Christian virtue of seeing and emphasizing the best in others, when that serves the cause of truth, and of facing life's situations with an attitude of hope and faith in God. Paul is encouraging the Philippians (and all Christians) to occupy their thoughts with that which has value and virtue and will strengthen their moral character. We are, however, crying anathema to the move to mitigate truth and God's correction by "positivizing" the two-edged sword of Holy Writ. To do so is not only a mockery of God, but it subtly absolves Christian leaders of accountability under the guise that to question their doctrine or to suggest a correction from Scripture would be "negative." This idea is prevalent among Christians today in spite of the well-known fact that the Bereans were commended as being "more noble" for questioning Paul's teaching and checking it out against the Word of God (Acts 17:11). It is our responsibility to hold the teachings and lives of today's Christian leaders up to the same searchlight of truth, even at the risk of sounding "negative."

Substituting "positive thinking" for the moral content of faith has left us with a pitifully shallow Christianity that is largely preoccupied with success. The mistaken belief that we ought to be immune from suffering has led to an unbalanced emphasis upon healing and miracles. Lacking is that thirst for holiness and for God that drew saints of old into an intimacy with Him and the genuine experience of His presence and power. Superficiality, an appalling lack of discernment, and all too often a dulled conscience seem to be the result.

What About the "Negative Confessions" of God and Christ?

Many of those deeply involved in what they call the "*positive* confession of the Word of God" consider the Bible to be "the foremost PMA (Positive Mental Attitude) book in the world." Yet reference to any exhaustive concordance will establish the fact that neither the word "positive" nor "mental" occurs anywhere in the Word of God. The "foremost PMA book in the world" doesn't even know such a concept! The Bible is in fact one of the more "negative" books ever written. Moreover, it is filled with examples of those who obtained God's blessing and deliverance through what today's "faith teachers" would condemn as a negative confession. As the Assemblies of God position paper against Positive Confession points out:

> King Jehoshaphat admitted he had no might against an enemy alliance, but God gave him a marvelous victory (2 Chron. 20). Paul admitted weakness and then stated that when he was weak, he was strong because God's strength is made perfect in weakness (2 Cor. 12:9-10).
>
> It was after the disciples recognized they did not have enough to feed the multitudes and admitted it that Christ marvelously provided a more than adequate supply (Luke 9:12-13). It was after the disciples admitted they had caught no fish that Jesus directed them to a most successful endeavor (John 21:3-6).
>
> These people were not told to replace negative confessions with positive confessions which were contrary to the fact. . . . Yet God

marvelously intervened even though they made what some would call negative confessions....

To teach that leaders in the early days of the church such as Paul, Stephen, and Trophimus did not live in a constant state of affluence and health because they did not have the light on this teaching is going beyond and contrary to the Word of God. Doctrine will be sound only as it is developed within the framework of the total teaching of Scripture.[3]

Foundational to the Positive Confession movement is the belief that there is a power inherent within words which causes whatever one says to come to pass, and that one must therefore be extremely careful only to make *positive* statements. E. W. Kenyon, who is the founder of this movement, taught that Jesus "was always positive in His message."[4] One need not read very far in the New Testament to prove that statement false. In fact, if it is true that we create what we speak, then we must charge Jesus with bringing disaster not only upon Himself but upon others as well. His numerous "negative confessions," such as "The foxes have holes, and the birds of the air have nests, but the Son of man hath not where to lay his head" (Matthew 8:20), must have been the cause of the poverty that plagued Him and His disciples. And the same must be said of His frequent statements to His followers that He was going to be crucified, even insisting upon this fact when Peter attempted to urge upon Him a more "positive" attitude (Matthew 16:21-23).

If "you get what you say," then Christ's numerous "negative confessions" not only brought upon Himself poverty, suffering, and death but brought it upon the entire world as well. Was not His prophecy of the coming destruction of Jerusalem a "negative confession" that caused this very tragedy to happen in 70 A.D.? And are not the prophecies of Jesus and His apostles concerning the great tribulation, the rule of Antichrist, and the coming Battle of Armageddon "negative confessions" that will bring these horrible events upon this world? And what about Isaiah, Jeremiah, Ezekiel, and the many other Old Testament prophets who made repeated "negative confessions" of judgment upon Israel and many other nations?

Even a superficial reading of the Bible would force us to

conclude that in order to be a prophet of God who is true to His Word it would be necessary to pronounce numerous "negative confessions." What are we to do with these prophecies? Are we to "confess" them as they are? And, if so, how can we call such an act a *"positive confession of the Word of God"*? Or are we to turn these "negative" prophecies around with a "positive confession" that will bring peace, prosperity, healing, salvation, and restoration instead of Armageddon? Or could it be, as we have already noted, that "positive" and "negative" are completely inappropriate terms when we are dealing with God's will and His Word?

The Power of Negative Thinking

Past revivals were marked primarily by repentance of sins. The current highly-promoted "greatest revival in history" is based upon a "positive confession" of our divine right to miracles. The healing of bodies seems to take precedence over the salvation of souls. Though many of the leaders would decry such an unfortunate result, it is their false teaching that has fostered this self-centeredness. As J. I. Packer points out:

> What, after all, do we mostly preach and teach and produce TV programs and video cassettes for each other about, these days? The over all answer to my question seems to be: success and euphoria; getting from God health, wealth, freedom from care, and constant happy feelings.[5]

The prevailing "be-positive-at-all-cost" attitude makes it extremely difficult to look beneath the surface of "church growth" and apparent "miracles" to face the painful truth. To do so would be "negative," and that is now the cardinal sin. Paul warned that those who are not lovers of truth would be given a "strong delusion" to believe Satan's lie (2 Thessalonians 2:9-12). The popular substitution of *positive* for *truth* is a perfect set-up for the prophesied delusion.

There is no escaping the fact that the Bible contains many "negative" pronouncements, including the solemn and specific warning that one of the primary characteristics of the last days will be religious deception such as the world has never before experienced. Jesus Himself continually made "negative" pronouncements concerning those who rejected the truth, and warned repeatedly of coming judgment. Nor is there even a hint that the proper response to prophecies concerning the rise of Antichrist, the great tribulation, and Armageddon is either political action or positive affirmation—or that the apostasy that we are told *must* come before Christ can return (2 Thessalonians 2:3) will turn out to be "the greatest revival in church history" if we all declare it to be so.

This is not a matter of difficult or questionable interpretation of obscure Scriptures, but something upon which God's Word seems to be unequivocally clear from Genesis to Revelation. The same God who pronounced *everything* good in the first chapter of the Bible warned Adam and Eve in the second chapter that the consequence of disobedience was *death*: "In the day that thou eatest thereof thou shalt surely die" (Genesis 2:17). Nothing could be more "negative" than that statement, yet it was *true*; and nothing could be more "positive" than Satan's promise that Eve would become a god through eating the forbidden fruit, yet it was *false*. Clearly, emphasizing the "positive" and rejecting the "negative" caused Eve to believe the serpent's lie. The issue then was *obedience*, and so it is today.

To insist that Christianity must always be "positive" is to mock God and lead souls astray. We must take heed to God's Word, allowing it first of all to cleanse our own hearts and then living by its precepts. Then we must warn and rescue as many as we can who are deceived by the popular delusions of our day. Even though the world is hastening to judgment, we are each to be a living example of the joy and victory that is ours in Christ.

Paul was inspired to write that *all* Scripture was given specifically "for doctrine, for reproof, for correction, for instruction in righteousness" (2 Timothy 3:16). These four elements are absolutely essential to biblical Christianity, yet they are largely absent from currently-published Christian books and seldom found in the sermons of today's new brand of "positive" preachers or on the popular Christian television talk shows. Much of Christian television majors in sensational testimonies, sentimental singing, and dramatic but usually futile attempts at healing;

but where are the *doctrine, reproof, correction,* and *instruction in righteousness*? What kind of Christianity can we have when these, the Bible's main themes, are missing?

In their misguided zeal to be "positive" at all times, many of today's Christian leaders have painted themselves into a corner where they have to ignore much of what the very Bible they claim to preach from has to say. By this subtle means the church, and Christian leaders themselves, have been robbed of the very corrective influence that God intended His Word to effect.

A Desperate Need for Correction

Correction is one of the most conspicuously absent yet essential ingredients needed in the church today. There are those who seek to avoid correction by hiding behind a misapplication of Christ's words, "Judge not that ye be not judged" (Matthew 7:1). It is conveniently forgotten that these words were spoken by the same One who warned the Jews to "judge righteous judgment" (John 7:24), told us to judge the fruit of prophets (Matthew 7:16) and promised His disciples that they would sit on thrones judging Israel (Matthew 19:28).

From the context and the remainder of Scripture it seems clear that Christ was warning us not to judge motives, because these are hidden from us. We must put the best reasonable interpretation upon what others say and do, not judging their hearts, which only God knows. However, we *must* judge doctrines and deeds.

Paul exhorted Timothy, "Reprove, rebuke, exhort with all longsuffering and doctrine." On what basis would one reprove or rebuke without having judged conduct or doctrine to be wrong? Such correction is a major theme throughout Scripture. Public teaching of false doctrine and publicly known sin must both be rebuked *publicly*. Paul reminded Timothy, "Them that sin rebuke *before all*, that others also may fear" (1 Timothy 5:20).

To the church at Corinth Paul wrote, "Let the prophets speak two or three, and let the others judge" (1 Corinthians 14:29). Public teaching, whether in sermons or songs or the operation of the gifts of the Spirit, must be judged publicly as to biblical authenticity and accuracy. This should be done by the pastor and elders at the time the teaching occurs in the local fellowship, though this seldom happens. It is even more essential, however, that the teaching pouring forth from the powerfully influential mass media—radio, television, magazines, and books—be judged and, if found wanting, be publicly corrected. That goes for this book and this author as well as all others.

Paul considered it necessary and proper to name publicly Hymenaeus and Philetus because of their publicly taught false doctrine which had "overthrow[n] the faith of some" (2 Timothy 2:17,18). How much more essential would public correction be if a modern Hymenaeus or Philetus as a best-selling author or popular Christian television personality were leading *millions* astray! Instead of giving priority to protecting the reputations of those whose teachings may be publicly questioned, should we not rather be concerned for the thousands and perhaps millions of people whom they influence? Such an attitude should surely characterize every leader who is truly a man or woman of God.

Those in control of most Christian television programming generally refuse to allow on their stations or networks Christian leaders who would question their views. Moreover, instead of judging within their own ranks, as Scripture says must be done, they decry correction as "divisive" and instead preach "unity" based not upon truth but upon the agreement not to disagree with one another. There is much talk of *love*, as though it somehow rules out *correction*. Yet the Bible teaches that love speaks the *truth* (Ephesians 4:15), which may very well be "negative." Real love corrects those who are loved: "Whom the Lord loveth he chasteneth" (Hebrews 12:6). Jesus Himself declared, "As many as I love, I rebuke and chasten" (Revelation 3:19). No wonder Solomon said, "Rebuke a wise man and he will love thee" (Proverbs 9:8)! A wise man desires and welcomes correction and loves the one who corrects, considering rebuke not an "attack" but a kindness. Inspired of the Holy Spirit, Solomon declared:

> Correction is grievous unto him that forsaketh the way, and he that hateth reproof shall die.
> Reprove not a scorner, lest he hate thee; rebuke a wise man, and he will love thee.
> The fear of the Lord is the beginning of wisdom, and the knowledge of the holy is understanding. . . but fools despise

wisdom and instruction (Proverbs 15:10; 9:8,10; 1:7).

The Biblical Example

From Genesis to Revelation, a major theme of the Bible is correction. This is because God loves us and desires to lead us from death and judgment into the eternal and abundant life available in Christ. Referring to the Old Testament narrative accounts of the history of Israel, Paul declared, "They are written for our *admonition*" (1 Corinthians 10:11). John the Baptist preached repentance and correction, and so did Christ. Much of what our Lord said was in the nature of reproof aimed directly at the religious leaders, but indicting also the typical Jew of His day. It is dishonest to focus only upon what one considers to be the positive aspects of Christ's ministry and to fail to take to heart and apply in our lives and churches the correction He brought.

Christ did not hesitate to call the religious leaders "hypocrites" and "whited sepulchres" and "blind leaders of the blind," and His own disciples "fools and slow of heart." He had obviously never taken a Dale Carnegie Course in "How to Win Friends and Influence People," and did not consider being positive the only or even the best way to present truth! The pastors, evangelists, and radio and television preachers who fail to press upon themselves and their audiences the corrective teaching of Christ because they don't want to be negative are not only ignoring the example He set but are repeating the very sin for which He rebuked the religious leaders of His day.

Much of the New Testament was written to correct error that had already crept into the church in the first century. The epistles of Paul, Peter, James, John, and Jude embody the major corrective doctrines of the church, which of course are still valid today. Leaders in the early church were expected to be involved in an ongoing corrective ministry. Unfortunately, many of today's most popular church leaders seem astonishingly unwilling either to judge the teaching of other leading Christians or to accept any correction themselves.

It is claimed by some that openly questioning or correcting the doctrinal teachings of church leaders is divisive, as though all division were bad and to be avoided. Yet Christ declared that He came to bring division (Luke 12:51), and it followed His ministry wherever He went (John 7:43; 9:16; 10:19; etc.). The division He brought was essential: It separated between truth and error, between light and darkness.

Romans 16:17, a favorite proof-text for those who cry *division* in order to avoid *correction*, is usually quoted only in part: "Mark them which cause divisions," as though "division" were the problem that is being dealt with. However, the verse actually says, "Mark them which cause divisions and offenses *contrary to the doctrine which ye have learned*," making it clear that the issue is sound doctrine. It is those who refuse to have their false doctrines judged who are causing the wrong kind of division, not those who "earnestly contend for the *faith*" (Jude 3), as we are admonished to do. Nor dare we compromise truth for the sake of avoiding controversy. J. I. Packer reminds us:

> First, there is nothing unscriptural about controversy when the good of souls requires it, as it did in the controversies of (for instance) Christ and Paul, and when the good faith of one's opponents is respected.
>
> Second, the motive of those who make a virtue of avoiding controversy is likely to be nothing nobler than the self-protectiveness of folk who are conceited and thin-skinned and, perhaps, unaware of the value of truth.[6]

"Touch Not the Lord's Anointed"

If there is to be a return to biblical Christianity, then no one in the church can claim immunity from correction. There is, unfortunately, a form of Christian guruism that has placed certain leaders on a pedestal of infallibility. To question anything they say or do is considered to be "touching" the "anointed of the Lord," which was forbidden in the Old Testament by both example and precept. Violators came under God's judgment. The psalmist wrote:

> He [God] suffered no man to do them wrong; yea, he reproved kings for their sakes, saying, Touch not mine anointed, and do my prophets no harm (Psalm 105:14,15).

The two words *wrong* and *harm* in this Scripture make it clear what God means when He says, "Touch not mine anointed." It has nothing to do with legitimate correction, which God in His love desires for all and especially for His "anointed." Who were these "anointed" and who fits this category today? In Old Testament Israel the prophets, priests, and kings were "anointed" to these offices by having poured upon them the special anointing "oil of the apothecary,"[7] after which they were known as "the anointed of the Lord." All three of these functions and offices— prophet, priest, and king—were to find their ultimate fulfillment in the promised Messiah. In fact, the title *Messiah*, of which *Christ* is the Greek translation, literally means "the anointed one."

In the New Testament, Christ's followers are identified with Him so closely that they, as members of His body, the church, carry on in His name these three offices of prophet, priest, and king. Every Christian is an "anointed one" because Christ, who is *the* Anointed One, has come to live in us and we are one in Him. And it is this "anointing" of the Holy Spirit that keeps us from being seduced by Satan's lies, if we will only heed His leading. John declared:

> These things have I written unto you concerning them that seduce you. But the anointing which ye have received of him abideth in you, and ye need not that any man teach you; but as the same anointing teacheth you of all things, and is truth, and is no lie, and even as it hath taught you, ye shall abide in him. . . that when he shall appear, we may have confidence, and not be ashamed before him at his coming (1 John 2:26-28).

Whatever it means to "touch not" the Lord's anointed applies to every Christian and not merely to a few top leaders. What does it mean? The term is first used by David in reference to King Saul. Chased by Saul and his army, David and his men were hiding in a cave when Saul came in to rest. David's men urged him to kill his pursuer under the rationale that surely God had delivered his enemy into his hand as prophesied. David was about to follow their advice when his "heart smote him" and he said to his men, "The Lord forbid that I should. . . stretch forth mine hand against. . . the anointed of the Lord" (1 Samuel 24:6). Later a similar incident occurred in which David could have killed Saul, but again he resisted the temptation, saying, "Who can stretch forth his hand against the Lord's anointed, and be guiltless?" (1 Samuel 26:9). The "wrong" and "harm" referred to in the prohibition of Psalm 105 against touching the Lord's anointed would have been, in David's case, to slay the king.

It is hardly accurate to teach that this Old Testament phrase means that we dare not question the teaching of a Christian leader. On both of these occasions, although David did not "touch" (kill) Saul, he did *rebuke* "the Lord's anointed" *publicly* in front of the army of Israel and his own men! A proper application of this Scripture would therefore require us likewise to rebuke publicly the "anointed of the Lord" for doing or saying what they ought not. Israel's leaders, whether prophet, priest, or king, were often rebuked publicly by those called of God to do so.

Paul rightly rebuked Peter publicly: "I said unto Peter *before them all*" (Galatians 2:14). By public example Peter had led many astray. It would have been entirely inappropriate for Paul to have had a private discussion about this with Peter. It was not a Matthew 18:15 matter ("If thy brother shall trespass [sin] *against thee*, go and tell him his fault between him and thee alone"). Peter had not offended Paul personally, but he had led *the church* astray. Paul was therefore not only obligated to correct Peter but to do so in a manner that would correct the situation that Peter's error had created in the church. Each Christian as an "anointed of the Lord" has the same obligation today. To establish an elite class of leaders whose teachings and actions cannot be questioned is to take the first step into cultism.

In the Hands of the Master Potter

The prevailing thinking of our age has made us imagine that correction is "negative" when in fact it is very positive. It would help to remember that any valued object is frequently dusted and polished. A skilled sculptor chisels the stone not to damage it but to shape it into a form of beauty. The artist steps back, gives his painting a critical examination, then brushes in more strokes to improve it. God is doing the same with us. And His Word is intended to be our guide in this ongoing process.

There is much talk of success and striving for excellence in the world around us (and much of that mentality has come into the church, mainly focused upon better organization and administration). But what about the work that God would do in our hearts? There are depths of humility and heights of joy and excellence that we have not even imagined, and God needs our willing cooperation and eager participation in the process. It is when we are most pleased with ourselves and think we need no more correction or improvement that we are actually farthest from what we ought to be. Andrew Murray wrote:

> In striving after the higher experiences of the Christian life, the believer is often in danger of aiming at and rejoicing in what one might call the more human virtues. Such virtues are boldness, joy, contempt of the world, zeal, self-sacrifice—even the old Stoics taught and practiced these. While the deeper and gentler, the more divine and heavenly graces are scarcely thought of or valued.
>
> These virtues are those which Jesus first taught upon earth—because He brought them from heaven—poverty of spirit, meekness, humility, lowliness. . . .
>
> The preacher of spiritual truth with an admiring congregation hanging on his lips, the gifted speaker on a holiness platform expounding the secrets of the heavenly life, the Christian giving testimony to a blessed experience, the evangelist moving on in triumph and made a blessing to rejoicing multitudes—no man knows the hidden, the unconscious danger to which these are exposed. . . .
>
> Just when we are most anxious to have our heart be the temple of God, we will find the two men coming up to pray. And the publican will find that his danger is not from the Pharisee beside him, who despises him, but from the Pharisee within, who commends and exalts. . . .
>
> Yes, even in the temple, when the language of penitence and trust in God's mercy alone is heard, the Pharisee may take up the note of praise, and in thanking God be congratulating himself. Pride can clothe itself in the garments of praise or of penitence.[8]

None of us is a finished masterpiece yet. We are all on the potter's wheel in the process of being shaped into the pattern He has planned. In the realization that there was so much more of God to know, so much more of His holiness and truth to understand, so much more of His unspeakable joy and comfort to experience by the indwelling Holy Spirit, Paul declared:

> Not as though I had already attained, either were already perfect; but I follow after, if that I may apprehend [grasp] that for which also I am apprehended of Christ Jesus.
> Brethren, I count not myself to have apprehended; but this one thing I do: forgetting those things which are behind and reaching forth unto those things which are before, I press toward the mark for the prize of the high calling of God in Christ Jesus (Philippians 3:12-14).

Christian psychology has convinced many of today's Christian leaders that the gospel needs to be tailored to the popular selfisms of our time in order to make it appealing to the secular mind. That is like treating cancer with aspirin: While the patient may feel better for a short time, the dosage has to be constantly increased and eventually the patient dies. The old-time evangelists were not so foolish. They relied upon God's Word and did not change its meaning to suit the temper of their times. Consequently they offered a solution that brought genuine victory. Here is the appeal that Spurgeon made to hearts desperate for a real solution to the sins that bound them:

> We want to be purified as well as pardoned. Justification without sanctification would not be salvation at all. It would call the leper clean and leave him to die of his disease; it would forgive the rebellion and allow the rebel to remain an enemy to his king. It would remove the consequences but overlook the cause, and this would leave an endless and hopeless task before us. . . .
> Remember that the Lord Jesus came to take away sin in three ways. He came to remove the penalty of sin, the power of sin, and last, the presence of sin. . . .
> Oh that you would do the gracious Lord the justice to believe that He can and will do this for you, great miracle though it will be! Oh that you would believe that God cannot lie! Oh that you would trust Him for a new heart and a right spirit, for He can give them to you![9]

3
Contending for the Faith

Beloved, when I gave all diligence to write unto you
of the common salvation, it was needful for me to write
unto you, and exhort you that ye should earnestly contend
for the faith which was once delivered unto the saints
(Jude 3).

WITH THE MANY RESOURCES of the modern world at
our fingertips, it is so easy to content ourselves with turning on
a Christian television program or flipping through the pages of a
Christian magazine or book to consult the opinions of the
experts, rather than to carefully think through the issues for
ourselves. Christianity was never intended to be a follow-the-
leader-blindly cult. It is the personal responsibility and privilege
of each individual Christian to be immersed in the Word of
God, to study it diligently, to meditate upon it, and to live
by it. The Christian life is a 24-hour-per-day and seven-days-
per-week full-time commitment—not a game to play on the side.
Nor is it a club to join that goes through its routine at certain
hours of special days in designated tax-exempt properties so
that those who faithfully (or even sporadically) attend can feel
the satisfaction of having done a duty and then get back to living
life in the real world.

A Sacred Trust

It was never God's intent that an elite corps of specialists would
be the sole proprietors of biblical truth, but that each Christian
would know for himself what he believes and why he believes

it on the basis of his personal study of the Word of God. "The Bible," Carl F. H. Henry has rightly said, "must become priority reading for us and for this generation."[1] Faith is an individual matter. Nor are pastors, evangelists, or theologians to be the only "defenders of the faith"; that is the solemn responsibility of each believer.

It is the Word of God that ministers true faith to our hearts: "Faith cometh by hearing, and hearing by the word of God" (Romans 10:17). This Word that God has spoken to man, which we dare not neglect or misinterpret, comprises *the faith* that all must believe in order to know God and to be saved from His judgment upon sinners.

The "saints" to whom this faith has been delivered to guard and disseminate are not a special class who have been granted this honorable title by official vote after their death. The New Testament epistles were written to the saints then living at Rome, Corinth, and Ephesus, and also to us today, for "called to be saints" is the designation of every Christian (Romans 1:7; 1 Corinthians 1:2; Ephesians 1:1; etc.). We are therefore to live sanctified, holy lives wholly for God. As J. I. Packer reminds us, "Holiness is commanded: God wills it, Christ requires it, Scripture prescribes it. A hurricane of texts and a barrage of theological arguments are ready to prove the point."[2] And to each of us, as *saints*, has been committed the sacred trust of defending the faith not only from attack by those outside the church but from an even more dangerous subversion by those within (Acts 20:28-32; Revelation 2:12-29; 2 Peter 2:1-3).

The Basic Issue

All Christians would agree to the supreme importance placed upon faith. The Bible assures us that we are "saved through faith" (Ephesians 2:8) and that the just "live by faith" (Romans 1:17), and it reminds us that "without faith it is impossible to please [God]" (Hebrews 11:6). Finally, we are commanded to take "the shield of faith," the Christian's essential defense against every weapon of his soul's enemy (Ephesians 6:16). Clearly, a correct view of faith is essential to biblical Christianity. Therefore to come short or to be confused in the area of faith is a very serious matter.

It is therefore understandable that in his plans to seduce the human race, Satan should make faith a primary object of his attack, seeking to destroy it or at the very least to discredit it in the minds of some people, or, as the Master Deceiver, to lull others into a false assurance, a deadly deception indeed. Unhappily, much of the present teaching about faith within the church has played into Satan's hands. Often those who emphasize faith the most seem to be the least biblical, twisting the Scriptures to fit their peculiar ideas. As a result, many Christians are so confused about faith that they are unable either to help sincere seekers or to refute the critics.

One of the most basic errors that is accepted not only in the secular world but within the church as well is that faith is some kind of force. One best-selling author and popular Bible teacher declares, "God's Word in your mouth produces a force called 'faith'...it generates a spiritual force called faith."[3] Many Christians who seek God's power to bless them will not allow His Word to correct them and have little concern for doctrinal purity. Chuck Swindoll laments that "Substance—time-honored biblical content—is increasingly conspicuous by its absence."[4]

The idea of an impersonal force is appealing because we can use it to our ends; but the personal God of the Bible wants to use *us*—for our good and to His glory. The first inward grace that genuine faith produces is *obedience*: submission to Christ's lordship, and not an obsession with power. David Wilkerson warns, "Christ is made a stranger in our midst—when we want His power more than His purity!"[5] One of the most popular "faith teachers" perverts Christ's Great Commission to go and under His authority teach all who would believe "to observe [obey] all things whatsoever I have commanded you" (Matthew 28:18-20) by paraphrasing it to read: "Jesus said, 'All power is given unto me; therefore, you take it and use it.'"[6] This "faith teacher" who says "faith is your servant" also calls faith a "force just like gravity"[7] that we can *use* because we are "part of God" and have *all* of His "capabilities."[8] In rebuke of such error, Tozer wrote:

> If we only believe hard enough we'll make it somehow. So

goes the popular chant. What you believe is not important. Only believe.

Back of this is the nebulous idea that faith is an almighty power flowing through the universe which anyone may plug into at will. When it comes in, out go pessimism, fear, defeat and failure; in come optimism, confidence, personal mastery, and unfailing success in war, love, sports, business and politics.

What is overlooked in all this is that faith is good only when it engages truth....[9]

The issue is truth: *What* and *in whom* one believes determines whether faith has been misplaced or not. "Faith never knows where it is being led," said Oswald Chambers, "but it loves and knows the One Who is leading."[10] True faith rests in God's love and care, relieving us of every burden and producing "the peace of God which passeth all understanding" (Philippians 4:7). The secular counterfeit of faith is called a "positive mental attitude." The PMA and success/motivation movement's influence is magnified by such best-sellers as *The Power of Positive Thinking*,[11] *The Magic of Believing*,[12] *Success Through a Positive Mental Attitude*,[13] and a host of other books of the same genre. Unfortunately, this seductive mixture of truth and error has invaded the church and a positive mental attitude has now been confused for faith. Take for example Norman Vincent Peale's "12 Magic Principles":

> When a negative thought comes, practice cancelling it with a positive thought and affirmation.
> Practice great affirmations like: "Life is good." "I believe." "People are wonderful." "God loves me." Such affirmations lift you into the area of infinite power.[14]

Truth is not at issue in such reasoning. Everyone, whether saint or sinner, pagan or Christian, without distinction of religious belief, is urged to "assert and dwell on your Divine origin. Say to yourself...'I am a child of God.' "[15] Rather than being based upon the truth of God's Word and objective reality, Peale's "magic" seems intended to create what is affirmed. The teaching that the earnest *belief* or *affirmation* that something will happen *causes* it to happen (or not to happen) has led many people to confuse metaphysical mind power with faith. Indeed, Peale plainly states: "Positive thinking is just another term for faith."[16] No wonder Charles Colson condemns "today's cheapened gospel that assures us our mental attitude can bring meaning and order" and compares it to the heresy of "first-century gnostics."[17]

Faith That Moves Mountains

Many sincere Christians imagine that faith is believing that what they are praying for will happen. That is not faith but presumption. If what we pray for comes to pass because we *believed* it would, then God in actual fact has played no real part in the answer to our prayer, but we have produced the results by the power of our own *belief*. There is a vast difference between believing that what I'm praying for will happen because I *believe it will happen* and believing that *God will make it happen* in response to my faith in Him. Recognizing this difference becomes crucially important if we are to understand what Jesus meant when He said:

> Have faith in God. For verily I say unto you that whosoever shall say unto this mountain, Be thou removed and be cast into the sea, and shall not doubt in his heart, but shall believe that those things which he saith shall come to pass, he shall have whatsoever he saith.
> Therefore I say unto you, What things soever ye desire, when ye pray, believe that ye receive them, and ye shall have them (Mark 11:22-24).

Many Christians mistakenly conclude that *faith* is a *power* which enables those who possess it to move mountains at command and to gain their every desire simply through a positive confession. That this is not true ought to be clear from the fact that Christ prefaces this entire statement with these words: "*Have faith in God.*" Rather than being a *power* that we direct, faith is confidence in God and in what *He* will do. The key element in faith is knowing the will of God. Surely no one would want to effect through the power of belief anything contrary to God's will, even if that were possible. Nor would God give anyone faith to believe what is not according to His will. To attempt to *believe* what we are not certain is His will would be presumptuous. Clearly I cannot have faith in God to command a mountain to move in His name unless I know when and where it is God's will to move it and that I am His chosen vessel to do so. Nor can I believe that I will receive what I pray for unless I know that it is God's will and that I am in a relationship of purity and obedience that will allow Him to bless me in this way (1 John 3:22; 5:14,15). Dave Wilkerson writes, "The church once confessed its sins—now it confesses its rights."[18] In full agreement with this reproof, Charles Colson elaborates:

> A popular daily devotional quotes Psalm 65:9, "The streams of God are filled with water," and paraphrases it, "I fill my mind to overflowing with thoughts of prosperity and success. I affirm that God is my source and God is unlimited."
>
> This is not just a religious adaptation of the look-out-for-number-one, winner-take-all, God-helps-those-who-help-themselves gospel of our culture; it is heresy.[19]

Faith and the Christian Media

The deadly error that faith is a force to tap into and use is widely disseminated not only in secular media such as the Star Wars film series, but surprisingly over Christian radio and television and in books and magazines. In any consideration of how the church can return to biblical Christianity, the tremendous potential of Christian media either to assist this corrective process or to accelerate the spread of heresy must be confronted.

Television is the most powerful branch of the media. It is therefore alarming to realize that the major Christian networks, rather than being under the direction of a representative group of church leaders, are controlled by a handful of individuals. They wield absolute authority over this unprecedented means of spreading either truth or apostasy and are insulated from correction from the body of Christ. Those who would challenge these leaders' views are generally banned from the networks and stations. (This is not to deny that there is also some excellent programming on Christian television, with solid biblical content that encourages viewers, promotes authentic worship, and

challenges Christians to a closer walk with God.) It is of course
the responsibility of each individual viewer—or the reader of
books such as this one—to discern for himself what is of God
and according to His Word and will, and what is not.

Regardless of how much or how little time the average viewer
spends watching Christian television, the potential is there to
influence the body of Christ far more powerfully than any other
means of communication. This is the only "church" that many
people ever attend, and for those who do frequent a local
fellowship, the pastor and elders in the average church can hardly
compete with the spectacle of television or correct in a 30-minute
sermon on Sunday morning false teaching that is being absorbed
for hours on a daily basis. To a lesser but still significant extent,
Christian radio, books, magazines, and films contribute to this
serious problem. If there is to be a return to biblical Christianity
by the church as a whole, it will have to take place within Christian
media as well as in local congregations.

Christian Television and Charismania

Most people are not aware that Positive Confession and Rhema
teaching, which dominate so much Christian television, far from
representing biblical Christianity, are not accepted by any mainstream denomination. Moreover, this false teaching has also
been rejected by major Pentecostal denominations (such as the
Assemblies of God).[20] *Faith* is indeed preached, but nearly always
as a power for gaining health and wealth and personal blessing.
The faith that has moral content—that demands holiness and
obedience and produces peace and joy—is all too often neglected.
And although *the Word* is emphasized, it is often twisted and
abused by those who claim to be its chief proponents.

The extremist charismatic teaching that dominates most
Christian television should not be confused with old-line Pente-
costalism, which generally opposes it. In his excellent masters
thesis at Oral Roberts University, Daniel Ray McConnell explained the heart of the problem:

> One looks in vain for the so-called "charismatic theology." It
> simply does not exist (and never did). The theological umbilical

cord to the Mother church has been cut and the charismatic baby is floundering around, searching in some strange and dangerous places from some pretty peculiar individuals for the doctrinal sustenance necessary for its own survival. Needless to say, the weaning process could be hazardous, indeed.[21]

When the exotic teachings and practices of what Chuck Smith calls "charismania"[22] dominate the airwaves, the situation becomes extremely hazardous for the entire church. Much of Christian television continues to pour forth a daily flood of teaching that most church leaders consider to be seriously in error. Protests of concerned pastors and viewers have brought no change, and confusion reigns in the body of Christ worldwide. The issue is of such importance as to warrant a careful consideration of the major heresies involved. In order to do so, it will be necessary to examine specific teachings of those who claim to adhere so closely to the Bible that they call themselves *"Word"* teachers. This brief but necessary diversion to document error is intended to enhance our consideration of biblical Christianity, which will stand out in even sharper focus in contrast to the erroneous Scripture interpretations that prevail in the Positive Confession movement.

The "Positive Confession of God's Word"

The fastest-growing segment of Christianity in recent years has been among churches connected with the Positive Confession movement or Faith movement. It does not yet constitute a new denomination, but it certainly represents innovative teachings outside of mainstream Christianity. McConnell points out that "any new religious movement [within Protestantism] must bear the scrutiny of two criteria: biblical fidelity and historical orthodoxy."[23] Regrettably, the Positive Confession movement fails on both counts. The historical roots of this movement (which Charles Farah has called "Faith Formula Theology")[24] lie in the occult and most recently in New Thought and its offshoot, the Mind Science cults. Its biblical basis is found only in the peculiar interpretations of its own leaders, not in generally accepted Christian theology. Its basic beliefs can be summarized briefly as follows:

1. **Faith is a force that both God and man can use.** "Faith is
   a force just like electricity or gravity,"[25] and it is the substance out of which God creates whatever is.[26] God uses faith,
   and so may we in exactly the same way in order to produce
   the same results through obedience to the same "laws of
   faith"[27] that God applied in creation. "You have the same
   ability [as God has] dwelling or residing on the inside of
   you."[28] "We have all the capabilities of God. We have His
   faith."[29]

2. **Faith's force is released by speaking words.** "Words are the
   most powerful thing in the universe"[30] because they "are con-
   tainers" that "carry faith or fear and they produce after their
   kind."[31] God operates by these very same laws. "God had
   faith in His own words...God had faith in His faith, because
   He spoke words of faith and they came to pass."[32] "That
   faith force was transported by words...."[33] "...the God-
   kind-of-faith...is released by the words of your mouth."[34]
   "Creative power was in God's mouth. It is in your mouth
   also."[35]

3. **Man is a "little god" in God's class.** "Man was designed or
   created by God to be the god of this world."[36] "Adam was
   the god of this world...[but he] sold out to Satan, and Satan
   became the god of this world."[37] "We were created to be gods
   over the earth, but remember to spell it with a little 'g.' "[38]
   "Adam was created in God's class...to rule as a god...by
   speaking words."[39] "Man was created in the God class....
   We are a class of gods.... God Himself spawned us from
   His innermost being."[40] "We are in God; so that makes us
   part of God (2 Cor. 5:17)."[41]

4. **Anyone—occultist or Christian—can use the faith-force.**
   Because man is a little god "in God's class: very capable of
   operating on the same level of faith as God"[42] and "because
   all men are spirit beings,"[43] therefore *anyone*, whether Christian or pagan, can release this "faith force" by speaking
   words if he only believes in his words as God believes in His.[44]
   "God is a faith God. God released His faith in Words"[45] and
   we must do the same: "Everything you say [positive or nega-
   tive] will come to pass."[46] "Spiritual things are created by
   WORDS. Even natural, physical things are created by
   WORDS."[47]

5. **You get what you *confess*.** The vital key is *confessing*, or
   speaking aloud, and thereby releasing the force of faith. "You

get what you say."[48] "Only by mouth confession can faith power be released, allowing tremendous things to happen."[49] "Remember, the key to receiving the desires of your heart is to make the words of your mouth agree with what you want."[50] "Whatever comes out of your mouth shall be produced in your life."[51] "They're [his two children] 30-some years of age today, and I don't believe I prayed more than half a dozen times for both of them in all these years. Why? Because you can have what you say—and I had already said it!"[52]

6. **Never make a *negative* confession.** The tongue "can kill you, or it can release the life of God within you...whether you believe right or wrong, it is still the law."[53] There is power in "the evil fourth dimension."[54] If you confess sickness you get it, if you confess health you get it; whatever you say you get.[55] "Faith is as a seed...you plant it by speaking it."[56] "The spoken word...releases power—power for good or power for evil."[57] Therefore, it is very important *never* to speak anything *negative* but only to make a *positive* confession—hence the name of the Positive Confession movement.

Distorted Views

While the leaders of Positive Confession seem to be sincere Christians and at times preach a clear biblical gospel, there can be no doubt that their errors are extremely serious and could indeed be fatal—if not for them, then certainly for some of their followers who take what they say to its logical conclusion. They have a wrong view of faith: Instead of trust in God as its object, it is a metaphysical force. They have a wrong view of God: He is not sufficient in Himself, but can only do what He does by using this universal faith-force in obedience to certain cosmic laws. They have a wrong view of man: He is a little god in God's class who has the same powers as God and can use the same force of faith by obedience to the same laws that God also must obey. They also have a wrong view of redemption and the cross of Christ, as we shall see later on. Obviously it is extremely serious to be wrong on such vital issues. Lloyd-Jones reminds us:

The man whose doctrine is shaky will be shaky in his whole

life. One almost invariably finds that if a man is wrong on the great central truths of the faith, he is wrong at every other point.[58]

The teaching that we are gods is growing among evangelicals and is leaving a devastating confusion in its wake. While some of those who teach this doctrine seem to both proclaim and disclaim it simultaneously, other leaders in the Positive Confession movement are affirming this teaching ever more boldly on radio and television.[59] In his latest book, one of the best-selling authors in this movement declares:

> Where did Satan get the title of being god of the world? He got it from Adam.... Adam was god over earth, but you spell it with a little "g." ...
> Some people have an image of God being 400 feet tall with arms as big as a building. But why would God make man a different size than He is? I'm convinced He made man just like Himself....
> We were created to be gods over the earth, but remember to spell it with a little "g."[60]

There is only one true God. He has said, "I am God, and there is none else" (Isaiah 45:22). Of course there are many false gods; that is what is meant by spelling god with a little "g." And *none* of them will escape God's judgment, for He has said of *all* gods:

> The gods that have not made the heavens and the earth,
> even they shall perish from the earth, and from under these
> heavens (Jeremiah 10:11).

Scripture-Twisting and Universalism

How can such error be possible when the leaders in this movement allegedly put such strong emphasis upon the Word of God? It has been accomplished by twisting God's Word to make it conform to their beliefs. For example, the phrase "God said," which occurs with each act of creation (Genesis 1:3,6,9,11,14,20,24,26), is cited as proof that there is power in *speaking words*.[61] This is neither biblical nor logical. On the contrary, what God said ("Let there be light...let the earth bring forth grass," etc.) came to pass not because God *said* it, but because it was *God* who said it. Anyone other than God could repeat the same words any number of times and nothing would be created. Moreover, God could create or move to action by simply *willing* it; He doesn't have to *speak* it. The power is in *God*, not in *words*. But by putting the emphasis upon *words*, it follows that man would be able to emulate God's mighty acts. If God does everything by faith in the power of the *words* He speaks forth, then surely man can do the same, since *words* are equally available for him to speak in "faith." The acknowledged leader of the Positive Confession movement writes:

> God had faith in His own words.... Jesus had faith in His own words, too....
> He had that God-kind of faith, then He said to the disciples—and to us—*You* have that kind of faith.[62]

Solomon wrote, "Death and life are in the power of the tongue" (Proverbs 18:21). A king such as Solomon—and he was writing to his son, who would become king in his place—had the power to condemn or to pardon. The same is true of a judge or jury today. A witness in court often has the same power. A gossiper can make life miserable and even destroy marriages and jobs. The "faith teachers," however, interpret Solomon's words to mean that there is some metaphysical force inherent in words that is released when they are spoken and will inevitably bring to pass whatever is said, whether positive or negative.

In the world of the occult, the metaphysical "mind power" of one's belief is reinforced by speaking it aloud. This act releases what occultists call the "creative power of the spoken word" and brings into existence whatever one says or decrees. This occult idea forms the basis for mantras, incantations, and hexes. Nevertheless, the faith teachers continue to expound upon this unbiblical and occult thesis and represent it to be the teaching of Scripture through their ministry in pulpit, radio, and television, and in books such as *The Tongue—A Creative Force*[63] and *You Can Have What You Say*.[64]

Hebrews 11:3 says, "*By faith we understand* that the worlds were framed by the word of God," but the faith teachers turn this declaration around to say, "We understand that it was *by faith that God framed the worlds*." By that simple twist, faith is not *man's belief in God* and what He has revealed, but *a force that God used* to make the universe and that man can also use by following the same "law of faith." Attention is subtly turned from *God* to *faith*, and the results are devastating. Among the thousands of letters received from readers of *The Seduction of Christianity*, the following is typical:

> No wonder my Positive Confession failed. I spent so many years of my Christian life trying to get *the faith that would move a mountain*, when all the time what I needed was *faith in the God who moves mountains*![65]

The most heretical element involved is the teaching that the power of belief is a universal force that works for *anyone* who follows "the law of faith." Whether one has a relationship with God through Jesus Christ is irrelevant when it comes to working "miracles" through the "laws of the fourth [i.e. spirit] dimension." Thus non-Christians and even occultists[66] can utilize this universal "law of faith" just as God allegedly did in creating the cosmos. The recognized leader of Positive Confession writes:

> Jesus said He had the God-kind of faith; He encouraged His disciples to exercise that kind of faith; and He said that *"whosoever"* could do it.
> Why did He say "whosoever"?... The reason is because all men are spirit beings....
> It used to bother me when I'd see unsaved people getting results, but my church members not getting results. Then it dawned on me what the sinners were doing. They were cooperating with this law of God—the law of faith.[67]

Getting Faith in Your Faith

This charismatic version of the metaphysics of the Mind Science cults is gaining increasing credibility in the church. It is an extremely serious heresy. The object of faith becomes *faith itself as a cosmic force*. Attention is devoted to and techniques are developed for *getting faith in faith* instead of *having faith in God*, as Jesus taught. To function as the gods that we were intended to be, we must develop faith in *our* faith just as God allegedly has faith in *His* faith.

Nowhere in the Bible are we told to have "faith in our faith." We have faith *in God*—total, absolute, unquestioning trust—because He is trustworthy and all-powerful. As W. H. Griffith Thomas says in his excellent commentary on Romans, "There is no value or merit in faith, for it derives its efficacy not from the person trusting but from the person trusted."[68] "Faith in faith" is not only unbiblical and a logical absurdity, but it destroys genuine faith in God. A. W. Tozer warned:

> Faith in faith is faith astray. To hope for heaven by means of such faith is to drive in the dark across a deep chasm on a bridge that does not quite reach the other side.[69]

In a 1986 book titled *How To Have Faith In Your Faith*, one of the leaders in the faith movement explains that because "faith in God comes by hearing the Word of God," therefore "faith in your faith comes by hearing yourself speak your faith."[70] In his booklet titled *Having Faith In Your Faith*, the foremost leader in the Positive Confession movement writes:

> That's what you've got to learn to do to get things from God: *Have faith in your faith.*
> It would help you get faith down in your spirit to say out loud: "Faith in my faith." Keep saying it until it registers on your heart. I know it sounds strange when you first say it; your mind almost rebels against it.[71]

Of course the mind ought to rebel against such teaching! But we are urged to put aside reason and common sense and the clear truth of God's Word, and begin instead to repeat this phrase over and over until we finally accept it. This is a brainwashing procedure that has led untold thousands of Christians into delusion and finally disillusionment, and has brought many to a denial of God and complete loss of faith in Him. They have repeatedly "confessed" aloud their healing and prosperity, failed to receive it, felt condemned for their lack of faith, and finally abandoned the whole thing. Many, on the other hand, have been delivered from this pernicious delusion by turning from *faith in faith* to *faith in God*. Typical is the following excerpt of a letter recently received:

As a former adherent to the Word of Faith teaching, my life was hell on earth for three years. This was complicated by the fact that I was in a sort of mystical "fog" during that time—totally out of touch with reality....

Three years ago when I left the "Word" church where I was organist, I was in a used bookstore one day and purchased an old Christian Science hymnal. I was amazed to learn that their songs would be perfectly appropriate in a "Word" church.

Since then, whenever I see one of my old friends from that church, I don't hesitate to tell them that their religion is a Pentecostalized form of Christian Science, which is the American counterpart to Brahmanism [Hinduism]....[72]

The Christian Science Connection

The leading faith teachers at times preach the simple gospel that Christ died for our sins. It is the mixture of seeming orthodoxy and outright error that makes their teaching so confusing. Although it seems to be a harsh charge to call the Positive Confession movement a charismatic form of Christian Science, which in turn is an Americanized version of Hinduism, that charge has been made by many and can be substantiated by simply comparing the similarities in their common beliefs. The leaders in the movement are aware of these similarities and deny the charge:

> You see, sometimes when I start teaching on this folks will say it sounds like *Christian Science*. One lady punched her husband in a service in Texas and said (My wife overheard them.), "*That sounds like Christian Science*."
>
> *It's not Christian Science.* I like what Brother Hagin says, "IT'S CHRISTIAN SENSE"![73]

Positive Confession is basically warmed-over New Thought dressed in evangelical/charismatic language. New Thought, which arose in America during the close of the last century, can in turn be traced to Phineas P. Quimby (1802-1866), whose "studies in mesmerism [hypnosis], spiritism and kindred phenomena... laid the basis for a new structure in the world of thought"[74] and who "was regarded as the founder of the [New Thought] movement."[75] This New England mesmerist, who healed Mary Baker Patterson (later Eddy) in 1862[76] must be credited with the genius of dressing ancient shamanism (witchcraft) in scientific terms to form what he called "the Science of Christ or Truth"[77] and what he later termed "Christian Science."[78]

There can be no doubt that Mrs. Eddy not only borrowed the term "Christian Science" from Quimby, but also derived from him most of the basic ideas that she later claimed were given to her by "revelation." These subsequently became the basis of the Mind Science cult she formed, known today as Christian Science.

Quimby's influence continues in the many Mind Science churches that now form the International New Thought Alliance. At its 1986 National Congress, the president of the Alliance, Unity Church of Christianity minister Blaine C. Mays, declared:

> Finally it's coming out. When one goes to hear them [Norman Vincent Peale and Robert Schuller] they are giving the New Thought message.
>
> Schuller's possibility thinking approach is nothing but New Thought religion, although the leader of the Crystal Cathedral in Southern California doesn't acknowledge it.[79]

It is no mere coincidence that, like Positive/Possibility Thinking, Positive Confession sounds so much like Christian Science. Their roots are undeniably the same. As McConnell notes, E. W. Kenyon, the true founder of Positive Confession, "did adhere to a religious scientism dangerously close to Christian Science."[80] Not only Charles Capps, but Frederick Price[81] and Kenneth Hagin also admit the confusing similarities but don't seem to understand the reason. Hagin writes:

> When I preach on the mind, it frightens some congregations. They immediately think of Christian Science.[82]

Contending for the Faith

So long as we seek faith as a power that we can use to secure blessings for ourselves or others, we are denying the true faith and playing into the hands of the one who will come with "all power and signs and lying wonders" (2 Thessalonians 2:9).

Paul warns that the opposition to the truth of God that we

must guard against and contend with in the last days will not come primarily from those who reject the supernatural, but from those who seem to work miracles. Referring to Jannes and Jambres, Pharaoh's magicians who "withstood Moses" by duplicating with satanic power the miracles that God did through Moses and Aaron, Paul declares that there will be similar miracle-workers who will "resist the truth: men of corrupt minds, reprobate concerning the faith" (2 Timothy 3:8).

It is clear from Scripture that genuine miracles will also continue in the last days. Otherwise anything that seemed miraculous would automatically be identified as coming from Satan. Because miracles have not ceased, we are warned that *discernment* will be needed to distinguish between God's true miracles and Satan's clever counterfeits. The warning is solemn, and we dare not ignore it. Again Paul reminds us that *truth* is paramount. *What* we believe is the issue, not simply *that* we believe. This is not because we cause what we believe to occur or to come into existence, but because we will either believe God's *truth* (the faith) or Satan's *lie*.

We must be very careful that we do not twist God's Word to suit our selfish or even well-intended desires or theories, but that we let it teach and guide us. And we must turn from any message that directs its primary focus upon man rather than upon God, which aims more at securing blessings for self than at crucifying self and glorifying God. With passion, Charles Colson writes:

> For the church, this ought to be an hour of opportunity. The church alone can provide a moral vision to a wandering people; the church alone can step into the vacuum and demonstrate that there is a sovereign, living God who is the source of Truth.
>
> BUT, the church is in almost as much trouble as the culture, for the church has bought into the same value system: fame, success, materialism, and celebrity.... Preoccupation with these values has also perverted the church's message. The assistant to one renowned media pastor, when asked the key to his man's success, replied without hesitation, "We give the people what they want."
>
> This heresy is at the root of the most dangerous message preached today: the what's-in-it-for-me gospel.[83]

We dare not—we must not—stand by in silence, afraid to speak for fear of offending or causing division, while *the faith* once-for-all committed to the saints is misrepresented. We must not compromise, for to do so does not help but hinder the cause of truth. Failure to contend earnestly for the faith dishonors God, and, while it may avoid hurt feelings and damaged egos, it destroys souls for whom Christ died. If the love of Christ rules our hearts, then we will earnestly contend for the faith that He has delivered to us.

4

Submission to Love

Thou shalt love the Lord thy God with all thine heart, and with all thy soul, and with all thy might. And these words which I command thee this day shall be in thine heart (Deuteronomy 6:5,6).

If ye keep my commandments, ye shall abide in my love, even as I have kept my Father's commandments, and abide in his love (John 15:10).

This is love, that we walk after his commandments (2 John 6).

When he [Jesus] was come near, he beheld the city [Jerusalem], and wept over it (Luke 19:41).

LOVE AND OBEDIENCE are inextricably intertwined in Scripture. Because God loves us, He wants us to keep His commandments, for they "are not grievous" (1 John 5:3) but are for our good (Deuteronomy 10:12,13). Real faith grows out of a love relationship with God. As we get to know Him and His love, we become confident that His way is best and that whatever He allows in our lives, even if painful or incomprehensible to us at the time, is first of all for His glory but will also bring blessing to us because we belong to Him. No longer do we want to get *power* from Him in order to command our circumstances to conform to what we would be pleased with, but we want to *obey* Him so that He can be glorified in us, "whether by life or by death" (Philippians 1:20). One of the least-understood truths of Scripture is that such obedience for the Christian is not enforced adherence to law but willing submission to a love so profound that we have not even begun to plumb its fathomless depths. That will take eternity:

> Eye hath not seen, nor ear heard, neither have entered into the heart of man, the things which God hath prepared for them that love him (1 Corinthians 2:9).
>
> Unto him that is able to do exceeding abundantly above all that we ask or think, according to the power that worketh in us (Ephesians 3:20).
>
> That in the ages to come he might show the exceeding riches of his grace in his kindness toward us through Christ Jesus (Ephesians 2:7).

As we have already seen, a major problem with Positive Confession, as with its secular, liberal, and occult counterparts (Positive Mental Attitude, Positive/Possibility Thinking, and Mind Science), is its self-centered orientation and therefore its shallow comprehension of the cause of suffering and death and its imposition of a simplistic solution upon the problem. As a result, God is sought for the *gifts* He gives rather than for *who* He is. Love is no longer pure but is polluted by self-interest. The main pursuit is blessing instead of the Blesser, gifts rather than the Giver, power instead of purity, healing rather than holiness. The thirst for possessions replaces thirst for God; yet even if possessions are obtained, prosperity makes a poor substitute for love. There is an attempt through formulas to establish God's kingdom upon a false basis and before its time—and with self as king.

The Roots of the Positive Confession Movement

Called by *Charisma* magazine "the grandaddy of the faith teachers,"[1] Kenneth Hagin is generally considered to be the founder of the Positive Confession movement. Most of today's leading "faith teachers" credit Hagin as their mentor, and it is his gospel that they preach. After them comes a growing number of young pastors and faith teachers (many of them graduates of Hagin's Rhema Bible Training Center in Tulsa, Oklahoma) who are doctrinally almost carbon copies of either Hagin or his most successful protege, Kenneth Copeland. These men and women generally make no secret of Hagin's influence upon their lives and ministries. Typical are the comments of Frederick K. C. Price: "Kenneth Hagin has had the greatest influence upon my life of any living man...his books...revolutionized and changed my life"; and Charles Capps: "Brother Hagin was the greatest influence of my life."[2] Kenneth Copeland confesses that Hagin's tapes revolutionized his ministry.[3]

Kenneth Hagin's gospel, however, is not original with him, but much of his teaching can be traced back to the writings of E. W. Kenyon, who first taught "the positive confession of the Word of God"[4] and must be recognized as the real founder of today's Positive Confession movement. It was Kenyon who first presented to the church the idea of "*now* faith,"[5] that faith "is a confession,"[6] that "what I confess, I possess,"[7] and that we create reality with the words of our mouths ("Faith's confessions create realities").[8] Kenyon also taught the basic principles that make Positive Confession possible: that man is a little god "in God's class"[9] and therefore can utilize the same universal forces that God does[10] and which are available to Christian and non-Christian alike. Laying the foundation for what Kenneth Hagin presents in *Having Faith In Your Faith*[11] (and which Paul Yonggi Cho later developed in more detail in his best-selling *The Fourth Dimension*),[12] Kenyon even acknowledged that Mind Science cultists could utilize these "spiritual laws":

> Natural man can develop his spirit until it becomes a force in him. We see this in Christian Science, Unity, Spiritualism and other psychological religions....
>
> Few of us realize that the greatest forces are not material, but spiritual.[13]

Numerous Kenyonisms have been popularized by Kenneth Hagin and mimicked by his followers. Kenyon's concept of "creative faith"[14] formed the basis for Hagin's teaching (some of which contains word-for-word repetitions of Kenyon) that *anyone* can develop these universal "laws of faith" to get what he wants.[15] Kenyon's teachings about "the power of words" and his warnings never to make a "negative confession" but only a "positive" one[16] not only deeply influenced Hagin but changed the thinking and ministry of many others who are recognized today to be the leaders of this movement. Charles Capps refers to Kenyon as "a man born before his time...with great revelation knowledge."[17] Another faith teacher confesses:

> Suddenly I was aware that my ministry was being influenced in an overwhelming manner by the writings of Dr. Kenyon.[18]

Most of those whom Kenyon influenced were not aware that they had embraced charismatic occultism (Farah calls it "charismatic humanism").[19] Yet the relationship of Positive Confession to New Thought's scientific shamanism is clear. Its similarities to the teachings of the Mind Science cults cannot be denied.

Kenyon and New Thought

It was probably during his attendance toward the end of the last century at "Emerson College of Oratory in Boston,"[20] a hotbed of New Thought at the time (one friend of the college said, "It ought to be called 'The First *Church* of Emerson' "),[21] that Kenyon first became acquainted with the metaphysical ideas that he later dressed in biblical language to form the foundation of today's Positive Confession movement.

McConnell declares, "That he [Kenyon] was taught its philosophy in the class rooms of Emerson College is a historical certainty."[22] In his definitive work on New Thought, in which he identifies Norman Vincent Peale as the one man "through whose ministry essentially New Thought ideas and techniques have been made known most widely in America,"[23] Charles S. Braden gives this brief summary of its major tenets:

> Three or four words pretty well identify the New Thought and those kindred movements that derive from it: health or healing, abundance or prosperity—sometimes even wealth—and happiness.[24]

"Sometimes even wealth" is an understatement when it comes to the prosperity that Positive Confession is said to bring. Hagin teaches that for a pastor or *anyone* to drive a Chevrolet instead of a luxury car isn't "being humble, that's being ignorant"[25] of God's "law of prosperity" that works for "whoever you are," saint or sinner. Even a non-Christian honors God by getting "into contact with that law.''[26] Missing completely what Jesus is saying, Gloria Copeland enthusiastically declares:

> You give $1 for the Gospel's sake and $100 belongs to you; you give $10 and receive $1000; give $1000 and receive $100,000. I know that you can multiply, but I want you to see it in black and white....
>
> Give one airplane and receive one hundred times the value of the airplane. Give one car and the return would furnish you a lifetime of cars. In short, Mark 10:30 is a very good deal.[27]

Those who promote this prosperity teaching become wealthy through heavy appeals for funds. They point to themselves as proof that their prosperity gospel works, as though money drops from the sky. In fact it has been given to them by those who have been persuaded to do so under the impression that they are planting a "seed-faith offering" that will return to them "100-fold." The prosperity teachers' followers, however, are at a distinct disadvantage in attempting to put this doctrine into practice without the large mailing lists and radio or television audiences of their mentors and imagine that their failure is due to a lack of faith. Billy Graham recently expressed the opinion that "some television evangelists" are setting a bad example by their emphasis on money and "ostentatious lifestyle." Graham stated with concern:

> They are hurting the cause of Christ. I think our lifestyle has to match our work.[28]

The Health-and-Wealth Gospel

There seems to be no shortage of covetous Christians eager to hear the "prosperity message." Perhaps some are sincerely deceived by the persuasive use of a few proof-texts and the authoritative manner of the faith teachers and are thus to be pitied. They naively overlook the obvious contradictions in the fervent and repeated reminders from leading faith teachers that say "I need you to continue...to support this ministry,"[29] don't forget to "enclose your seed-faith offering in the envelope."[30] Disillusionment comes when they discover too late that their "seed-faith" offerings, instead of returning money to their own pockets as promised, are only making wealthy those who invented and are propagating this false doctrine. Those who drop out, however, are quickly replaced by others equally eager to get rich from "giving to God."

To expect a financial return is not biblical *giving* but secular *investing*. While it is legitimate to place money in a savings account to draw interest, there is no eternal reward for doing so. And to give to charity or a Christian ministry in order to get a monetary reward here upon earth is to rob oneself of an eternal reward in heaven. We cannot have it both ways. Jesus said:

> Lay not up for yourselves treasures upon earth, where moth and rust doth corrupt, and where thieves break through and steal; but lay up for yourselves treasures in heaven, where neither moth nor rust doth corrupt, and where thieves do not break through nor steal; for where your treasure is, there will your heart be also (Matthew 6:19-21).

Paul declared that giving "all my goods to feed the poor" and even giving "my body to be burned" would bring no heavenly reward unless done out of pure love. And he explains that love seeks nothing for itself and expects nothing in return (1 Corinthians 13:1-8). Attempting to justify the "seed-faith" concept, one of the leaders in this movement stated on a widely-viewed Christian talk show in early 1986 that if we do not expect to get *money* multiplied back to us when we give money to God's work, we are "mocking God." This, he explained, was the meaning of "God is not mocked: for whatsoever a man soweth, that shall he also reap" (Galatians 6:7).[31] The next verse, however, contradicts such an interpretation:

> He that soweth to his flesh shall of the flesh reap corruption; but he that soweth to the Spirit shall of the Spirit reap life everlasting (Galatians 6:8).

Money is clearly not the subject of this Scripture. Yet the regular cohosts of the network program added their amens of approval to this twisted interpretation. This same leader in the "faith movement," whose teaching has influenced thousands and perhaps millions of people in the church, when asked by *Time* magazine with evident surprise whether he wasn't "tithing to *get*," replied:

> Yes, yes, yes! A thousand times yes! I want to get healed, I want to get well, I want to get money, I want to get prosperous![32]

The "health-and-wealth gospel," as it has been called by critics, neglects almost entirely any teaching on holiness and other important biblical themes. Paul declared that those who suppose "that gain is godliness" are "destitute of the truth" (1 Timothy 6:5) and went on to warn against seeking wealth. Yet the prosperity teachers claim that God has impressed upon them the great importance for these days of conducting "prosperity seminars" and teaching "God's laws of prosperity."[33] They have one major proof-text: "Beloved, I wish above all things that thou mayest prosper and be in health, even as thy soul prospereth" (3 John 2). Ken Sarles points out that the term John uses "does not refer to financial wealth but simply means 'to go well' "[34]—which is in fact the way the New International Version translates it: "that all may go well with you." Gordon Fee elaborates:

> This combination of wishing for "things to go well" and for the recipients' "good health" was the standard form of greeting in a personal letter in antiquity. To extend John's wish for Gaius to refer to financial and material prosperity for all Christians, of all times...is to abuse the text, not use it.[35]

"Prosperity" is mentioned only two more times in the entire New Testament, which seems hardly an adequate basis for a "prosperity gospel," much less for teaching that every Christian's divine right is to be wealthy. In 1 Corinthians 16:2 financial prosperity is included in the meaning, but in Romans 1:10, where Paul (using the same Greek word) speaks of his desire to make "a prosperous journey" to Rome, he is clearly not hoping to become wealthy on that trip but refers to the blessing of God upon his ministry. This would also seem to be what John has in mind, for he plainly states that his greatest joy comes from knowing that his "children walk in truth" (3 John 4).

Truth is indeed the issue and is mentioned more than 100 times in the New Testament. Biblical Christianity requires majoring on what the Bible emphasizes rather than building doctrines and ministries upon the tenuous foundation of a few verses, particularly where there are clear warnings against the very thing being promoted, as is the case with wealth. We must take great care not to read into Scripture what we want it to say.

For Paul, God's blessing upon his life and ministry never involved a *financial* reward, but rather the opposite: "weariness and painfulness, in watchings often, in hunger and thirst, in fastings often, in cold and nakedness, in stripes [floggings] above measure, in prisons more frequent, in deaths oft" (2 Corinthians 11:23-33). The same was true of the other apostles. It is an insult to them (and to the Holy Spirit who inspired them) to teach that a major theme of their writings is financial success, without which we are lacking in faith.

Redemption and the Cross

There is something even worse than the unscriptural emphasis upon health and wealth—it is the unbiblical view of the cross that accompanies such teachings. The doctrine of redemption (along with the teaching that we are gods) represents the most serious heresy of the Positive Confession movement.

Just before He died on the cross, Jesus cried in triumph, "It is finished!" (John 19:30). Down through history the church has always understood this to mean that *the work of redemption was finished.* E. W. Kenyon, however, taught that Christ was merely announcing "the end of the Abrahamic covenant"[36] and that the Aaronic "priesthood was finished."[37] "But Christ did not mean that He had finished His Substitutionary work...."[38] Reflecting Kenyon's influence, Kenneth Copeland teaches:

> The cross of Calvary...is where the final redemptive work of Jesus began.
> When Jesus cried, *It is finished!* He was not speaking of the plan of redemption. There were still three days and nights to go through before He went to the throne....
> Jesus' death on the cross was only the beginning of the complete work of redemption.[39]

It was just after this cry of triumph "with a loud voice" that

Jesus declared with confidence, "Father, into thy hands I commend my spirit" (Luke 23:46). Kenyon, however, taught that Jesus wasn't in His Father's hands at all, but in the hands of Satan in hell: "When Jesus died, His spirit was taken by the Adversary [Satan], and carried to the place where the sinner's spirit goes when he dies."[40] There He took on the very nature of Satan and was tortured for three days and nights: "He became one with Satan in spiritual death to make us one with God in spiritual life."[41]

It is blasphemous to suggest that Satan had to torture Christ in order to effect our redemption. That would make Satan as much our Savior as Christ Himself. Our redemption would then depend upon whether Satan tortured Christ to the full extent. How can we be sure that he did so? Shall we thank him if he did?

The Bible always links redemption with what happened on the cross. It is never even implied, much less taught, that redemption took place in hell. Paul declared that he would glory in nothing except "the cross of our Lord Jesus Christ" (Galatians 6:14). We are told that Christ "became obedient unto death, even the death of the cross" (Philippians 2:8). There is no hint that He also died spiritually in hell at the hands of Satan. We have "redemption through his blood" (Ephesians 1:7; Colossians 1:14) and not by reason of tortures which Satan inflicted upon Christ. His blood was shed on the cross, not in hell, and it is explicitly stated in Scripture that He "made peace through the blood of his cross" (Colossians 1:20). The song of the redeemed in heaven throughout eternity will forever be to Him "that loved us, and washed us from our sins in his own blood" (Revelation 1:5; cf. 5:9). What a contrast these and many other similar Scriptures present to Kenneth Copeland's assurance that "When His blood poured out, it did not atone..."![42] Could this false view of redemption cost those who believe it the very salvation that Christ accomplished on the cross?

Healing and Miracles

There is another teaching within the Positive Confession movement that comes from Kenyon and is wreaking havoc in many lives: "It is wrong for us to have sickness and disease in our bodies....[43] It is not the Father's will that any die of disease. Sickness does not belong to the body of Christ."[44] Kenyon taught that we must confess that we are healed even though we still have the symptoms of disease.[45]

There are sufficient verifiable healings today to show anyone with an open mind that God still does miracles. Take for example Barbara Cummiskey, whose body, though ravaged from years of multiple sclerosis, an incurable disease, was instantly healed on June 7, 1981. God spoke to her in a quiet voice that Barbara heard "over her shoulder": "My child, get up and walk." As Rodney Clapp reported in *Christianity Today*:

> Barbara Cummiskey, her doctors admit, should never have gotten well, but not only did the MS leave... Barbara's caved-in lung dormant for years... was completely healthy and functioning. The chronic lung disease, also "incurable," was gone. So were the hand and feet tumors.
>
> Even if the woman somehow recovered from MS, there should have been permanent nerve damage. There was none... health was entirely restored instantaneously.[46]

That the vast majority of those who are prayed for are not miraculously healed, however, demonstrates that something is seriously wrong with the Positive Confession concept and serves as an indictment of the mixture of outright fraud, exaggeration, wishful thinking, gullibility, and self-centered carnality that characterize so much of the "healing" scene today. All of the talk about "healings and miracles" with so little to show for it gives fuel to the arguments of the skeptics and eventually erodes the faith of those who were misled for a time. How disillusioning it is to see through the froth of promotion to the actual results! And how instructive to know that Barbara Cummiskey's healing came without the involvement of any "faith healer" or "Positive Confession." She had no explanation as to why it had happened, no formula to give anyone else. Said Barbara:

> God never promised me I'd understand everything. Not when I was sick. Not now. He just says, "Love me, my child, and accept me."[47]

No one involved in "faith healing" is better known or more highly regarded by the leading charismatics than Oral Roberts, who began his ministry in Enid, Oklahoma, in 1947. One would expect to find more than ample evidence for "faith healing" at Roberts's City of Faith medical center. It was built at the specific command of a "900-foot Jesus" who, during a seven-hour conversation with Roberts,[48] promised cures for cancer and other diseases if his "prayer partners" would each contribute 240 dollars and thereby provide the funds to finish this huge medical complex. The donors came through with more than the 150 million dollars required. According to Roberts, "God told me to...merge His healing streams of prayer and medicine."[49] After the City of Faith had been in operation for a number of years, *Health* magazine made the following statement as the result of a special study of healing:

> Surprisingly, however, [City of Faith] hospital spokesmen have no faith-healing statistics to offer and are even unwilling to say that combining prayer with medicine cures more frequently or hastens healing any more quickly than medicine itself.[50]

No faith-healing statistics? Yet prayer letters from Oral Roberts soliciting "urgent help" for support have declared that "the City of Faith" (described as late as July 1986 as "a state-of-the-art shell, roughly half of it sitting empty"[51]) is helping patients like no other hospital "by merging prayer and medicine."[52] Declaring that "we minister God's healing power in so many ways to thousands of people," this same funds appeal offered to donors the hope of "your own miracle" as their reward for a "seed-faith offering."[53]

Obvious and Serious Discrepancies

There seems to be some discrepancy between the loose talk of "miracles" by the "trainload"[54] in promotional material sent out to stir the donors to give yet more and the careful language of those involved at the medical center. For example, Duie Jernigan, director of Oral Roberts's City of Faith prayer partner ministry, has admitted, "There are no more miracles at the City of Faith than any other hospital. Just as many patients die."[55]

That shocking admission stands in stark contrast to the extravagant claims of healings and miracles that continue to come forth not only from Oral Roberts but from many other leaders in the so-called "faith movement." And now in his desire to share the miracles with even more people, Roberts is building a 15-million-dollar "Healing Center" adjacent to his City of Faith that will include a "Seed Faith Center," where visitors can apply to their own "practical needs" Roberts's "concept of planting a 'seed of faith' to obtain results in spiritual, physical and financial needs."[56]

In January 1986 Roberts called together 27 of the top leaders of the charismatic movement to form Charismatic Bible Ministries in what participants considered to be "one of the greatest moves of unity" in history.[57] "Signs and wonders as confirmation that the gospel is being fully preached" is the major emphasis of the newly formed group. Says Roberts, "I personally do not believe that the gospel can be *fully* preached without signs and wonders."[58] If that is the case, we would be forced to conclude that the Wesleys, Whitefields, Finneys, and Moodys of the past, who saw thousands of people saved without "signs and wonders," didn't fully preach the gospel.

Moreover, such a requirement would also mean that today's major evangelists such as Jimmy Swaggart and Billy Graham are not fully preaching the gospel. Of course the same would also have to be said for the ministry of Oral Roberts and his City of Faith, where the promised miracles seem conspicuously rare.

An Appeal to Face the Facts Honestly

When honestly questioning whether something is genuinely from God is condemned as being "negative" and is labeled as unbelief, the church is set up for all manner of deception. And the climate is doubly conducive to delusion where healing and speaking in tongues are badly overemphasized and "miracle" crusades are advertised as though God will perform on command.

As a further example, a major healing ministry in the Los Angeles area saw 80 "miraculous healings" one Saturday evening in a crusade that had those attending applauding the Lord with joyful fervor. What a time it was for strengthening one's faith!

And what a disillusioning experience for the young man who, as part of this ministry, followed up these "miracles" over the next two weeks. Instead of the testimonies he expected to obtain, he discovered that *not one* of the 80 had actually been healed! Yet many of them had sincerely testified to "healings" that evening in front of thousands—being themselves deceived into an apparent temporary psychosomatic loss of their symptoms by the mass enthusiasm.

While many more examples similar to the above could be given, there is no intention to deny that God is still doing miracles today. However, we must have the moral integrity to reject the counterfeit at the same time that the genuine is defended. The faith to believe that God can and will do today the same miracles that the early church experienced is hindered rather than helped by hailing as miraculous what is actually fraud or else temporary psychosomatic relief of minor ailments generated by mass enthusiasm. That kind of dishonesty can only lead to growing disillusionment and finally an abandonment of the faith altogether.

Where "signs and wonders" are regarded more highly than purity of doctrine and life, the passion for "miracles" can become a snare. Referring to Fuller Theological Seminary's MC510 course, "Signs and Wonders," Ben Patterson wrote:

> What do you do with the people who are not healed? This question was foremost in the minds of many of the faculty. Did Satan win one? If so, then Satan holds a commanding lead in the game, because the majority of people who are prayed for do not, in fact, get well physically.
>
> A subtle, but powerful, pressure therefore builds in the Signs and Wonders mentality to see miracles where there are none. Some faculty members were outraged at what they felt were wild, unsubstantiated reports of healings coming out of the meetings of MC510.[59]

The Need for Holiness and Obedience

Concerning the gifts of the Spirit, A. W. Tozer wrote: "Those who deny that the gifts are for us today and those who insist upon making a hobby of one gift are both wrong, and we are all suffering the consequence of their error."[60] Although this is still a controversial topic, the majority of evangelical Christians, while understandably cautious, are willing to concede at least the possibility of the gifts for today on the basis that God can do in any age whatever He wills. The condition for blessing, however, has not changed:

> Behold, the Lord's hand is not shortened, that it cannot save, neither his ear heavy, that it cannot hear; but your iniquities have separated between you and your God, and your sins have hid his face from you, that he will not hear (Isaiah 59:1,2).

When God's power was bared fully at the beginning of Israel's journey from Egypt to Canaan, to gather sticks on the Sabbath or to mock one's parents was punishable with death. Had that standard been maintained, miracles would have continued, but most of Israel would have died. God therefore withheld His judgment—but the holy presence that accompanied His mighty works was also withdrawn, and miracles became few and far between, as they are today.

So it has been with the church. The only "slaying in the Spirit" that can be substantiated from Scripture was the death of Ananias and Sapphira. Yet their sin was not so grievous by today's standards. They gave to the Lord a far larger percentage of all they had than most of us do today, but they exaggerated, claiming to have given all when they had actually held some back. They died for their sin of exaggeration—yet how many exaggerated testimonies are still being told! We want God's miracle-working power, but are we willing to pay the price? His holy presence does not come in response to seminars and techniques. The argument over whether the gifts of the Spirit are for today will only be answered in power too obvious to deny when we begin to "hunger and thirst after *righteousness*" (Matthew 5:6) instead of after prosperity, and when we put holiness ahead of healing.

The Need for Balance

Questionable manifestations of what is purportedly miraculous power from the Holy Spirit abound today because millions of

Christians seem to have little knowledge of God and His Word and even less discernment. As a result, they are content with the weekly whipping up of frenzied enthusiasm in many congregations and "miracle crusades" across America and are seemingly favorably impressed by the exhibitionism of many "faith healers." As one reviewer of a popular book which suggests that signs and wonders are essential for what it calls "power evangelism" has observed:

> Fakery and manipulation are easy when one is operating in the realm of the supernatural. False claims are difficult to test. . . .
>
> Furthermore, the masses are easily excited by charismania, by an overemphasis on the spectacular, to the detriment of the ongoing works of charity. A generation whipped up to a frenzy by high-tech show biz may well demand charismatic Christianity and be bored with anything else.
>
> But we must be careful not to tailor our presentation to market requirements.[61]

While the importance of the gifts of the Holy Spirit for the church today should not be minimized, we must be equally careful not to give them an emphasis that the New Testament does not. In doing so we become unbalanced and vulnerable to heresy, which usually results simply from carrying some truth to an extreme. We are warned, "Despise not prophesyings" (1 Thessalonians 5:20), but we are equally warned in the very next verse to "prove all things." Failure to follow this command encourages the many false declarations, whether alleged prophecies, interpretations of tongues, or words of knowledge, that pour forth continually in the name of the Lord. Unfortunately, where they fail to come to pass correction is not administered for fear of being negative.

No true prophecy will contradict or add to or take from the Bible. We are not to gullibly accept everything a self-proclaimed prophet prefaces with "Thus saith the Lord." We are instructed, "Forbid not to speak with tongues" (1 Corinthians 14:39); but that is no license to ignore the specific restrictions placed upon this gift or to assign to it a function or value that cannot be supported from Scripture. Although we are to desire spiritual gifts, our purpose must be to glorify Him and to serve and bring blessing to others through whatever gifts the Lord grants. And always our passion must be love for the Giver rather than for the gifts.

Dave Wilkerson raises these solemn questions:

> How many of us would serve Him if He offered nothing but Himself? No healing. No success. No prosperity. No worldly blessings. No miracles, signs, or wonders.
>
> What if—once again we had to take joyfully the spoiling of our goods? . . .
>
> What if—instead of painless living, we suffered cruel mockings, stoning, bloodshed, being sawn asunder?
>
> What if—instead of our beautiful homes and cars, we had to wander about in deserts in sheepskins, hiding in dens and caves?
>
> What if—instead of prosperity, we were destitute, afflicted, and tormented? *And the only better thing provided for us was Christ?*[62]

Power Evangelism

The overemphasis upon and obsessive seeking after the *power* of the Spirit has caused many to forget that He is the "Spirit of *truth*" who leads us into "all *truth*" and the *"Holy* Spirit" who purifies our lives to God's glory. *Power* has thus taken on a very narrow meaning. The power that is manifested in miracles is more highly regarded than the power of truth to change hearts and deliver from bondage to sin. Dave Wilkerson writes:

> Satan is not afraid of power-hungry saints, but he trembles at the sound of a praying saint![63]

Sound doctrine loses its importance, while experiences are eagerly cultivated and made the basis for understanding God's will and even for interpreting His Word. Those in charge of Christian media who promote this pseudospirituality must take much of the responsibility for popularizing the error that *signs and wonders* are essential to a full proclamation of the gospel. In contrast, Scripture clearly says:

> I am not ashamed of the gospel of Christ, for *it* is the power of God unto salvation to every one that believeth, to the Jew first and also to the Greek (Romans 1:16).

> The preaching of the cross is to them that perish foolishness; but unto us which are saved it is the power of God.... It pleased God by the foolishness of preaching to save them that believe (1 Corinthians 1:18,21).

The idea that "power evangelism" requires miracles has not been the understanding or the emphasis of the church in the past. Paul declared that "the power" is in the preaching of the cross. Even in the book of Acts there were instances of powerful gospel preaching with many pagans converted (Paul *"so spoke* that a great multitude...believed"—Acts 14:1) without any miracles being performed. There were other occasions when great miracles occurred, yet the crowd's reaction was to beat and imprison Paul and his companions or force them to flee. Of God's power to change lives Spurgeon wrote:

> The power lies in the grace of God and not in our faith.
> Great messages can be sent along slender wires, and the peace-giving witness of the Holy Spirit can reach the heart by means of a threadlike faith which seems almost unable to sustain its own weight.
> Think more of Him to whom you look than of the look itself. You must look away even from your own looking and see nothing but Jesus and the grace of God revealed in Him.[64]

Tragic Consequences of Positive Confession

There is a deeper purpose that God wants to work in our hearts than miracles can produce. And often the desire for healing can stand in the way of that molding and maturing that God in His love wants to effect in our lives. Our insistence upon a miraculous healing when there is medical means available is like refusing to look before crossing a busy street and insisting that God must prevent any cars from hitting us. In response to an angry letter from a pastor of a Positive Confession or "Word Church," Jimmy Swaggart replied:

> Let's look at the "name it and claim it philosophy."
> Just the other day a dear pastor told me of a prominent Brother in his church (incidentally, a man with whom I am acquainted) who watched his daughter die because of this unscriptural philosophy.

He had been taught by some of the men you have named [and defended] that if we pray for someone's healing and then confess that the individual is healed, there is no way that person cannot be healed. Consequently, we should not confess that they are sick, neither should we seek the help of a doctor (if a healing has not come), but should continue to confess the healing.

The poor Brother continued to confess the healing; the little girl died. He sat with head in hands, out of his mind, telling his pastor, "I killed my baby!"[65]

Similar tragedies have occurred countless times to sincere Christians who have tried to put into practice what they have been taught about "faith." One widely publicized case was that of Wesley Parker, whose parents withheld needed insulin from him, even when he sank into a diabetic coma. They persisted in denying the symptoms, as they had been taught, and confessed his healing. He died nevertheless. How heartbreaking to read the story in the book *We Let Our Son Die!*[66]

It is ironic that the insistence upon health and wealth so often brings just the opposite. Christ's teaching that His disciples must endure persecution and accept the path of suffering and the cross is the very antithesis of Positive Confession. Indeed, in some ways this teaching is the enemy of the cross. Charles Farah deplores "its emphasis on the centrality of man's desires, aspirations and ambitions; its eager and unabashed lust for wealth...its emphasis on the practical sovereignty of man as over and against the sovereignty of God."[67] In the closing paragraphs of his thesis on the *Kenyon Connection*, Dan McConnell says with obvious sorrow:

The crass materialism of the doctrine of prosperity propagated in the Faith Movement has made a mockery of the cross and the call of Christ to self-denial and servanthood.

...neither Kenyon nor Hagin probably ever realized that what made their teaching distinctive and attractive was its cultic obsession with health and wealth.[68]

A Striking Contrast

Happy are those who have obeyed the command to deny self, take up the cross, and follow their Savior and Lord. They have a faith that rests in God's love even in the face of what would otherwise appear to be tragedy of unbearable proportions. Recently a close friend, a young and apparently healthy mother of only 33 years of age who was living a vital Christian life of service to others, was suddenly taken by a massive heart attack. It was all the more a shock because it was the last thing even a medical expert would have expected. Her young husband, now left to raise two small boys, read the following statement at the funeral:

MY ONE REQUEST

I want you to know that everything in this funeral is intended to be conveyed with my sweetheart's personality and purpose of life in mind. The songs of the soloist were from her favorite album, the selections of the organist, her best-loved hymns, and the minister, the man who performed our wedding ceremony 5 years and 36 days ago.

I want to clarify, as I know Michelle would want me to, that this will not be a ceremony full of empty words that are sanctimoniously uttered before we finally acknowledge the defeat of death and another young life for reasons unknown to us tragically wasted. For myself, my boys, and our family we cannot deny the tragedy of Michelle's passing and the great void left in our lives, but I refuse to view any part of Michelle's life or death as wasted.

She saw purpose in her life. She did not just live life to the fullest, though she did. She was not just committed to being the best wife, mother, sister, daughter or friend one could be, though she was, but her purpose was to know and love the Lord Jesus Christ with all her heart and to express His image as best she could to all she came into contact with.

I know few people who live or have lived their lives with the purpose and vitality of Michelle. How then can I feel that any purpose would be served in her untimely death when it seemed life had so much more to offer? I submit to you that we *all* are the purpose in her death, if we will only soften our hearts and be sensitive to the voice of God expressed in memory of Michelle Youree Mellinger in this service.

I entreat you to consider carefully all that is said and done here today, as I know Michelle not only endorsed it but believed it and lived it. We have been *touched* by her life; now let us be *moved* by her death.

What a contrast between the "positive confession" of the father who sought to deny the truth and change the facts of physical disease to suit his desires (but ended in inconsolable grief) and the submission to God's mysterious but loving and wise will on the part of the young man who had so suddenly lost his dearly loved wife of 5 years and 36 days. His declaration, courageously read at the funeral, was the incomprehensible triumph of a faith that could not be shaken. Even in the face of such a loss, unlike those who sorrow because they have no such hope, he remained confident of God's loving care.

In spite of the sorrows and sufferings of this life, the Christian has the assurance that "all things work together for good to them that love God, to them who are the called according to his purpose" (Romans 8:28). It was clear to all who attended that never-to-be-forgotten funeral service that the bereaved young husband was utterly convinced that he was submitting to God's perfect wisdom and love, even though events were beyond his comprehension.

What is the stuff of which such faith is made? It comes from a confidence that when all seems dark and we cannot understand, that even then, as Charles Colson says, "God often uses what we least expect for His divine purposes."[69] More than a hundred years ago, in a sermon preached at the Metropolitan Tabernacle in London, Charles Spurgeon declared:

> Do you think we love God for what we get out of Him, and for nothing else? Is that your notion of a Christian's love to God? This is how the ungodly talk, and that is what the devil thought was Job's case. Says he: "Does Job fear God for naught? Hast thou not set a hedge about him, and all that he has?" (Job 1:9,10). The devil does not understand real love and affection; but the child of God can tell the devil to his face that he loves God if he covers him with sores and sets him on the dunghill, and by God's good help he means to cling to God through troubles tenfold heavier than those he has had to bear, should they come upon him.
>
> Is He not a blessed God? Yes, let the beds of our sickness ring

with it: He is a blessed God. In the night watches, when we are weary, and our brain is hot and fevered, and our soul is distracted, we yet confess that He is a blessed God. Every ward of the hospital where believers are found should echo with that note.

A blessed God? "Yes, that He is," say the poor and needy... and so say all God's poor throughout all the land. A blessed God? "Yes," say His dying people, "as he slays us we will bless His name. He loves us, and we love Him; and, though all His waves go over us, and His wrath lieth sore upon us, we would not change with kings on their thrones, if they are without the love of God."[70]

5
Unbelief Has Many Faces

Jesus answering saith unto them, Have faith in God (Mark 11:22).

When the Son of man cometh, shall he find faith on the earth? (Luke 18:8).

CONSIDERED BY MANY to be of paramount importance yet scorned by many others, "faith" is a topic surrounded not only by perpetual controversy but by great misunderstanding. Oddly enough, many Christians seem to be nearly as confused as atheists on this subject. For example, both believers and unbelievers generally consider reason to be the enemy of faith, when in fact they are close partners. Indeed, without a questioning attitude "faith" is mere credulity.

Most critics of Christianity mistakenly equate faith with an irrational belief, which, in spite of contrary evidence, doggedly hangs on to a pet superstition out of stubborn loyalty and pride. Ridiculing faith as anti-intellectual and therefore beneath serious consideration, the skeptic scoffingly insists that faith requires a person to abandon scholarship, critical thinking, and common sense. Nothing could be further from the truth. C. H. Spurgeon, known as "the prince of preachers," declared:

> Faith is not a blind thing, for faith begins with knowledge. It is not a speculative thing, for faith believes facts of which it is sure.
> It is not an impractical, dreamy thing, for faith trusts and stakes its destiny upon the truth of [God's] revelation.[1]

Only a complete fool puts his confidence in what is obviously false. It could be equally serious to put "faith" in someone or something without sound reason for doing so. To prevent such folly is the essential role of the God-given qualities of skepticism and reason. Indeed, the critical faculties must be properly used to their fullest extent if one is to arrive where faith would lead. With a lawyer's clarity Irwin H. Linton suggests, "There is a place for skepticism as well as a place for faith; and in considering an investment or embracing a religion, skepticism should come first."[2] The proverbial "blind leap of faith" is a caricature: True faith is never blind, although the counterfeit always is. If heeded, A. W. Tozer's advice would keep many people who call themselves Christians from falling for false doctrines:

> A bit of healthy disbelief is sometimes as needful as faith to the welfare of our souls. It is no sin to doubt some things, but it may be fatal to believe everything.
> Faith never means gullibility. Credulity never honors God. . . . Along with our faith in God must go a healthy disbelief of everything occult and esoteric.[3]

Faith and Freedom

The freedom to think for ourselves, to weigh all of the evidence carefully, to make up our own minds without being pressured, is essential to genuine faith. One of the primary marks of a cult is the denial of this freedom by various tricks of persuasion so that eventually the cult member has surrendered his autonomy to the point that the "guru" or "prophet" does his thinking for him. Unfortunately, almost any church can, either wittingly or unwittingly, exert the same kind of pressure so that members conform to group thinking rather than coming to a deep and carefully-thought-out conclusion themselves.

"Is it faith," John Calvin asks, "to understand nothing, and merely submit your convictions implicitly to the Church?" Decrying such an attitude, Calvin reminds us that "faith consists not in ignorance, but in knowledge." Being "prepared to embrace every dictate of the Church as true" is not the way to obtain salvation.[4] Far too many churchgoers imagine they can escape moral responsibility by letting the clergy do their thinking for them, and that attending church and going along with its rules puts them "in the faith." Denouncing such misconception, Calvin emphasizes once again: "Faith consists in the knowledge of God and Christ (John 17:3), not in reverence for the Church."[5]

There are probably far more persons than one imagines within most large churches who have been talked into assenting to something which they never really believed and who scarcely know how to rid themselves of the sham that makes their lives so miserable. The weak person who compromises his professed Christian standards when faced with peer pressure in the world may very well have adopted his Christian ways through peer pressure from family or friends. We must be very careful not to force false decisions upon those who do not fully understand the issues or are not ready to make a genuine commitment. Jesus Himself set the example of discouraging mere enthusiasm or lip profession by the way in which He responded to some who seemed to be so eager to follow Him (Luke 18:18-25; Luke 9:57-62).

Faith and Daily Life

In his open contempt of Christians for placing faith in what they cannot "prove," the atheist condemns himself. Modern civilization involves numerous benefits that can be reaped only by trusting those who know what we don't and by believing what we can neither understand nor verify. Millions of men and women untrained in pharmacy exercise sufficient faith in pharmacists to ingest with complete confidence the prescriptions they prepare. And those who know little of either accounting or law nevertheless believe and follow advice that they cannot fully comprehend.

It would indeed be foolish to respond to a doctor's diagnosis and recommended remedy with the atheist's standard objection: "I never believe anything that I can't personally prove!" Obviously, it would take too long to acquire the medical knowledge necessary to understand fully the doctor's advice. Atheism's principles don't apply well to daily life.

Unfortunately, some people attend church for social or family reasons and profess to something they don't really believe because it would be embarrassing to back out. Others do so because they are too proud to admit their doubts when everyone else seems so sure of what they believe. Unbelief has many faces, often hiding behind a mask of pretended faith that begins to fool even the person wearing it. We betray our real beliefs, however, with our lives. Spurgeon put it like this:

> Faith is the root of obedience, and this may be clearly seen in the affairs of life...a captain trusts a pilot to steer his vessel into port...a traveler trusts a guide to conduct him over a difficult pass...when a patient believes in a physician, he carefully follows his prescription and directions.
>
> Faith which refuses to obey the commands of the Savior is a mere pretense and will never save the soul.[6]

It is one thing to hope for heaven if hell is the only alternative, and to grasp at Christianity as an insurance policy to cover contingencies after death in case the Bible turns out to be true after all. It is something else, however, to live right now as though we *really* believe what we recite and sing. Obedience to God in the affairs of everyday life is the test. Boice reminds us that "we cannot know the Scriptures until we are willing to be changed by them."[7] What William Law wrote with his incisive pen more than 200 years ago applies equally well today:

> It is primarily for the lack of a sincere intention to live in accordance with the prayers they pray and the faith they profess that such an incongruous mixture of sinful folly and professed devotion to Christ fills the lives of so many who call themselves Christians.
>
> Without an honest, determined purpose of heart, Daniel could never have been the man of God that he was; and without this sincere intention to deny self and take up the cross to follow Christ in the course of daily life, the early church would never have been a fellowship of saints and glorious martyrs.
>
> So it is that for lack of this basic intention to surrender all to Christ, the church today is an open fraud of mere lip profession to that faith and divine love that once burned as a fire from heaven in those who "turned the world upside down."[8]

How is this faith which once "turned the world upside down" to be developed? Biblical faith grows out of an intimate, moment-by-moment relationship with God. Christians are weak in faith, suggests Boice, because "they have forgotten what God is like and what He promises to do for those who trust Him."[9] Only those who know Him well can genuinely trust Him and believe and obey His Word. Jesus declared that eternal life consists in *knowing* God (John 17:3). Stafford points out that there is a major problem in some of the methods that are being offered today for getting in touch with God, which subtly have the opposite effect:

> My third objection is that all these spiritual emphases tend to turn their reference point from God to man. They ask, "How can I shape myself, my mind, my faith, and my activities to meet God?"
>
> God becomes a force to be tapped into, a center for emotional orientation, an image to manipulate in your mind, a particular kind of feeling that grips the heart.
>
> Attention turned toward ourselves, toward what is happening with us, is subtly but surely different from turning toward God himself.
>
> And by placing the focus there, we bypass the more fundamental question, "How will God come to me?"[10]

The Necessity of Faith

If we must trust fallible people for what we can neither understand nor prove in order to benefit from modern medicine or technology, how much more reasonable it is to acknowledge that *faith* is necessary if we are to benefit from what *God* knows and is willing to do for us. It is not a mark of intelligence but of folly to refuse to receive the blessings that God offers us because we were not an observer when He created the universe or when Christ was crucified and resurrected. We must decide on the basis of the evidence—and there is an ample amount of such evidence— whether God can really be trusted. The necessity to know God personally for ourselves and not merely to know *about* Him through a church cannot be emphasized enough.

Obviously there is much that the infinite God wants us to know and experience about Himself which cannot be fully communicated to our limited understanding. Those who are too proud to admit this will never know God, for it is to *faith* that He reveals Himself. And if it is foolish to believe in God, then what must be said of those who trust doctors and accountants and even boast that they believe in themselves!

Only God is worthy of one's total trust and obedience—and that is what real faith is. If God does not exist, there is no true faith at all, and without the capacity to trust such a God there could be no real love either.

The search for love and happiness is universal, but no university offers degrees in these subjects, nor can science help us attain them. Our own experience of these joys and other powerful emotions convinces us that they are not a delusion, in spite of the inability of any instrument or laboratory to measure or verify what we *know* to be real. It is clear that science can give us no help in loving or being loved. It can provide *things* and *methods*, but not the spiritual reality we seek. To seek ultimate satisfaction from the products of God's creation rather than from God Himself is to consign ourselves to a feast of fools that can only increase our spiritual hunger.

Faith and God's Love

The universe points beyond itself to God, its Creator. Persuasively, all the wonders of nature cry: "Plan—Planner; design—Designer; law—Lawgiver; creation—Creator, infinite and eternal." We may shrink from the clear implications of the overwhelming evidence, but reason demands that God has neither beginning nor end, that He created the entire universe out of nothing, that He knows every thought which every person who ever lived or will live has thought or will think, that He knows where every subatomic particle in every atom ever was or ever will be.

It is even more staggering, however, to realize that this infinitely great God loves each of us deeply and personally. We can be confident that God is loving, compassionate, and kind. These attributes, when reflected in man, no matter how dimly, are acknowledged to be the ultimate virtues, qualities which cannot be explained by evolution. They *must* reflect the nature of the God who created us in His image.

Moreover, love must be an essential personal attribute of our Creator. It cannot be some inexorable cosmic law or principle like gravity or electricity, for that kind of "love" would never satisfy us. We know that the God who made us cannot be an impersonal First Cause. Philip Yancey said it well:

> The Bible shows God's power to force a Pharaoh to his knees and reduce mighty Nebuchadnezzar to a cud-chewing lunatic. But it also shows the impotence of power to bring about what God most desires: our love.
>
> When his own love is spurned, even the Lord of the universe feels in some way like a parent who has lost what he values most, or a mother hen who sits helpless as her brood flees toward danger....
>
> When we tame him, in words and concepts, and file him away under alphabetized characteristics, we can easily lose the force of the passionate relationship God seeks above all else.
>
> After two weeks of reading the entire Bible, I came away with the strong sense that God does not care so much about being analyzed. Mainly, he wants to be loved.[11]

It is not anger or a desire to control us but *God's love* that longs for our faith-response. He is not interested in pressuring us into believing something that isn't true; and those who use such tactics are not serving God but their own misguided interests. Faith grows out of a love relationship; you trust those whom you love. If we truly love God, we will trust Him to guide our lives. Jesus said, "If a man love me, he will keep my words" (John 14:23). Those who claim to be Christians but habitually live for self instead of for God betray their lack of love and trust in daily life no matter how "faithfully" and often they perform their religious rites. William Law drives the point home:

> If you will but stop to ask yourself why your brand of Christianity is hardly recognizable as related to that which primitive Christians knew, your own heart will tell you that it is primarily because you never thoroughly intended to live as they lived and to die as they died....
>
> Did you but have this intention to please God in all your actions, as being the happiest and best choice for life in this world, you would then find yourself as unwilling to deny Christ with your life as you are now unwilling to deny Him with your lips.

And would you but add to this intention a simple faith in the
promises of God in Christ, you would find yourself living in the
same denial of self and as contrary to the world as fishermen
apostles did in their day.[12]

The Faith of Fools

The God of the Bible is no mere human invention. If God does
not in fact exist, man could no more invent Him than those who
live and die in a world of total darkness cut off from all else could
invent the concept of light. Yet we can pervert the revelation that
God gives. We must be very open to allow God to reveal Himself to
us however He may choose to do so, but at the same time we
must be very careful not to interfere in the process lest the "God"
we worship be our own creation. The human heart is deceitful,
and our imagination can even dress its own rebellious fantasies
to look like Deity. Unbelief truly has many faces.

One way we can be kept from the delusion that mistakes self
for God (the ultimate lie that is deliberately pursued in the East
through such practices as Yoga and is called "self-realization")
is to pay close attention to the revelation that God has given of
Himself in His Word. All that He reveals about Himself in
Scripture rings true to all of the evidence and to our hearts. Yet
at the same time, such a God is completely beyond our limited
comprehension. If He were not, He could not possibly be our
Creator. All of the evidence demands that we believe in Him,
that we take this step of faith, even though mortal mind staggers
at the dizzying thought of infinity.

The alternative to the existence of God, however, is not just
staggering but completely irrational. Atheism is not simply *beyond*
reason but *contrary* to reason. We know that the sun has not
existed from infinity past. If it had, it would have burned out
by now. Since the same is true of every other star, the universe
of necessity had a beginning. Should we accept the notion that
life and intelligence sprang spontaneously from dead, empty
space? Could the incredible design and structure of even one cell,
much less individual human personality and all of our thoughts
and emotions, be the accidental product of a cosmic explosion
some 18 billion years ago? It would take far more faith to believe

that than to believe in a Creator—but such a belief would be patently absurd.

The atheist has his "faith," his unprovable belief. All of the evidence, however, points clearly in another direction. Encyclopedias are not produced by explosions in printshops. How then should we account for the human brain, that incredibly designed bionic computer? And what about the spirit or mind that runs the brain? (Mere machines don't reason and love and care.) The cry of the psalmist speaks truth to our hearts: "The heavens declare the glory of God!" (Psalm 19:1).

The First Step of Faith

No wonder Einstein admitted that the more science discovers about the universe, the more we are forced to a conclusion concerning its origin that "only faith can grasp." Reason and the evidence force us to *believe* what we know full well we will never be able to *explain*: that God, who has no beginning and is infinite, created the universe out of nothing. Could it also be true that such a God is not only able but eager to reveal Himself to all who seek Him? Reason and the evidence point in that direction also. We are over our depth, led beyond scientific knowledge of mere facts to the assurance of a faith that causes us to willingly relinquish the warped delusion of self-importance in confrontation with the grandeur of God. Spurgeon proclaimed:

> It [the knowledge of God] is a subject so vast that all our thoughts are lost in its immensity; so deep that our pride is drowned in its infinity.
>
> Other subjects we can comprehend and grapple with; in them we feel a kind of self-content, and go on our way with the thought, "Behold, I am wise." But when we come to [the knowledge of God], finding that our plumbline cannot sound its depth, and that our eagle eye cannot see its height, we turn away with the solemn exclamation, "I am but of yesterday and know nothing."
>
> But while the subject humbles the mind, it also expands it.... Nothing will so enlarge the intellect, nothing so magnify the whole soul of man, as a devout, earnest, continuing investigation of the great subject of the Deity.[13]

If there were no God, then the existential viewpoint would be true: Nothing would make sense. A watch, for example, derives all of its meaning from the fact that it was manufactured for the purpose of telling time. Without someone to use and value it for that purpose, the most intricate and expensive timepiece would be no more than a senseless conglomeration of atoms. The same would be true of man if he were merely part of an impersonal universe produced by blind chance.

It is only in relation to *our Creator* that we as humans have any significance or purpose, and His eternal intent is beyond our finite understanding. Therefore it takes *faith*—and reason itself demands this—to get to know God and begin to experience what He has planned for us. Repeatedly the Bible asserts, "The just shall live by faith" (Habakkuk 2:4; Romans 1:17; Galatians 3:11; Hebrews 10:38). Those who imagine they can pursue a meaningful path independent of God need to face the evidence, abandon their egos, and follow conscience and reason. After carefully examining the evidence as a lawyer, Linton came to this joyous conclusion:

> To doubt is not sin, but to be contented to remain in doubt when God has provided "many infallible proofs" to cure it, is.
>
> From many years of experience and observation, I believe that the most joyous and morale-building experience possible is the discovery that Christianity's proofs are as overwhelming as its prospects and promises; that Christian faith is not a thing desperately to be clung to (often in spite of intellectual doubts and protests) like a life ring thrown to a drowning man, but may be as a result of investigation such an established conviction as to become like a strapped-on life belt with its inescapable security.[14]

It is not a "blind leap" but the highest act of reason to rest in the assurance of God's unchangeable character and infinite love. Nor is it a great sacrifice but an unspeakable privilege to cast ourselves upon His mercy and care, determining with all our hearts to do His will. Only a fool would try to get God to bless his own plans. Far better to let God reveal His will and to follow where He leads. Inspired of God, Jeremiah wrote:

O Lord, I know that the way of man is not in himself; it is
not in man that walketh to direct his steps (Jeremiah 10:23).

The Limitations of Science

Justice and truth as well as love, joy, beauty, and all of life's
most wonderful experiences are beyond the ability of science to
explain. Readily we exclaim with rapture over the beauty of a
sunset sky or read meaning in a loved one's eyes. The simplest
child can revel in the experiences provided by a universe that is
so marvelous as to overwhelm even the most brilliant intellect
with feelings of inexpressible wonder. We look in vain to science,
however, either to affirm or to deny the reality of these emotions.
So it is with everything in life that touches us most deeply: What
our hearts know to be real our intellects cannot explain. As Blaise
Pascal said in *Les Pensees*, "The heart has its reasons that reason
doesn't understand."

Moreover, if science could ever succeed in explaining and
remaking man, it would have destroyed him. If man through
science and technology could gain control of God's universe and
determine his own destiny, then not only would God be dead,
but man as well. In *The Abolition of Man,* C. S. Lewis wrote:

> For the wise men of old the cardinal problem had been how
> to conform the soul to [God's] reality. . . . For magic and applied
> science alike the problem is how to subdue reality to the wishes
> of men. . . .
> I am not supposing them [these manipulators] to be bad men.
> They are, rather, not men (in the old sense) at all. They are, if
> you like, men who have sacrificed their own share in traditional
> humanity in order to devote themselves to the task of deciding
> what "Humanity" shall henceforth mean. "Good" and "bad"
> applied to them are words without content. . . .
> Man's final conquest has proved to be the abolition of Man.[15]

The United Nations Pavilion at the 1986 Expo in Vancouver
was a monument to this very folly. It portrayed the problems
of threatened ecological collapse and nuclear war, then lamented
in the words of the late Buckminster Fuller that "spaceship Earth"
had not come equipped with an "operator's manual." Such a
manual is provided by the designer and manufacturer of a product

to assist in its proper use for the intended purpose. This is exactly
what the Bible uniquely claims to be, and those who deny the
existence of the Creator must forever mourn the absence of a
manufacturer's instruction manual.

Nor can science at its most ingenious explain the purpose of
man's existence. It can analyze the physical universe and make
inferences from its intricate design, but it cannot provide the
ultimate answers needed to slake man's undeniable spiritual thirst.
David knew where that thirst could be quenched:

> O God, thou art my God; early will I seek thee. My soul
> thirsteth for thee, my flesh longeth for thee in a dry and
> thirsty land where no water is....
>
> Because thy lovingkindness is better than life, my lips shall
> praise thee. Thus will I bless thee while I live: I will lift up
> my hands in thy name (Psalm 63:1,3,4).

The Thirst for God

Our deepest emotions tell us that we were made for God and
that something has gone terribly wrong in our relationship. And
because of this breach between man and God, all else is amiss.
No matter how wonderful our experience of love, joy, or peace,
we recognize it as a mere shadow of something infinitely higher
from which we have become separated and for which we long,
even as the psalmist did. He panted after God as a deer "for
the water brooks" (Psalm 42:1). As Hugh Black said so many
years ago:

> It is sooner or later found that the most perfect love cannot
> utterly satisfy the heart of man. All our human intercourse, blessed
> and helpful as it may be, must be necessarily fragmentary and
> partial.
>
> The solitude of life in its ultimate issue is because we were made
> for a higher companionship. It is just in the innermost sanctuary,
> shut to every other visitant, that God meets us. We are driven
> to God by the needs of the heart.[16]

If God does indeed exist, as both our hearts and heads tell us,
then who would not want to know Him? That intimate "knowing" ought to be the passion of every true believer. And because

God is infinite, the friendship and fellowship that He offers is of infinite depth and duration also. Could anyone imagine a heaven with any greater joy than an eternal unfolding of ever-deeper revelations of God and His love in intimate communion with Him? He wants to begin that process now, and has promised:

> Ye shall seek me and find me when ye shall search for me with all your heart (Jeremiah 29:13).

The love and joy and eternal companionship that we long for, and the ultimate secrets of the universe that man's intellect seeks through science, are all hidden in the heart of the Creator, and nothing else will satisfy the heart of man. Beyond any doubt, there must be a meeting of these hearts in order for creation to reach its fulfillment and man his destiny. It was Hugh Black, again, who expressed it so beautifully:

> There have been implanted in man an instinct and a need which make him discontented till he find content in God...[for] without God life is shorn of its glory and divested of its meaning.
>
> So the human heart has ever craved for a relationship, deeper and more lasting than any possible among men, undisturbed by change, unmenaced by death, unbroken by fear, unclouded by doubt.[17]

Beyond Science

A movie was presented to those visiting the U.N. Pavilion at Expo 86. Appealing for peace in a troubled world, the film asked, "Why must there be good and bad, right and wrong, us and them?" As one exited the theater a further appeal for international cooperation met the eye, with this heading in large, bold print: FOR THE COMMON GOOD.

Ironically, those who insist upon *absolutely* no absolutes cannot live by the standard of no standards. Like every other false religion, humanism has its priests also, who take it upon themselves (having denied that there can be any "good or bad") to impose upon the rest of us what they have decided is "for the common good."

Blind egomania refuses to see that it causes and perpetuates its own problems. The fulfillment of our deepest longings and the resultant joy and satisfaction which that fulfillment brings can only come when we allow the Creator who built these capacities within us to have His way in our lives. And if we are to know God, and the love and joy and eternity of experiences He offers of Himself and His unbounded universe, then we must take that step of *faith*. Our hearts bear full witness to the biblical declaration:

> Without faith it is impossible to please him, for he that cometh to God must believe that he is, and that he is a rewarder of them that diligently seek him (Hebrews 11:6).

True faith and true science are not rivals, but deal with different realms. Faith involves that which science can neither verify nor disprove. To mix faith with science is to destroy both. This is the great error of Christian Science and Christian psychology, both of which pretend to be a "science of mind." As we have seen, Positive Confession with its reliance upon laws of prosperity and healing is merely another form of the same error.

The mind of man is not a physical thing but is a reflection of the God in whose image we were made. That image has been darkened and deformed by sin, but those who open their hearts to receive Jesus Christ as Savior and Lord are given the "mind of Christ" (1 Corinthians 2:16). The secret of the Christian life is not in struggling to be perfect, nor in our own strength attempting to apply certain moral principles, but in allowing Christ to express Himself through us.

The God who created us in His image exists beyond the scope of scientific laws. Therefore, human personality and experience, which come from God and not from nature, must forever defy scientific analysis. No wonder psychotherapy, which pretends to deal "scientifically" with human behavior and personality, has failed so miserably! No human being has the power to define from within himself, much less to dictate to others, what constitutes right or wrong behavior. Only God can set such standards, and if there is no Creator God, then morality is nonexistent. This is why psychology's "scientific" standards of "normal" behavior are arbitrary, changeable, meaningless, and inevitably amoral.

The fact that we have concepts such as justice and truth, and that we recognize right and wrong, is sufficient evidence to show that we have been made in the image of God. Man's moral conscience points to a dimension of experience beyond rational understanding, for which man was made by his Creator. This is the realm of faith, a faith untouched by the skeptics' scoffing because its existence is beyond their most ingenious arguments to either prove or disprove. This is why A. W. Tozer wrote:

> The modern vogue of bringing science to the support of Christianity proves not the truth of the Christian faith but the gnawing uncertainty in the hearts of those who must look to science to give respectability to their faith.[18]

Love Transcends Science

In His grand design for those created in His image, God implanted in man the capacity for faith, hope, and love. Mankind everywhere recognizes these three as the very essence of humanness, and their absence as a diminishment of those qualities we call human. It is the sublime qualities that distinguish humans from all animals—sense of purpose, feelings of compassion, respect for truth, recognition of right and wrong, appreciation of music and art.

If *everything* could ultimately be explained in scientific terms, then love itself would be a natural process governed by scientifically explicable laws and would thus be of no more significance than a yawn or a gastrointestinal pain. Yet humanists, in their rejection of God and worship of science, ignore the obvious evidence and instead persist in their search for a scientifically designed utopia. In *Walden Two*, behaviorist B. F. Skinner has his hero Frazier (who speaks for him) declare the following humanist religious dogma:

> The one fact that I would cry from every housetop is this: the Good Life is waiting for us. . . .
> At this very moment we have the necessary techniques, both material and psychological, to create a full and satisfying life for everyone.[19]

Thankfully, that dream is an obvious delusion, founded upon false premises. In spite of great accomplishments, the attempts

of science to interfere with nature have brought us to the brink
of ecological collapse. The problem only worsens as man's
control increases. How much greater is the tragic disaster when
science attempts to tamper with the soul and spirit, the mind
and emotions of man! Science has not yet been able to duplicate
a flower or even a blade of grass, much less the human brain.
Do we imagine, nevertheless, that at some point in the distant
future science will at last have gained the capacity to improve
upon God's creation? It is a vain hope. But even if we could
achieve the ultimate goal of creating that long-sought super-
man, he and all those who lived after him would be but the
mere creatures of science. Can anyone be such a fool as to
imagine that such a state would be better than being the creatures
of God? C. S. Lewis explained the fallacy well:

> If any one age really attains, by eugenics and scientific educa-
> tion, the power to make its descendants what it pleases, all men
> who live after it are patients of that power.... Man's conquest
> of Nature, if the dreams of some scientific planners are realized,
> means the rule of...the Conditioners over the conditioned...the
> world of post-humanity which...nearly all men in all nations are
> at present labouring to produce.[20]

Surprisingly, even religion can become an attempt to interfere
with God's universe. Prayer is too often a religious technique
cloaked in pious language for getting our own way. And if a *religious* science could achieve answers to our prayers and give us
control over our own destiny by *laws* that even God must obey,
then we would have realized the ultimate in power and thus the
ultimate in destruction. By making God Himself subject to cosmic
laws, Religious Science or Positive Confession reduces Him to
an impersonal force or principle and His love to an inexorable
cosmic process. In so doing, it extends the abolition of man, to
which Lewis referred, to the abolition of God. He has become
a pawn in our hands. This is not *faith in God* but an attempt
to play at being gods.

The Fruit of the Spirit

Significantly, the Bible declares that "love, joy, peace, longsuffering, gentleness, goodness, faith, meekness, and temperance"

are "the fruit of the Spirit" of God (Galatians 5:22,23). Those who lack these qualities have not only a sense of emptiness but also of guilt. Why *guilt*? This can only be the inevitable consequence of separation from the God who designed us for something that we all know should be ours but which we sense is strangely missing in our lives. The Bible says that sin causes us to "come short" of the glory of God, a glory that we were designed to reflect as beings made in His image. We are all rebels, and we know it; we are determined to make life "work" either by religious or by scientific principles that we as little gods can use to our own ends. How lamentable a goal it is to attempt to develop faith in order to gain *power*! Oswald Chambers warned:

> We are apt to imagine that if Jesus Christ constrains us, and we obey Him, He will lead us to great success. We must never put our dreams of success as God's purpose for us; His purpose may be exactly the opposite....
> His purpose is that I depend upon Him and on His power now. ...if we realize that obedience is the end, then each moment as it comes is precious.[21]

Faith has a far more worthy object than the acquisition of power or personal success or even of doing great exploits for God. Peter spoke of the "trial of faith" that is "more precious than gold": It praises and honors God and submits to His holy will in spite of prison and death, and in so doing it brings eternal "praise and honor and glory" to God (1 Peter 1:7). True faith opens the door to the otherwise unseen and unknown world of God's kingdom and to His rule in our hearts and over our lives. Faith sees God for who He really is, bows to His majesty, surrenders to His purpose, and turns us into the instruments of His holy will. It is Chambers again who reminds us:

> If we believe in Jesus, it is not what we gain but what He pours through us that counts. It is not that God makes us beautifully rounded grapes, but that He squeezes the sweetness out of us.
> Spiritually we cannot measure our life by success, but only by what God pours through us, and we cannot measure that at all.[22]

The fruit of the Spirit does not come by work but by faith, not by our efforts to bring it forth through obedience to laws or meticulous application of certain principles but by our surrender to the work of God in our hearts and lives. And it is faith alone which puts man in touch with God and opens to his heart a universe of reality that cannot be understood with the finite mind. Charles Swindoll points us back to the one passion we all ought to have:

> I am more convinced than ever that life's major purpose is not knowing self...but knowing God.
>
> As a matter of fact, unless God is the major pursuit of our lives, all other pursuits are dead-end streets.... They won't work. They won't satisfy. They won't result in fulfillment. They won't do for us what we think they're going to do.[23]

Faith Is Not Gullible

The Bible does not argue the existence of God. It begins with the assumption that all men, whether they admit it or not, know what is self-evident: "In the beginning God created the heavens and the earth" (Genesis 1:1). Moreover, the Scriptures assert that those who deny God's existence or worship false gods have willfully rejected what both common sense and conscience have perceived and are thus without excuse for their rebellious perversion:

> The invisible things of him from the creation of the world are clearly seen, being understood by the things that are made, even his eternal power and Godhead, so that they are without excuse: because that, when they knew God, they glorified him not as God, neither were thankful, but became vain in their imaginations, and their foolish heart was darkened.
>
> Professing themselves to be wise, they became fools....
> For this cause God gave them up unto vile affections (Romans 1:20-22,26).

In spite of the overwhelming reasons for trusting and obeying God, the life of faith is not an easy road. Many doubts lie in wait along the way. Paul exhorted Timothy to "fight the good fight of faith" (1 Timothy 6:12). Doubts are frequently an indication that we are trying to get God to bless our plans instead of surrendering to His will. If we are not surrendered to God's will, then we perceive "faith" as a means of getting an answer to our prayers. Trying to get that kind of "faith" can cause us to believe what is not true. Nothing is more destructive of true faith than the attempt to create a mental attitude of "believing."

If we go either deliberately or unwittingly beyond God and His Word and the evidence He has provided, we will be beset with doubts. That is God's way of getting us back on track. The common mistake that many Christians fall into at this point is trying to regain faith by determining to "believe" and adopting various techniques of positive/possibility thinking, positive confession, visualization, or similar methods to implement belief. Instead, one needs to reexamine *what* and *in whom* one believes—and *why*. Therein lies the problem and the solution. Do we want to use God to bless our plans, or do we genuinely want to let Him use us to fulfill His will?

Unfortunately, what passes for faith among religious people, including many who call themselves Christians, is frequently exactly what the skeptic considers it to be: mere credulity born of selfish desire and defended by pride. Blind fanatical commitment to religious dogmas and a stubborn refusal to face the clear teaching of Scripture is all too often passed off as faithfulness to God. This is one of the most seductive and deadly forms of unbelief. Atheism and agnosticism are only two of many ways *not* to believe in God. All of the others are false forms of "faith." Gullibility is one of these many faces of unbelief.

A professed "faith" is very often a devious excuse for clinging to one's prejudices and often serves as the ideal rationale for rejecting the truth in a religious attempt to fulfill one's own desires instead of bowing to God's will. Agnosticism is an open admission of doubt; but in its most deceptive form unbelief wears the mask of "faith." This is the pseudo-Christianity that causes some people to flee the church. Either way, they have been robbed of what God really wants for them.

Popular Misconceptions About Faith

Both the secular and religious worlds are glutted with false but widely held concepts that represent popular counterfeits of genuine faith. The familiar illustrations of having "faith in a chair" for support or "faith in an airplane" are not only inadequate but misleading as well. One *assumes* that a chair will give the needed support because chairs usually do. But chairs have also been known to collapse for one reason or another, and if that should happen, such an unlikely event would do little to change one's view of chairs. As for planes, everyone recognizes that flying even the best of aircraft with even the best of pilots represents at best a calculated risk. Passengers with faith in God pray to *Him* for His protection when they fly, because no one has true *faith* in airplanes. Believing, no matter how sincerely, will not keep a plane aloft. But if God should fail, even once, His claims would be forever nullified.

Many well-meaning persons equate faith in God with belief in general and imagine that the results it produces are caused by a "placebo effect" which releases healing substances in the brain or subconscious forces that cure the body.

The theory seems to work, at least to some extent, for millions of people. Witness the many self-help groups, such as Alcoholics Anonymous and a host of others, which teach that all one needs to do is believe in a "higher power," call it Buddha, Jesus, the Star Wars Force, or whatever suits one best. These are all broad-minded cosmic placebos ("God as you conceive Him to be"), and the various religious myths are only important as a means of arousing the "placebo effect." Allegedly, *belief* releases the power, which is controlled by the subject's positive or negative thinking and speaking.

To suggest, however, that all that is necessary is to believe in some vague "higher power" or "God as you conceive Him to be" would be like saying that all that is necessary for a successful marriage relationship is for each person to believe in the existence of the opposite sex. Is it narrow-minded, dogmatic fundamentalism to desire to know one's husband or wife personally? Is it fanaticism to expect to have definite marriage, family, business, or social relationships with specific persons? Should we expect less of our relationship with God? Jesus said that "life eternal" is knowing "the only true God" in and through His Son (John 17:3).

Unbelief Has Many Faces

In his best-seller *Seeds of Greatness*, behavioral scientist and popular Christian motivational speaker Denis Waitley calls faith both a "positive power" and a "negative power."[24] To strengthen one's faith he suggests: "Don't run around with the Henny Pennys who are looking up, chanting, 'The Sky is Falling!'. . . Get high on yourself. . . . Use positive self-talk on a daily basis."[25] In his entire chapter on "faith," Waitley never once mentions God or even hints that faith involves believing in and obeying Him. His list of "Questions About Your Faith" include: "Are you lucky?. . . Would others view you as an optimist?"[26]

Unfortunately, secular success/motivation concepts have been erroneously equated with faith and brought into the church. In its classical and biblical sense, faith must have an object. One can only have faith *in something or someone*, and true faith can only be in God, for He alone is worthy of our complete trust and obedience. Faith that has for its object some unidentified "higher power" has been placed in a substitute for the one true God and is thus the most deceitful form of atheism. W. H. Griffith Thomas, theologian and widely respected preacher and Bible teacher of the early part of this century, had this to say:

> Faith can be analyzed as including (1) renunciation of self; (2) reliance on God. These two aspects sum up its meaning.
> Faith implies the cessation of self-dependence and the commencement of dependence upon another.[27]

Faith is not a "positive" or "negative" force, nor does it trigger such a force. It simply opens a person to whatever is offered by the object in which faith is placed—and woe to those who misplace their faith. The important question is *what* and *in whom* one believes. The Bible leaves no room for ambiguity on the subject of faith. Faith is always *in God* and it inevitably results in obedience to Him and to His Word. Anything else is unbelief, no matter how loudly it protests otherwise. Unbelief does, indeed, have many faces.

The Signs-and-Wonders Mentality

The overemphasis upon healing and miracles has given birth to one of the major delusions of our time: the popular belief now held by many sincere Christians that most if not all skeptics would be convinced if only they could see some genuine miracles. This is, however, clearly not the case. It is a grave mistake to conclude that God's truth lacks convicting power that only miracles can supply. Lack of faith is unbelief that derives from man's basic rebellion against God, and it cannot be automatically created by seeing miracles. The rebel convinced of God's miraculous power remains a rebel until he has surrendered himself to Christ. And until that time, though he may seem to have become a Christian, his basic interest will remain self and his motive will be to use God's power to his own ends.

No people saw more miracles than the children of Israel, who were led out of Egypt by Moses and Aaron, yet this generation was constantly rebellious against God and His Word. The Red Sea opened spectacularly before them as Moses extended his rod over its waters; then the waters drowned their enemies behind them. They were led by a pillar of fire and a cloud that literally showed them when and where to go. They heard God speak with an audible voice from Mount Sinai out of the midst of the spectacular flames and smoke engulfing its summit. Water issued miraculously from solid rock to quench their thirst and manna supernaturally condensed from the dew each morning to feed them. In 40 years of wandering in the wilderness their sandals and clothes did not wear out. Nevertheless, the Israelites, who saw daily signs and wonders more dramatic and convincing than any other people, stand out in the pages of Scripture as the classic example of unbelief and rebellion. Of them God said:

> All day long have I stretched forth my hands unto a
> disobedient and gainsaying people (Romans 10:21).

Of Moses, who led God's people in their exodus, the Scripture says, "There arose not a prophet since in Israel like unto Moses, whom the Lord knew face to face" (Deuteronomy 34:10). No prophet since that time, except for Christ Himself, has been so powerfully used to display to the world God's miraculous power, yet Israel repeatedly complained and rebelled against this unique man of God. The Pentateuch, the Five Books of Moses, ends with this declaration of the ways in which Moses excelled:

> In all the signs and wonders which the Lord sent him to do in the land of Egypt to Pharaoh, and to all his servants, and to all his land, and in all that mighty hand, and in all the great terror which Moses showed in the sight of all Israel (Deuteronomy 34:11,12).

The Bible makes it equally clear, however, that miracles are not the necessary sign of a true prophet of God. The call for Israel to repent in preparation for receiving her Messiah was, significantly, accompanied by no miracles, even though John the Baptist, God's chosen messenger for this task, came "in the spirit and power of Elias [Elijah]...to make ready a people prepared for the Lord" (Luke 1:17). We thus learn the interesting fact that, although God did many signs and wonders through Elijah, miracles were not an integral or essential part of the "spirit and power" that characterized his ministry.

We are told that John the Baptist, the "Elijah" who prepared the way for Christ, "did no miracle" (John 10:41). Yet Jesus said of him: "Among those that are born of women there is not a greater prophet than John the Baptist..." (Luke 7:28). That declaration gives an entirely different perspective on miracles than is presented by charismatic leaders today.

With Christ it was exactly the opposite. There could be no question about the numerous miracles that Jesus did, yet these did not convince the Jews of the truth He proclaimed. In fact, the convincing quality of His miracles only hardened the hearts of the Pharisees and made them all the more determined to do away with Him. In contrast to the "healers" who are exposed as frauds today, the religious leaders wanted to kill Jesus because His miracles were genuine:

> Then gathered the chief priests and the Pharisees a council and said, What do we? for this man doeth many miracles.
> Then from that day forth they took counsel together for to put him to death (John 11:47,53).

A Biblical Perspective on Miracles

While it is true that genuine miracles have been a means of helping some people to believe, true faith is a matter of the heart and not the head. Submission to God is a moral issue, not an intellectual one. The "devils [demons] also believe and tremble" (James 2:19), but they still persist in their rebellion. No one needs a miracle to believe in God: Conscience and the witness of creation have already convinced even the professed atheist of that. What we need to be convinced of is that God really loves us and that therefore His way is best. This deep conviction will cause us to surrender willingly and completely into His hands and to love Him with our whole heart. Only then will we obey God for His sake alone and not for what we hope to get out of that relationship. One of today's leading "faith healers" writes that we have a divine right to ask, "Lord, what's in it for me?"[28] In contrast, Oswald Chambers quotes Jeremiah 45:5—"Seekest thou great things for thyself? Seek them not"—then comments:

> There is nothing easier than getting into a right relationship with God except when it is not God whom you want but only what He gives.
> If you have only come the length of asking God for things, you have never come the first strand of abandonment, you have become a Christian from a standpoint of your own.
> "I did ask God for the Holy Spirit, but He did not give me the rest and the peace I expected." Instantly God puts His finger on the reason—you are not seeking the Lord at all, you are seeking something for yourself.[29]

No miracle, no matter how spectacular and convincing, can cause any person to love God or to submit to His will. In fact, miracles very often have just the opposite effect. It was because Jesus did miracles that the multitude wanted to "take him by force, to make him a king" (John 6:15). They had no intention of submitting to His lordship. What they wanted was a figure-head "king" who could overthrow the Romans, heal them when they were ill, and feed them miraculously when they were hungry. This carnal attitude is encouraged by the fund-raising appeals emanating from the computers of so many "faith" teachers, who would sanctify covetousness by offering miracles from God in exchange for "seed-faith" offerings to support their ministries.

There were no doubt many people in the crowd who cried "Away with him, crucify him!" that fateful day who had been healed and fed by Jesus but would not accept His indictment of their sin nor His remedy for their souls. Those who once followed Jesus because of the miracles He performed eventually turned back and "walked no more with him" (John 6:66) because they would not accept His teaching concerning the giving of His flesh and blood for them.

One expects unbelief from atheists and agnostics, but not from Christians. The extent to which those who sincerely call themselves believers are practicing unbelief in the name of faith and in the name of God is indeed disturbing. We have unmasked some of the faces of unbelief, but there are many more. One of these is so seductive that its mask must be torn away if there is to be any hope for the church to return to biblical Christianity.

6

Too Glorious to Be Easy

We have this treasure in earthen vessels, that the excellency of the power may be of God, and not of us. We are troubled on every side, yet not distressed; we are perplexed, but not in despair; persecuted, but not forsaken; cast down, but not destroyed; always bearing about in the body the dying of the Lord Jesus, that the life also of Jesus might be made manifest in our body (2 Corinthians 4:7-10).

WE HAVE SEEN that, whether one is a Christian or an atheist, the benefits of modern science and technology can only be received by having confidence in other people who have specialized knowledge that we can neither understand nor prove for ourselves. There is nothing wrong with a Christian consulting a Buddhist physician or a Muslim lawyer if a Christian of comparable competency is not available. So it is with the laws of aerodynamics or physics or chemistry—they work the same for everyone.

In *spiritual* matters, however, a Christian must *never* turn for help to a rival religion. One would suppose that the distinction between the physical and spiritual, and between Christianity and all other religions, would be easily recognized. Yet that is not always the case. The physical brain is not the same as the nonphysical mind, but they are often confused because the two are so closely related. Medicine deals with both brain and mind (many seemingly physical ailments are psychosomatic), so a good physician tries to buoy his patients' spirits. Solomon said, "A merry heart doeth good like a medicine" (Proverbs 17:22). It is, of course, true that nerves and glands and digestion work better and one's general state of health is benefited when one is happy. As we have also seen, however, a Christian must be careful not to substitute a positive mental attitude for faith in God.

Emotional problems, such as depression, could be the result of either a physical or a spiritual problem, or both. Here again, caution is required. Though closely related to the body, the mind and emotions involve the soul and spirit. These three—mind, soul, and spirit—are so closely related that for all practical purposes to deal with one is to involve all three. Psychology claims to deal not only with the mind but with the *psyche*, which is the Greek word for soul and brings us into the realm of the spirit. It is easy to see, then, how psychology could open the door to religious practices hostile to Christianity that might not be recognized as such and could therefore gain unwitting acceptance in the church as "Christian psychology."

Some Obvious Inherent Dangers

It would be foolish to speak of Christian chemistry or Christian medicine, yet the term Christian psychology is commonly accepted. Why? The impression is given that psychology legitimately deals in the same areas of concern as the Bible and can therefore be united with Christianity—a claim that no other profession makes. In one of his many best-selling books, one of today's most popular television pastors tells of attending the World Psychiatric Congress in Madrid, Spain, in 1967 and describes how thrilled he was that the speakers talked of faith and hope and love. "I was jubilant, of course!" he writes,[1] as though psychiatrists who use such words must therefore be affirming the Bible. Later in the book he declares:

> A widespread tension has too long existed between psychologists and theologians. Both disciplines should be committed to the healing of the human spirit. Both can and must learn from each other....
> What we need is a theological restructuring which synergizes scientific and spiritual truth as related to the human being.[2]

The subtitle of the book referred to is *The New Reformation*, and the basis of that "reformation" is made very clear. Psychology is recognized as dealing with the *spirit* and is thus placed on a par with Christian theology. Something tantamount to a merger between the two is suggested through a "restructuring"— of *theology*, of course. One is nonplussed to observe that after a Christian leader perceptively points out that Christian psychology of necessity involves a restructuring of theology, he then goes on to recommend this as the basis for a *new reformation*! The dangers inherent in such thinking ought to be obvious.

We have already seen that science cannot deal with spirit, for the latter is nonphysical. Any system that attempts to deal with spiritual matters is by very definition a *religion*, regardless of what it is called. Psychology is clearly a religion, and its hostility to Christianity is a matter of record so well-known that we need not even document it here. Of course, not *everything* in psychology is anti-Christian (nor is *everything* in Buddhism or Hinduism anti-Christian), yet it would be not only folly but dishonoring to God and a denial of the sufficiency of the gospel and of Scripture to look to any of these, or any other rival religion, to either support or supplement our Christian faith.

In *The Myth of Psychotherapy*, psychiatrist Thomas Szasz points out that through the acceptance of psychotherapy "the cure of (sinful) souls, which had been an integral part of the Christian religions, was recast as the cure of (sick) minds."[3] The mind was seen as purely a function of the body in the early days, because Freud was a physician. However, Freud's "medical model" didn't work and has since been abandoned by all but hard-core Freudians, to be replaced by a spiritual or pseudo-spiritual model, with the meaning of "spiritual" still in flux.

Lawrence Le Shan, past president of the Association of Humanistic Psychology, who has suggested that psychotherapy will probably be known as the hoax of the twentieth century, has also explained that its spiritual roots lie in Eastern mysticism:

> The basic model of man that led to the development of [Eastern] meditational techniques is the same model that led to humanistic psychotherapy.[4]

Like Positive/Possibility Thinking, Positive Confession, and the Mind Science cults, which are all closely related, psychology is a secularized religion of the mind. In spite of this fact, its adherents perpetuate the deceitful myth that psychotherapy is scientific.

A Contradictory Pseudoscience

Early in December 1985, 7000 participants (3000 were turned away for lack of space) gathered in Phoenix, Arizona, for the "Evolution of Psychotherapy Conference." Billed by its organizers as "probably the largest gathering ever devoted to the practice of psychotherapy," the prestigious convention drew participants from 29 countries. One of the major features was the presence of psychology's remaining living masters, such as Carl Rogers, Rollo May, R. D. Laing, Joseph Wolpe, Albert Ellis, Bruno Bettelheim, and Thomas Szasz.[5]

The huge convention presented a strange dichotomy: On the one hand was the shocking display of confusion and contradiction; on the other hand, in apparent blindness to the bankruptcy of their profession, there was the enthusiastic and competitive planning by participants for the expansion of their influence upon a gullible public that eagerly looks to them for answers which they obviously don't have. *Los Angeles Times* staff writer Ann Japenga reported, "The heroes were there to evaluate where psychotherapy has come in 100 years and where it might be going—except they really could not agree on either."[6]

The convention failed to settle differences among psychotherapy's hundreds of rival sects and bring some semblance of order to the chaotic muddle of literally thousands of conflicting theories and therapies. Three out of the four members of the prestigious panel on schizophrenia declared that "the disease was nonexistent."[7] Called by *Time* magazine "the favorite shrink of student rebels in the '60s,"[8] R. D. Laing insisted that schizophrenia "did not exist until the word was invented," and described schizophrenics as "brave victims who are defying a cruel culture."[9] Szasz, who calls mental illness a "myth" (the mind, being nonphysical, cannot be *sick*), labels schizophrenia a fiction. He declared bluntly that while it was "useful" for the parents of President Reagan's would-be assassin "to think of their son as a schizophrenic...he's really just a bum."[10]

The disagreements over schizophrenia were typical of the confusion and rivalry among psychologists and psychiatrists. The entire field today is a nightmare of competing theories and practices that not only offer little real help, but are in many cases actually damaging. According to a recent article in *Time* magazine titled "Madness in Their Method":

> Everyone knows that a good deal of psychotherapy does not seem to do well. What everyone does not know, says Psychoanalyst Robert Langs, is that a common factor in failed therapies is the "madness" of the therapists....
>
> He uses the word to indicate the inner turmoil and contradictions that are present in everyone. But his conclusion is anything but tame: the average consumer of therapy is likely to be influenced by the emotional problems of therapists. ... many patients are more damaged by their therapists than they realize, and some actually end up seeking out one disturbed therapist after another....[11]

The Answer Within

Referring to the Phoenix conference, John Leo of *Time* magazine wrote, "The closest thing to a central idea was that the patient, or client, already has the answer to the problem deep within, and the therapist simply helps bring it out."[12] Nothing could be better calculated to keep mankind from getting in touch with God. Such folly has spawned a generation of lost souls whose major purpose in life seems to be to "find" themselves. Were the church, through the influence of Christian psychology, not so busily in pursuit of the same illusive selfisms, she could proclaim with a clear voice to the lost:

> Seek ye the Lord while he may be found, call ye upon him while he is near; let the wicked forsake his way, and the unrighteous man his thoughts; and let him return unto the Lord, and he will have mercy upon him, and to our God, for he will abundantly pardon (Isaiah 55:6,7).

Of today's 10,000 therapies, most aim at unlocking an infinite inner wisdom and power. The success rate is low and at best temporary, causing dissatisfied customers to switch from therapy to therapy—and the therapists to dabble ever more deeply into occult techniques. Reflecting his own involvement in occultism and Eastern mysticism, Carl Jung called the self the "God within us." When humanists refer to the "God" or "Divine" within, they don't mean the Holy Spirit indwelling sinners saved by grace through Christ's death and resurrection; they mean a deified self that replaces the God of the Bible. It is a false gospel that offers no real hope.

At the Phoenix conference, in spite of the trade-show enthusiasm and the hero worship, the disillusionment was difficult to hide. In referring to his "current personal struggle with depression," Laing implied that he has recurring bouts with a nemesis that he has yet to conquer. Christians who turn from God and His Word to psychotherapies for help with depression forsake "the fountain of living waters" to drink from the polluted and unsatisfying and even harmful "broken cisterns, that can hold no water" (Jeremiah 2:13). Laing then shared something that was proving, for him at least, to be "of greater help than anything psychotherapy offers": *Humming a favorite tune to himself!* And what was his magic tune? "Keep Right On to the End of the Road."[13] No, laughter would be entirely inappropriate; we ought to weep. One cannot help but think of the Scripture warning:

> There is a way which seemeth right unto a man, but the end thereof are the ways of death (Proverbs 14:12).

It is difficult to understand how a pseudoscience that has been so thoroughly discredited by its own practitioners could continue to be held in high esteem by anyone, much less by those who profess to be indwelt by the Spirit of Christ. The church needs no help from this bankrupt profession. Instead of looking to the warped theories of Freud et al, we need to get back to the Bible, which claims to have provided through God's grace and power

> all things that pertain unto life and godliness, through the knowledge of him that hath called us to glory and virtue...
> that by these ye might be partakers of the divine nature, having escaped the corruption that is in the world through lust (2 Peter 1:3,4).

A Growing Seduction

In spite of their impotence to provide any lasting help, psychotherapies by the thousands have become almost as much a part of life as motherhood and apple pie. Consequently, the average Christian is not even aware that to consult a psychotherapist is much the same as turning oneself over to the priest of any other rival religion. Of course when it is practiced by a Christian, psychology is given an unwarranted legitimacy that deceives the unwary. Fallacy is still fallacy, and it is no less dangerous even when proclaimed or practiced by Christians. Through the naive acceptance of psychotherapy as a "scientific" supplement to biblical truth which has been passed off as "inner healing" or "Christian psychology," the church has been afflicted with spiritual schizophrenia. Tozer explains:

> It is in this matter of how to deal with man's proud and perverse and sinful human nature that we discover two positions within the framework of Christianity.
> One position is that which leans heavily upon the practice of psychology and psychiatry. There are so-called Christian leaders who insist that Jesus came into the world to bring about an adjustment of our ego.... So, there are thousands of referrals as the clergymen shift our problems from the church to the psychiatric couch.
> On the other hand, thank God, the Bible plainly says that Jesus Christ came to bring an end of self—not to educate it or tolerate it or polish it!...
> In true repentance and in self-repudiation, we may turn our backs on the old self life.... We have the right and the power...to cross over to spiritual victory and blessing...walking joyfully under the banner of the cross of Jesus Christ from that hour on.[14]

There is no emotional problem that psychology attempts to deal with for which the Bible does not claim that God Himself offers a complete cure that can be received by faith. To trust in God and obey His Word is to be delivered from the anxiety that seems to hang over this world like a cloud. Elisabeth Elliot knew the terror of anxiety and despair during those hours of waiting, only to learn that her husband, Jim, and his four companions had been sent to heaven with Auca spears. She experienced frailties and fears of another kind as she undertook that perilous jungle journey to live with her husband's killers and eventually saw them won to Christ. In a recent interview she said:

> During all the years that I have recounted the [Auca] story and reflected on it in the light of subsequent experience, one lesson above all others shines: *God is God.* If He is God, He is worthy of my worship, my trust, my obedience.
>
> I am only a child, He is my Father. He will not explain everything, but I may find rest in His glorious will. His will is infinitely, immeasurably, ineffably beyond my largest notions of what He is up to, but I will find rest nowhere else.[15]

Strangely enough, however, a substantial number of Christians find themselves living under the same cloud of anxiety that plagues the world, and they don't seem to know how to get back into the sunshine of God's love. Many seek psychological help because it seems to offer an escape from the pain that often accompanies spiritual growth. Martin and Deidre Bobgan remind us:

> The value system in the Bible may involve self-sacrifice, pain, and relinquishment.
>
> However, by following the teachings of Scripture one finds truth and gains true freedom (John 8:31,32,36).[16]

Southern California's Henrietta C. Mears, whose life and ministry affected so many people, had this to say in Bible study material used by the Billy Graham Evangelistic Association:

> Do not pray for an easy task. Pray to be stronger!
>
> The greatness of a man's power is the measure of his surrender. It is not a question of who you are, or of what you are, but whether God controls you.[17]

Too Glorious to Be Easy

"The Christian," says D. Martyn Lloyd-Jones, "is a man who can be certain about the ultimate even when he is most uncertain about the immediate."[18] That fact should bring an inner peace that the world knows nothing about and no psychological technique can provide. Yet so many Christians live in uncertainty and doubt, afraid to testify boldly for their Lord lest their faith be challenged or they lose the "acceptance" which they have been told is essential for emotional stability. There is only one explanation for this strange contradiction: Many who call themselves Christians have not found the release from all anxiety that comes from surrendering all to Christ; they are still bound up in themselves.

It is impossible to trust God to preserve one's life, health, job, or whatever has not first of all been surrendered to Him. One will always be fearful of losing what has not been surrendered completely to Christ. "If you give God your right to yourself," wrote Oswald Chambers, "He will make a holy experiment out of you. God's experiments always succeed."[19] Too many Christians do not yet seem to know that complete deliverance from all anxiety comes from fully believing that they have been bought with the blood of Christ and are therefore not their own. William Law said it so powerfully:

> To think that you are your own, or at your own disposal, is as absurd as to think that you created yourself. . . .
> Whenever a man allows himself to have anxieties, fears, or complaints, he must consider his behavior as either a denial of the wisdom of God or as a confession that he is out of His will.[20]

The very truth they claim to believe is denied by the self-centered complaints of many who call themselves Christians. Much of the "Christianity" being taught today does not come from the Bible, but represents a Christianization of the latest secular ideas popular in the world. Many of the "heroes" looked up to by today's Christians and often seen on Christian television are the antithesis of the humility and dependence upon God rather than self that is so evident in the lives of Bible characters. The average Christian is led to believe that the secret to the success exuded by those he admires is to develop a comparable self-confidence and "positive" self-image. Frustrated in the attempt, many Christians become unhappy and, at the urging of a friend or recommendation of their pastor, end up in "counseling," seeking to repair their shattered self-image, which they sincerely believe to be their problem. Many become the unwitting victims of a psychologized Christianity which is so self-oriented that it either compounds the problem or, most destructive of all, produces false cures based upon diagnoses and treatments that were unknown and unneeded in the church until very recently.

Even from a secular point of view, psychotherapy doesn't work—not even for the therapists themselves. Christians who naively—and no matter how sincerely—turn to this bankrupt and godless system both dishonor their Lord and rob themselves of the true joy and victory that can be found only in trusting Christ alone. Fifteen years of research went into Bernie Zilbergeld's *The Shrinking of America: Myths of Psychological Change*. In an interview, Zilbergeld (himself a clinical psychologist) pointed out:

> A survey of seven medical specialties by *Medical Economics* found that psychiatrists came out on top in more categories of marital problems, including sexual problems, than practitioners of any other specialty.
>
> Anyone who keeps company with counselors knows that, no matter what they may be like with their clients, in their personal lives they are no freer than others from pettiness, depression, poor communication, power struggles, anxiety, bad habits, and other difficulties. Nor are the organizations, departments, or clinics that they run.[21]

We would not minimize the sad fact that many of the sheep in Christ's flock are weak and bruised and in need of help that too often they are not receiving. If we are to return to biblical Christianity, then clearly we must take seriously the scriptural command to "comfort the feebleminded, support the weak, be patient toward all men" (1 Thessalonians 5:14). Does it not seem odd, however, that the early Christians thrived under rejection and triumphed over severe persecution, whereas today's Christians are given months and sometimes years of counseling to overcome rejection and abuse? We must not ignore genuine needs, but we must be equally concerned that the correct solution is offered. We do well to remember what Oswald Chambers wrote:

> God has frequently to knock the bottom board out of your

experience if you are a saint in order to get you into contact with Himself.

God wants you to understand that it is a life of *faith*, not a life of sentimental enjoyment of His blessings. . . .

Faith by its very nature must be tried, and the real trial of faith is not that we find it difficult to trust God, but that God's character has to be cleared in our own minds. . . .

"Though He slay me, yet will I trust Him"—this is the most sublime utterance of faith in the whole of the Bible.[22]

Don't Water Down Christianity

The ministry of the Holy Spirit is too often either neglected or misrepresented. To be filled with the Spirit is a command to all Christians and not an option for those who want a "higher life" than the norm. And to be filled with the Holy Spirit is also to be filled with Christ—with His life and with a love for other people that causes us to forget ourselves and our problems and enables us to witness with holy boldness and to expend ourselves for God. Life can become a burden too heavy to bear until we turn it all over to Him and let Him, in the power of the Holy Spirit, live His life through us. Christianity is *Christ* living in us; it is altogether miraculous. In counseling those who are hurting, we must be careful not to misrepresent the Christian life either as to its pains or its power. C. S. Lewis reminded a group of clergymen:

> Do not attempt to water Christianity down. There must be no pretence that you can have it with the supernatural left out.
> So far as I can see Christianity is precisely the one religion from which the miraculous cannot be separated.[23]

Those who have been through deep trial testify that their experience has strengthened their faith; but those who are pampered need ever-larger doses of "unconditional" acceptance. Consider the condition of Geoffrey T. Bull at the climax of hard years of mental and physical torture in prisons in China after World War II, during which time his Communist captors had done all they could to brainwash him into denying his faith in Christ:

> My mind had been so battered and was now so fatigued that

I hardly knew how to think. Yet, as in that dark cell my vision cleared, I could not explain it nor did I need to do so.

I knew that I believed my Saviour risen from the dead. I knew He was the Son of God. I knew He had shed His blood for me.

I had been shaken, torn and wounded but I was conscious still that round about me were His everlasting arms. I knew within my heart the witness of His Spirit, triumphant still, standing yet inviolable to all the foe's assault.

I knew that underneath my feet, impregnable, unshaken and strong as ever, was the Rock of Ages, Jesus Christ my Lord.

And there as I sat, from the very well springs of my soul surged up the words that God is pleased to honour above all human utterance, "I believe."[24]

We must be careful that the support we give does not lead the counselee deeper into the morass of self-indulgence and self-pity. Chambers warns, "Beware of any belief that makes you self-indulgent; it came from the pit, no matter how beautiful it sounds."[25] We grow strong in trial; therefore we must be careful that the counsel and help given will bring the person through the trial of his faith with his roots deepened in Christ, rather than enable him to escape the very challenges that God intends for his good. "The Christian way is a difficult way of life," Lloyd-Jones reminds us all. "It is too glorious to be easy."[26] Every counselor ought to heed this advice from Richard S. Taylor:

> Sometimes instead of gushy affirmation people need to be helped to face up to reality. At times true love will give not saccharin but shock treatment.
>
> At times, instead of trying to talk people out of their self-deprecation we should agree with them; then try to get them to confess their worthlessness to God, and turn from the sin which is at the root of such feelings.[27]

"Yea, though I walk *through* the valley of the shadow of death, I will fear no evil, for thou art with me," wrote David. He did not plead to be given another path that would bypass that terrible valley, but only that God be with him through his trial. Today's Christianity too often seems to be more concerned with escaping every problem and experiencing only health, wealth, and success than with knowing God. Yet often it is only in times of distress that He can break the hold of that which has captured our affection away from Him, perhaps without our even knowing it.

Individual Responsibility

Today's popular and easy Christianity would scarcely be recognized by those early believers who forfeited all to follow Christ and daily faced prison or death as a consequence. It is a Christianity that seeks the world's approval and thus fears to rebuke it. Forgotten is Christ's clear call to separation from the world (John 15:19; 17:14). As Boice says, "They have allowed their minds to become conformed to the 'spirit of this age'...."[28]

Unfortunately, most of us are part-time Christians and full-time something else. As a result, we bring into the church many of the methods and ideas we have become accustomed to out in the world. We trust our physician or accountant, so we think it should work the same way in matters of religion: There must be some *professional* whom we should trust as the expert who understands the things of the Spirit which we don't have the time or capacity to learn.

God will not tolerate such an approach. We cannot abdicate our moral responsibilities to someone else, no matter how godly, who will then do our Bible study and prayer and thinking for us. Christianity involves a *personal* relationship with God through Jesus Christ. We must each know God and His Word for ourselves. Our faith is in *God and His Word*, not in some expert who studies, lives, and interprets it all for us. Of course there are those who are gifted to teach, and we are to "obey them that have the rule [leadership]" over us, but only to the extent that they themselves are submitted to the leading of the Holy Spirit and are teaching and following the Word of God.

Each of us is individually responsible to judge whether what we are being taught is biblical. We are not to believe or to follow anything that our own individual consciences by the leading of the Holy Spirit indicate is not in accordance with God's Word. We are to obey God through men, but not men who do not truly speak and live for God. Many verses in the Bible make this clear. Here are a few:

If any man obey not our word by this epistle, note that man and have no company with him (2 Thessalonians 3:14).

Peter and the other apostles answered [the religious leaders] and said, We ought to obey God rather than men (Acts 5:29).

Be ye followers of me, even as I also am of Christ (1 Corinthians 11:1).

The anointing which ye have received of him abideth in you, and ye need not that any man teach you (1 John 2:27).

If any man think himself to be a prophet, or spiritual, let him acknowledge that the things that I write unto you are the commandments of the Lord (1 Corinthians 14:37).

The New Professionals

It may not be so difficult for most Christians to understand that they must, as the Bereans did with Paul's teaching, personally check out from the Word of God whatever is taught by their pastor or other preacher or teacher. A new category of "clergy," however, never before known throughout history, has recently been granted leadership within the church. This new source of authority carries with it peculiar dangers that must be dealt with if Christianity is to survive.

"What you need is *professional* counseling!" That phrase is being heard increasingly and is usually spoken with a sense of great assurance and urgency. It often comes from pastors who feel inadequate to handle what they now perceive to be *psychological* problems—a new category unknown to Jesus or the apostles. The church has unwittingly opened its doors to the very enemy that could destroy many lives. After his years of research, Zilbergeld warns that "one of the most consistent and important effects of counseling is a desire for more counseling... [and] it is no longer unusual to meet people who are looking for...a therapist to resolve problems caused in a previous therapy." He goes on to explain why *professional* help is not the answer:

There is absolutely no evidence that professional therapists have any special knowledge of how to change behavior, or that they obtain better results—with any type of client or problem—than those with little or no formal training. In other words, most people can probably get the same kind of help from friends, relatives, or others that they get from therapists.

Second, as we have seen, people are not all that easy to change.[29]

Such research findings should encourage those involved in Christian counseling to rely upon God's Word, the leading of the Holy Spirit, and the love of Christ expressed in and through them rather than upon "professional" techniques. And the average Christian should be encouraged to know that taking the time in love and compassion to hear someone out and then to help in simple ways is effective. The Bible and not psychology has the answers to life's problems.

Sincerely dedicated to Christ and to helping others, most Christian psychologists would affirm the sufficiency of Scripture. However, in actual practice they deny that the Bible has all the instruction needed for Christian life. Freud and Jung and a host of other humanists must also be consulted. The knowledge gained from such godless sources and dressed up in biblical language becomes the new "truth" that no one without a degree in psychology, no matter how godly or mature in the faith, can possibly challenge. After 19 centuries it was discovered that the pastor and his staff and godly elders were incompetent to meet the need for a new kind of counseling that requires psychological specialists hitherto unknown in the church.

There are varying degrees of error among Christian psychologists, many of whom have much to offer. However, to whatever extent they rely upon psychology's false theories and practices either as a substitute for or supplement to the solutions offered in Scripture, they are leading people astray. Obviously the acceptance of "truth" that is a blend of Scripture and psychology means that the Word of God is no longer the final authority. That fact represents a major barrier on the road back to biblical Christianity.

Back to the Word of God

One day each of us must stand alone before God and give an account of himself. Although the advice of a godly pastor or Christian counselor can be invaluable, none of us will be able to excuse ourselves from personal moral accountability for our own actions by saying that we took the advice of our pastor or some great church leader or Christian psychologist. Scripture explicitly states, "The *Lord* is my Shepherd." Everything that this or any other book says, no matter by whom written, must be checked against Scripture. The instruction that God gave through Isaiah is still applicable:

> To the law and to the testimony: if they speak not according to this word, it is because there is no light in them (Isaiah 8:20).

How can we know whether someone (and that includes this author) is speaking according to the Word of God if we don't know the Bible thoroughly for ourselves? We can't. It is as simple as that. There is no way to get around that fact. So if nothing else is understood, let it be clear that this book is primarily a call for each reader to get back to the Bible for himself.

Nor is there any substitute for *living* the Word. We will not be able to adequately understand the Bible until we have committed ourselves to obey it by putting God's truths into practice in our daily lives no matter what the cost. God has said, "My ways are not your ways," but instead of being glad that His thoughts are so high above ours, we often attempt to reinterpret His Word to conform to our desires. Of course it is done with protestations of our love for Him and perhaps clapping of hands and shouts of victory, but there is a hollow ring that betrays the absence of the One we claim is present. Were He truly in our midst in power, as we boast that He is, the show-biz atmosphere would quickly turn into holy reverence and awe. Real worship and praise—which may indeed involve outward displays of emotions—comes from hearts that have first trembled at God's Word and stand in awe of Him. Carl Henry has said:

> The resurgent evangelical movement has too much tamed its fear of God; it sometimes performs triumphally as if it had the Lion of the Tribe of Judah by the tail, and as if Christ were serving us rather than our serving Him.[30]

It is tragic that Christ is so badly misrepresented to the world by some of those who claim to speak and act for Him. Too often

Christianity is presented as merely a superior way to achieve the same ambitions as the world pursues. What a pity that so shallow a Christianity seems to satisfy so many who sing so lustily about the cross!

Christianity is far more glorious than most of us even suspect— much too glorious, in fact, to be as easy as many would like it to be. Knowing nothing of pleas for "acceptance" and "unconditional love," the Christians of Paul's day got along victoriously without psychotherapy in spite of heavy trials and persecutions. "The saint realizes that it is God who engineers circumstances," wrote Chambers; "consequently there is no whine, but a reckless abandon to Jesus."[31] Consider these stirring words that Paul wrote under the inspiration of the Holy Spirit to cheer on the church at Corinth in its struggle against paganism:

> We then, as workers together with him, beseech you also that ye receive not the grace of God in vain. . . .
>
> But in all things approving ourselves as the ministers of God, in much patience, in afflictions, in necessities, in distresses,
>
> In stripes, in imprisonments, in tumults, in labors, in watchings, in fastings;
>
> By pureness, by knowledge, by longsuffering, by kindness, by the Holy Ghost, by love unfeigned,
>
> By the word of truth, by the power of God, by the armor of righteousness on the right hand and on the left. . . .
>
> Be ye not unequally yoked together with unbelievers; for what fellowship hath righteousness with unrighteousness? And what communion hath light with darkness?. . .
>
> And what agreement hath the temple of God with idols? For ye are the temple of the living God; as God hath said, I will dwell in them and walk in them; and I will be their God, and they shall be my people.
>
> Wherefore come out from among them and be ye separate, saith the Lord, and touch not the unclean thing; and I will receive you,
>
> And will be a Father unto you, and ye shall be my sons and daughters, saith the Lord Almighty (2 Corinthians 6:1-18).

7

Is All Truth God's Truth?

Then said Jesus to those Jews which believed on
him, If ye continue in my word, then are ye my disciples
indeed; and ye shall know the truth, and the truth shall
make you free (John 8:31,32).

WE HAVE EMPHASIZED that if the church as a whole
is to return to biblical Christianity, then each individual Christian will have to make that journey for himself. We are not
to follow Christian leaders except to the extent that they follow
Christ. This means that each of us has to know and follow
the Bible for himself, contending without compromise for
the faith that has been committed to us as saints to proclaim
and live. At this point an important question arises: Is it really
practical in this modern world for the Bible to be our guide
for daily living?

Of course God's Word is to be "a lamp to our feet and a light
to our path" (Psalm 119:105). But what does that mean from
a practical standpoint? After all, we live in a world that has
advanced technologically far beyond the relatively simple society
of the psalmists and apostles. The Bible isn't a medical manual,
nor is it a handbook for making out an income tax return. How
can it be a practical guide for us today? In studying the Bible,
we must remember:

1. The Bible doesn't claim to cover every subject, but whatever it says about any subject is without error, because the
entire Bible is inspired of God and therefore infallible. In those
areas that are not the primary focus of the Bible, we may

look outside its pages for counsel, but nothing should be accepted that is not in *agreement* with what the Bible says related to that subject or which violates general principles in God's Word.

2. When it comes to our relationship with God through Christ, what the Christian life consists of, how that life is to be lived, and the power for doing so, the Bible claims to offer the only and complete truth.

We must look to no other source for what God declares that He alone can supply. Whatever claims to supplement that of which God says He has given us *all* can only be a counterfeit, no matter how closely it seems to be in agreement with God's truth.

A Seductive Challenge

The Bible has been called the "manufacturer's handbook," given to man by his Creator. It is man's guide to repentance, reconciliation, and the knowledge and worship of the God who loved and redeemed him—and who desires to lead him into the happy fulfillment of all that God intended him to be and do and experience of Himself and His creation. The Bible promises that those who heed its counsel will be "perfect [mature, complete, fulfilled], thoroughly furnished unto every good work" (2 Timothy 3:17). Therefore, as Jay Adams points out in his excellent book *The Biblical View of Self-Esteem, Self-Love, and Self-Image*:

> Any system that proposes to solve human problems apart from the Bible and the power of the Holy Spirit (as all of these pagan systems, including the self-worth system, do) is automatically condemned by Scripture itself.[1]

Adams, of course, is referring to so-called "psychological problems," and explaining why the basic premise of "Christian psychology" puts it in direct conflict with Scripture. Isn't Adams being narrow-minded? After all, scientific discoveries in such fields as medicine, for example, have undeniably deepened our understanding of certain Scriptures. Then why not accept the same help from the field of psychology,* which claims to be the study of the psyche or soul? If it is legitimate for a Christian to go to a doctor who treats physical illness, then why isn't it just as legitimate to go to a doctor who treats mental illness? There are four basic prohibitive reasons. We have dealt with them already, but it may be helpful to summarize them here:

1. Medicine deals with the body (including the brain), which is physical and not covered exhaustively in the Bible. But psychology claims to treat the soul and mind, which Christians agree are nonphysical or spiritual. There is no such thing as a *mental* illness; it is either a physical problem in the brain (such as a chemical imbalance or nutritional deficiency) or it is a moral or *spiritual* problem.

2. Medicine is a *physical* science; psychology can only claim to be a *spiritual* science. But this is an impossible contradiction of terms. Psychology is a religion trying to pass itself off as a science. In fact it is a pseudoscience riddled with contradiction and confusion.

3. The Bible isn't a *scientific* manual but a *spiritual* one. It doesn't claim to provide everything we need in the way of medical advice, but it does make that kind of specific claim concerning the soul or spirit of man. Psychotherapy by very definition contradicts that claim and must be rejected for that reason if for no other.

4. The only possible rationale for supplementing the Bible with the findings of psychology would be if psychology were a physical *science* such as medicine or physics. We have already seen that to arrive at a scientific explanation for human personality, behavior, happiness, and fulfillment would destroy mankind, for the very qualities "scientifically explained" would thereby have become *natural* processes governed by scientific laws and would thus be meaningless.

Violating a Basic Principle

We must be careful not to approach the Bible with our own

---

* There is a certain segment of psychology that is scientific. It deals with such matters as learning theory, sensation, perception, and problem-solving. We are not referring to those areas but to psychotherapy, which is the area that most directly impacts the church.

prior opinions in an attempt to find verses that we can somehow use to justify what we already want to believe. Succumbing to this temptation has probably brought more problems into the church than anything else. On the contrary, we must let the Bible teach and change us. If the Bible is truly God's Word, then it will tell us what we didn't and couldn't otherwise know, and our lives will be transformed if we believe and obey.

Christian psychology is one of the most alarming examples of a wrong approach to Scripture: It is based upon predetermined psychological theories that are imposed upon the Bible. Nor were these ideas developed by sincere Christians; in most cases they were the contrivance of humanists hostile to God's Word, men who were seeking solutions to human problems outside Scripture and without God. This is not a wild accusation, but a fact that Christian psychologists cannot deny. The suggested "new reformation" has in fact been in process for some time, with accepted theology being challenged and changed by psychology. One of the leaders in that new and growing movement writes:

> Under the influence of humanistic psychologists like Carl Rogers and Abraham Maslow, many of us Christians have begun to see our need for self-love and self-esteem. This is a good and necessary focus.[2]

The author of this quote acknowledges that it was psychologists opposed to the gospel who originated theories that gave Christian psychologists a new interpretation of Scripture, one which neither they nor any other Christians before them had ever derived from the study of the Bible. Yet they now expect fellow Christians to gladly embrace these beliefs.

Trivializing Christ

As a result of the influence of psychology, the pure gospel and the practical application of the cross in daily life have been undermined. One of the most astonishing new teachings that has resulted is that *"the cross will sanctify the ego trip."*[3] (Emphasis is in the original.) The new reformation now underway requires a new interpretation of the cross:

The classical interpretation of this teaching of Christ on "bearing our cross" desperately needs reformation....

The cross Christ calls us to bear will be offered as a dream...an inspiring idea that would incarnate itself in a form of ministry that helps the self-esteem-impoverished persons to discover their self-worth through salvation and subsequent social service in our Savior's name....

So the proclamation of possibility thinking is the positive proclamation of the cross!...

Christ was the world's greatest possibility thinker. Do we dare to follow him?[4]

To call Christ a "possibility thinker," even the "greatest," trivializes who He is and what He accomplished. Like positive thinking, possibility thinking is an amoral term that can apply equally to saint or scoundrel. And to turn our daily taking up of the cross and our fellowship with Christ in His sufferings (Philippians 3:10; Colossians 1:24) into "an inspiring idea" that will build up our self-esteem and sense of self-worth is an insult to the One who hung upon the cross in agony and to Paul and the other early Christians, who were *persecuted* because of "the offense of the cross" (Galatians 5:11). Paul's indictment of those who compromised "lest they should suffer persecution for the cross of Christ" (Galatians 6:12) is equally applicable today. This new psychologized cross is an insult also to those Christians who down through the years have sincerely and meaningfully pledged in song to "cling to the old rugged cross" and "its *shame and reproach* gladly bear." Contemplation of the cross has always raised one's esteem of Christ, not of oneself, and has filled worshipers with gratitude for the worth of His blood, not with thoughts of self-worth.

It is not at all uncommon for well-meaning pastors to build their sermons around psychological theories. The new reformation is subtly bringing theology into line with psychology, and the results are devastating. The long-accepted adage that "the chief end of man is to glorify God" has now been rewritten to read, "The chief end of God is to glorify man." Sinners are no longer called upon to repent, but to awaken to their potential. No wonder J. Vernon McGee, whose highly respected Bible teaching ministry has spanned the globe for decades, sounds the alarm:

I see that this matter of psychologizing Christianity will absolutely destroy Bible teaching and Bible churches.[5]

A Most Appealing Delusion

Of all that the world has to offer, nothing appeals quite so seductively to the church as psychology's promise of rephrasing the gospel in popular selfist terminology that the world can understand and accept. One Christian leader exclaims enthusiastically, "If the gospel of Jesus Christ can be proclaimed as a theology of self-esteem, imagine the health this could generate in society!"[6] This kind of message has done anything but generate health in the secular world, and it certainly is not the gospel that Christ and His apostles preached. Nevertheless, the impression is given that here at last is the real key for evangelizing the world. Sadly, this misunderstanding seems to be growing. Those who pollute the pure water of life from God's Word with the contaminated streams of psychology are highly honored for having done so.

"Christian psychology" represents the most dangerous and at the same time the most appealing and popular form of modernism ever to have invaded the church. Those who refused the temptation to adjust biblical interpretation to agree with Darwin eventually succumbed to the even-more-deadly delusion of integrating Freud, Jung, Mesmer, and Maslow into Christianity. Many of today's staunchest evangelical and fundamentalist leaders, in order to be relevant and professionally respected, are preaching a form of Religious Science, apparently without even recognizing it. Psychology, which entered the church as a Trojan horse, now wields such a powerful and all-pervasive influence in our Christian world—in seminaries, Bible schools, Christian colleges, mission organizations, radio/television programming, denominational leadership, and most other Christian institutions and churches—that to call Christian psychology into question is taken as an attack upon Christianity itself. This is all the more astonishing when one realizes that, in actual fact, "Christian" psychology doesn't even exist.

What Is Christian Psychology?

Most Christians mistakenly assume that the term "Christian

psychology" refers to a cohesive and identifiable body of knowledge. Brief reflection will make it clear why this is not the case. Was there ever a Christian who was recognized as the founder of a particular school of psychology known as "Christian"? Of course not. University psychology textbooks list many schools of that burgeoning discipline, but not even textbooks used in Christian colleges list "Christian psychology." Certainly Jesus Christ didn't found a school of psychology! It would be as much an insult and as destructive an error to call Him a psychologist as it was for Mary Baker Eddy to call Him a scientist.

One may be, for example, a Rogerian therapist, a Freudian psychoanalyst, a Jungian analyst, or the follower of any one (or combination) of numerous schools of psychology (such as behavioristic, humanistic, transpersonal, or existential), all of which have many divisions within them. But *Christian* psychology? It is a term which everyone uses, but what does it mean? In a book that contains not one warning of any danger that might be involved, two of the most highly regarded Christian psychiatrists take what they describe as the "Christian eclectic approach."[7] By this they mean that what they consider to be the best secular methods to be found in every school of psychology are borrowed for use in a biblical context. They state:

> In addition to an awareness of the holistic nature of man, the Christian counselor must have both a broad knowledge of the great variety of [psychotherapeutic] approaches which are available and a sensitivity as to which approach is most suitable for each counselee...we take the best from each of the major categories of psychotherapy.[8]

In reading the elaborate brochures promoting the psychological and psychiatric clinics and services offered by Christian professionals in this field, one finds nearly everything from hypnosis to gestalt, but very seldom even a hint that what is being offered is *Christian*. And when the term Christian psychology is used, what is meant is simply one kind or another of secular psychology dressed up in biblical terms and passed off as something unique in itself. Consider the following statement from a paper presented to a professional gathering of Christian psychologists:

We are often asked if we are "Christian psychologists" and find it difficult to answer since we don't know what the question implies. We are Christians who are psychologists but at the present time there is no acceptable Christian psychology that is markedly different from non-Christian psychology.

It is difficult to imply that we function in a manner that is fundamentally distinct from our non-Christian colleagues. Is there a distinct Christian dentistry, or surgery, or history or grammar?

...as yet there is not an acceptable theory, mode of research or treatment methodology [in psychology] that is distinctly Christian.[9]

The admission that Christian psychology is not "markedly different from non-Christian psychology" and that Christian psychologists do not "function in a manner that is fundamentally distinct from" non-Christian psychologists probably comes as a surprise to most Christians. And well it might! Then why refer to *Christian* psychology at all? Whether intentionally or not, a false impression has been fostered in the church that needs to be corrected.

A Clear Denial

While a distinctive *Christian* psychology doesn't exist, it is the hope of most Christian psychologists to eventually bring such a discipline into existence by integrating psychology and Christianity. It ought to be clear that this would form both a new psychology and a new Christianity. For those who believe that Christianity and the Bible upon which it is founded need no improvement, such a thought is anathema. Yet such a syncretism is considered highly desirable by many Christian leaders today. One writes with concern, "Are we aware that theology has failed to accommodate and apply proven insights in human behavior as revealed by twentieth-century psychologists?"[10]

The obvious implication is that Christianity is somehow deficient and that psychology has found answers to spiritual problems that are missing from the Bible. This attitude is encouraged by statements such as the following from two leading Christian psychologists: "Both the Bible and psychology have a great deal of subject matter in common. Both study the attitudes and behavior of the human race."[11] But the Bible is not a *study*; it states God's diagnosis of our hearts and provides the complete and only answer through the redemption in Christ Jesus, His indwelling presence and power through the Holy Spirit, and the guidance of His Word. Psychology is still *studying* the matter and has come to no definitive conclusions upon which all psychologists can agree—and even if they could, it would be irrelevant to Christianity, which needs no help from psychology.

A scientist may provide some interesting insights into the inner workings of the atom, and a psychiatrist may offer fascinating information about how the brain functions, both of which would make us more appreciative of the power and creative genius of God. But to say that *theology*—the knowledge of God and of man's relationship to Him—needs to be adjusted by such information is another matter. Yet this is the claim that is being made repeatedly: that *theology*—the basic tenets of Christianity, the *spiritual* truths pertaining to man's well-being—needs to be revamped due to discoveries in the field of psychology. It is a clear denial of the sufficiency of Scripture and must therefore be unacceptable to any true Christian.

All Things That Pertain to Life and Godliness

Christian psychologists seem to overlook the fact that God promises in His Word to provide, through faith and the indwelling Holy Spirit, everything that psychology pretends to offer, and far more beyond that. To the fearful, God gives His "perfect love [that] casts out fear" (1 John 4:18) and the spirit of "power, and of love, and of a sound mind" (2 Timothy 1:7). Is someone suffering from anxiety? The Christian is *commanded* (and apparently it is a command that is possible for all to obey) to "be anxious for *nothing*," and is promised that if he will commit everything into God's hands and trust Him, then God's peace that "passes all understanding" will keep his heart and mind through Christ Jesus (Philippians 4:6,7).

The Christian psychologist complains that we are passing out Bible verses like prescription pills. It is alleged that we don't understand the deep wounds festering in the subconscious mind caused by traumas in childhood and that we therefore have no sympathy for the hurts which such persons suffer. We are accused of being uninformed in the area of psychology and are told that believing biblical promises and obeying Scripture commands doesn't work for those who need *psychological* help.

On the contrary, the Bible is filled with examples of men and women, young and old, who suffered traumas and trials such as many of those now seeking psychological help have never even imagined. It was out of their faith in God and their experience of His faithfulness through the deepest tribulations, and under the inspiration of the Holy Spirit, that the Scriptures were written. It is an insult to God and His Word to say that help is now needed from another source, particularly when the lives of those who conceived these humanistic theories pale beside the shining heroes and heroines of the faith.

What the psalmist wrote was not mere theory; he proved it himself, and so can we today: "God is our refuge and strength, a very present help in trouble; therefore will not we fear" (Psalm 46:1,2). We "have the mind of Christ" (1 Corinthians 2:16); indeed, Christ has become our very life (Colossians 3:4). *All* that we need has been provided in God's Word and may be experienced through the indwelling Spirit of Christ as we fellowship with a local body of caring believers. Surely psychology cannot improve upon the following:

> The fruit of the Spirit is love, joy, peace, longsuffering, gentleness, goodness, faith, meekness, temperance; against such there is no law. And they that are Christ's have crucified the flesh with the affections and lusts (Galatians 5:22-24).

Jesus said, "Except a corn of wheat fall into the ground and die, it abideth alone; but if it die, it bringeth forth much fruit" (John 12:24). The "fruit of the Spirit" can be produced in our lives only when we are willing to die to self in Christ—there are no formulas, no techniques, no shortcuts. To look to psychology for spiritual help is not only begging bread and fish of that which can only give stones and scorpions, but is treading on dangerous ground in view of the clear injunction against adding to or taking away from biblical revelation. Yet that is precisely the seduction of Christian psychology.

A Basic Fallacy

Christian psychologists claim that "both psychology and theology offer a great deal toward an understanding of the human race."[12] Psychology attempts to *explain* scientifically and thereby provide an *understanding* of human behavior under the amoral assumption that *ignorance* and not *sin* is the problem. If we only *understood*, then we could change our behavior to conform to our understanding.

This is a delusion that denies the root of the problem—man's sin nature and rebellion against God. A moral choice has been made that must be repented of before God. He alone can give cleansing for sin. More than that, He alone can give the *power* to live a new life through Christ's indwelling Spirit. All of the *understanding* in the world will not provide the power to change one's behavior: A new moral choice is demanded. And if that choice is made without recognizing one's obligation to God and without accepting His remedy, then the result will either be failure to make a lasting change, or, what is even worse, outward success that produces self-righteousness.

Inherent in the very idea of *Christian* psychology are two seriously erroneous implications: 1) Psychology speaks with an authority equal to the Bible; and 2) psychology offers truths (it is claimed that all truth is God's truth) that are missing from the Bible, yet are necessary if we are to be the whole persons that God intended us to be. Evangelical pastors are indicted for failing to keep up with and integrate into their ministries the theories of secular psychology:

> The typical conservative minister [is] 20 or 30 years behind his liberal colleague in being aware of the contributions of psychology to the understanding of personality.[13]

The Need for a Thorough Purging

While there are some Christian psychologists who use only Scripture in their counseling, their designation of themselves as "psychologists" is unfortunate. That word has an established meaning, which can only create confusion by the honor it seems to bestow upon a godless system that does not merit any association with Christianity at all. Unfortunately, there are also Christian psychologists who accept and practice almost every kind of psychology and therapy invented. By this means godless beliefs and practices which have already proven to be ineffective and have numerous critics among secular psychologists and psychiatrists themselves have been brought into the church. In order to return to biblical Christianity, the church must purge itself of psychological theories and terminology, and thus divest itself of the rival religion which it has taken to its bosom.

But instead of purging out the leaven, the church is granting increasing credence and honor to psychology. Christians are asked to accept psychology as the new source of truth and put it on an equal footing with God's Word. Yet psychology is as unstable as water. Its false gospel continually changes as its conflicting theories ebb and flow and its gurus come and go. Nevertheless, these illegitimate prophets who are worshiped in the secular world are influencing Christianity. Martin L. Gross comments:

> Today, the M.D. psychiatrist and his first cousin, the Ph.D. psychologist, have appointed themselves the undisputed Solomons of our era. . . .
> The new seer delivers his pronouncements with the infallible air of a papal bull, a stance which intimidates even the most confident of laymen.[14]

We are expected to rejoice that the Bible has been discovered at long last to be in agreement with humanism. Best of all, this means that we no longer need to go about with a hangdog look and poor self-image, but can now hold our heads high before the world, and especially in academic circles. All this because a "new reformation" that psychologizes Christianity has uncovered new interpretations of Scripture never before known in the history of the church, thus bringing Christianity into line with the theories of men such as Rogers and Maslow.

So goes the litany, with apparent disregard for the increasing admissions by the psychologists themselves that psychotherapy is really bankrupt. R. D. Laing, one of psychology's most respected leaders, recently gave his opinion that *not even one* "fundamental insight into relations between human beings [had] resulted from a century of psychotherapy."[15] Yet the discredited "truth of psychotherapy" has brought fundamental new insight into "God's truth"! Before believing that suspicious scenario, we would do well to heed the many non-Christian psychologists and psychiatrists who are issuing warnings, such as the following by internationally respected psychiatrist and author E. Fuller Torrey:

> Psychiatry has been willing to sanctify its values with the holy water of medicine and offer them up as the true faith of "Mental Health." It is a false Messiah.[16]

"All Truth Is God's Truth"

Should we not consider it odd that God has apparently inspired men such as Freud, Jung, and now more recently Maslow and Rogers with "truths" hidden to the apostles and prophets and all of the leaders in the entire history of the church until the present time? No, we are told reassuringly, this is not to be considered strange at all. What we allegedly need to understand is: "All truth is God's truth." This specious phrase is put forth whenever questions are raised and is generally accepted without further thought by those inquiring.

What is meant by *truth* is seldom elaborated. Are we talking about *scientific facts* involving the brain and body, or about *God's truth* involving the soul and spirit? Jesus said, "Thy Word *is* truth," not *part* of the truth. Psychotherapy deals with a subject upon which God has spoken with finality and about which He claims to have communicated in His Word the *whole truth*. There are no parts of this truth missing from the Bible and left in limbo, only to be discovered somewhere in the secular world. To suggest that there is such a lack contradicts the clear testimony of Scripture and the consistent teaching of the church for centuries, a church that withstood the Roman arena and the Inquisition and left the stamp of victorious Christian living and the blood of her martyrs upon the pages of history long before Freud or his successors came upon the scene.

It is one thing to say that it was inspiration from God, at least in a general sense, that led to the discovery of polio vaccine or atomic theory. It is quite another matter to say that God inspired

Freud with insight into methods of diagnosing and treating the soul and spirit of man. And it is equally dangerous to suggest that anti-Christians have been inspired to fill in a missing portion of the truth that God Himself declares He has already revealed in its fullness in His Holy Word. The very idea of a *Christian* psychology violates basic biblical principles, and increasing numbers of those once involved are beginning to see this and to reject this false religion. Typical of many responses received to *The Seduction of Christianity* is the following excerpt from a letter:

> I am delighted that there is something coming on the [book-store] shelves telling the truth.
> I majored in psychology, but am ashamed of it. After becoming a Christian, I realized that psychology is a false religion, but sure have a hard time convincing anyone of that fact.[17]

Paul wrote, "...the things of God knoweth no man but by the Spirit of God." It is clear in the context that he is not talking about scientific discoveries made by atheists through an insight into nature or the witness of moral conscience that God gives to all men. Paul is referring not to *natural* but to *spiritual* truths, which he specifically states are revealed by God only to true believers. The Bible clearly claims to be written to those who belong to the Lord, and the truth it communicates is called "the things of the Spirit of God." We are told in unequivocal terms:

> ...the natural [unsaved] man receiveth not the things of the Spirit of God, for they are foolishness unto him; neither can he know them, because they are spiritually discerned (1 Corinthians 2:14).

Undermining of Biblical Authority

How can "God's truth" be communicated to humanists who have rejected even the witness of creation and conscience? Are such persons really God's chosen vessels to reveal heretofore undiscovered spiritual truths to the body of Christ? According to the Bible the only "truth," in this sense, that the unsaved person can understand is that he is a sinner and needs a Savior. Until he is born again of the Spirit of God through faith in Christ, he cannot understand the "things of God" that are "spiritually discerned."

God's truth, says Paul, is only understood by the "spiritual man" who has been born of God's Spirit into the family of God. It is only such, Paul declares, who "have the mind of Christ" (1 Corinthians 2:16). To the unsaved Jesus said, "He that is of God heareth God's words; ye therefore hear them not because ye are not of God" (John 8:47). Yet we are asked to believe that a part of God's truth heretofore unknown to those who are of God and who have the mind of Christ has lately been discovered by those who are not of God, and that this new insight ought to be incorporated by the church into its understanding of the Word of God. Before we accept such an unbiblical and illogical thesis we need better justification than the plea "All truth is God's truth"!

The Christian life is not a grit-your-teeth and hold-your-breath roller-coaster ride. It is Christ living His resurrection life in those who have opened their hearts to Him. To suggest that psychotherapeutic techniques lately discovered by Freud et al are now necessary in order for today's Christian to experience the abundant life in Christ is destructive of the very faith that the proponents of this teaching say they are trying to enhance. Such is the inevitable result of interpreting the Bible on the basis of predetermined outside opinions. Martin and Deidre Bobgan point out where this eventually leads in their excellent book *How To Counsel From Scripture*, with the following quotation from a secular psychologist:

> Psychology has become something of a substitute for old belief systems. Different schools of therapy offer visions of the good life and how to live it, and those whose ancestors took comfort from the words of God and worshipped at the altars of Christ and Yahweh now take solace from and worship at the altars of Freud, Jung, Carl Rogers, Albert Ellis, Werner Erhard, and a host of similar authorities.[18]

A New Priesthood for the Church

As soon as the door was opened for the "truths" of psychology to shed further light upon Scripture, a subtle process began that is bearing its deadly fruit in the church today. If "all truth is God's truth" and psychology is part of that truth, then it must be given equal authority with the Bible. Of course Christian psychologists deny this: They assure us that no psychological theory will be accepted that contradicts the Bible. But in actual practice "psychological truth" is imposed upon the Bible and becomes the new grid through which Scripture is now to be interpreted. We are plainly told by some Christian psychologists that theology must be brought into line with psychological theory. Abraham Maslow's "hierarchy of needs" has even been baptized into the church and dressed in biblical language, in spite of the fact that Jesus taught the opposite. (Maslow puts food, clothing, shelter, etc. first; Jesus puts them last and says to seek the kingdom of God and His righteousness *first*.)[19] This plain truth is reinterpreted by the new experts, and anyone without training in psychology is disqualified from taking issue with them.

We are today confronted with an almost-impossible situation in the church. In spite of their desire to benefit the body of Christ, Christian psychologists, themselves deceived by their faith in what they believe to be helpful supplementary truth, have brought beliefs and practices into the church which are, in fact, destructive of the very faith most of them sincerely desire to defend. The responsibility for this seduction does not rest alone with Christian psychologists, however, but must be shared by those who have willingly accepted new truth that comes from sources outside of and contradicts the Bible.

As a consequence, Christians no longer can say, "To the law and to the testimony," but must now include Freud and Jung et al in assessing orthodoxy, since "all truth is God's truth." We can no longer be like the Bereans and search the Scriptures alone to see whether what is being taught is right, because some humanistic psychologist may have recently come up with a new theory that changes entirely the generally accepted understanding of a biblical passage. Since we can't possibly keep abreast of all such developments, we will have to trust the new ruling priests among us—the "professionals," the Christian psychologists.

Imperceptibly but inevitably, psychological theory by this

process gains authority over the Bible and the church. Christian universities and seminaries develop large and growing psychology departments in order to keep up with "current trends." The study of psychology has even become a prerequisite for a degree in theology. Another reader of *Seduction* writes:

> I want to thank you for taking the risk of writing such a book.... When I arrived on the college campus for 4 years at _____ [a well-known Christian university], my desire was to study psychology in order to become a counselor.
>
> When I did a little inquiring...I experienced a great disappointment. Somewhere I had picked up the erroneous idea that psychology on a "Christian" college campus was taught from the Scriptures based on who God says we are.
>
> Boy, was I wrong![20]

The New Christianity

No church staff of any size is any longer considered to be complete without at least one psychologist. Pastors begin to believe that they are not competent to counsel from the Bible without going back to seminary for an advanced degree in psychology. They are competent to *preach* or *teach* the Word of God if they have a degree in theology, but incompetent to *counsel* from the Word of God without a degree in psychology. This new state of affairs (which would disqualify the great spiritual counselors of the past) simply cannot be supported from the Bible. Yet it is being accepted almost without challenge, and those who do speak out are accused of causing division or of speaking from ignorance. Another reader of *Seduction* writes:

> I've been a Christian for about fourteen years, spending much of that time preparing for full-time Christian work.... Since I planned to become a pastor, it seemed natural for me to major in psychology.
>
> So that's what my degree is in.... Before I was a junior, I realized what a mixed-up hodgepodge of senseless trash I was studying. My typewriter faces a bookshelf loaded with dozens of texts on psychology and counseling, none of which I would reread or recommend anyone else to read.[21]

A whole new vocabulary of psychological jargon is now needed to explain an endless new category of problems tagged with labels not found in the Bible and unknown to the church in its entire history. These new phrases now roll glibly off the tongues of pastors who are sincerely trying to "be relevant" and to "communicate." We are being told that, although no one understood it that way before, the Bible has all along been talking about Freud's "id, ego, and superego," Jung's "collective unconscious, individuation, and integration," Rogers's "nondirective, client-centered counseling,"[22] Glasser's "*Reality Therapy*,"[23] Maslow's "hierarchy of needs and self-actualization,"[24] and even Janov's "Primal Pool of Pain."[25] The following quotation from the pastor/author who reportedly has the largest Christian television audience in America is typical of the new Christianity's selfist-psychology vocabulary that was unknown to the church until a few years ago and seems strangely at odds with Christ's command to "deny self and take up the cross and follow me":

> Self-love is a crowning sense of self-worth. It is an ennobling emotion of self-respect...an abiding faith in yourself. It is sincere belief in yourself.
> It comes through self-discovery, self-discipline, self-forgiveness and self-acceptance. It produces self-reliance, self-confidence and an inner security, calm as the night.[26]

Spiritual or Psychological?

Spiritual problems that were once dealt with through biblical counseling by caring fellow believers have now become *psychological problems* that require psychological solutions administered by a new class of "professionals." One of the leading inner healers explains that this new Christianity deals with *psychological* problems and solutions previously unknown to the church:

> I was born again of the Spirit...I became a "new creation"....
> But my "soul" part is another matter.
> The Greek for "soul" is *psyche*. My soul is my *psych*ological nature...this part of me is in the process of *being* made whole, day by day....
> This book is specifically talking about the healing of the *soul*...
> [emphasis in original].[27]

She then proceeds to discuss "a vast area called the unconscious" that Christians "are not able to reach directly" but which mysteriously governs our behavior in ways we aren't even aware of because "everything that happened to you, even from the time you were a tiny baby, is recorded in your memory" and has then "sunk into the subconscious."[28] In his devastating critique of psychology, Martin Gross, who does not approach this subject from a Christian point of view, discusses this Freudian invention that forms the basis for most Christian psychological counseling and inner healing:

> If science and statistics are not on the side of psychotherapy, and if shamanism and witch doctoring do as well, what is holding up its inordinate prestige? As in other major unscientific movements, its true support is a *religious idea* which has captured the mass imagination.
>
> *One of the most powerful religious ideas of the second half of the twentieth century is the Great Unconscious....*
>
> We can control our present and our future, we are told, *only* if we learn the mysteries of psychology and psychiatry which can unlock the Unconscious. Like the primitive witch doctor, the modern therapist promises to do this... [emphasis in original].[29]

Again we see the sad result of interpreting the Bible on the basis of predetermined beliefs—and, unfortunately in the case of psychology, beliefs that cannot be agreed upon among the "experts," and which have not been proven (and in many cases have actually been proven not to work). Christian psychology is an attempted balancing act, with one foot upon the solid Rock, Christ Jesus, and the other on the sinking sand of humanism.

The next chapter in the book on inner healing referred to above is titled "Do You Need Soul Healing?" The author has already defined "soul" as the "psychological nature," so what the book is really about is "psychological healing." Those who practice inner healing, or healing of the memories, are often very sincere and earnest Christians seeking to help other people. However, their ministries are built upon the contradictory and passing theories of psychology, not upon the eternal and never-changing truth of God's Word. What they offer is in fact psychotherapy thinly coated with a Christian veneer to make it acceptable in the church.

A Vital Issue

In summary, by accepting a "new interpretation" of the Bible that comes from outside and cannot be supported by the Scriptures themselves, the church has embraced an alien gospel administered by a new class of priests supported by humanistic authority. With its own vocabulary and rituals and academic knowledge, this new clergy has gained authority over those who know only God and His Word and are thus no longer qualified to *counsel* from Scripture. That long-established function has taken on new meaning: It now involves the diagnosis of *psychological* problems and *psychological* solutions and must therefore be under the direction of those trained in this art. No one can appeal to the Scriptures as a means of correcting this new priestly class, because they alone hold the keys to a vital part of "God's truth" that supplements the Bible.

In fairness to the Christian psychologists, most of them have been motivated by the genuine desire to help the many hurting people who are not receiving the care and guidance they ought to have from their brothers and sisters in the body of Christ. One of the most desperate needs within the church is for personal and family and marriage counseling—but it must be *biblical* and not *psychological*. For this need to be supplied, the church must be willing to support biblical counselors who can thereby provide the necessary help without charging for it. Many young people sense a call of God upon their lives to work in this vital area, but the only possibility for support is to charge a fee—which means that they must be licensed by the state and therefore conform to secular standards of education and competency. The church must provide adequate training in biblical counseling, yet at the present almost nothing of this nature is available. Christian colleges and seminaries have succumbed to the pressure to be accredited by secular agencies, and the academic courses in "pastoral counseling" are therefore generally heavily weighted with psychology.

It would be unthinkable for the state to license and impose such control over those who *preach* and *teach* from Scripture.

Yet we consider it normal for those whom we expect to *counsel* from the Bible to be regulated in this way. Only when the church considers *counseling* of individuals to be as important as *preaching* to and *teaching* congregations will biblical counseling take its rightful place in the church. Until then the best of sermons will still leave many practical needs unmet and hurting people will unfortunately continue to turn to psychologists for lack of the real solution being put into practice by the local church.

The healing of broken lives, moreover, cannot be accomplished by an hour of counseling once or even several times a week. It can take place only in the context of the caring and loving family of God, the body of Christ concerned for the welfare of each member. There ought to be older couples, mature in the Lord and leading exemplary, Spirit-filled lives of leadership, who will give the time and expend the effort to take under their wing younger couples who may be having marital or financial problems. Again it is an individual matter: Revival begins with each of us. We dare not wait for someone else to say or do what is needed, but each of us before the Lord must step out in the leading and power of the Holy Spirit to fulfill that ministry to which God has called us. God's Word enjoins us:

> Warn them that are unruly, comfort the feeble-minded, support the weak, be patient toward all (1 Thessalonians 5:14).
>
> Blessed be God, even the Father of our Lord Jesus Christ, the Father of mercies and the God of all comfort; who comforteth us in all our tribulation, that we may be able to comfort them which are in any trouble by the comfort wherewith we ourselves are comforted of God (2 Corinthians 1:3,4).
>
> Bear ye one another's burdens and so fulfil the law of Christ (Galatians 6:2).

We are spending considerable time on this issue because it is vitally important that we understand how we got to the present impasse. If we are to return to a biblical Christianity, then we must undo what has already been done. We must cease adding to and taking away from the Bible. God has specifically forbidden this and has prescribed heavy penalties for it, yet we have violated His command and are reaping the inevitable results.

8

The Roots and Fruits
of Selfism

When the woman saw that the tree was good for food,
and that it was pleasant to the eyes, and a tree to be desired
to make one wise, she took of the fruit thereof and did eat,
and gave also unto her husband with her, and he did eat
(Genesis 3:6).

THE PROHIBITION AGAINST taking from or adding to
God's Word is consistently implied throughout Scripture, and
at times it is stated explicitly, as in the following admonition by
Solomon: "Every word of God is pure.... Add thou not unto
his words, lest he reprove thee, and thou be found a liar"
(Proverbs 30:5,6). No other reason should be needed for rejecting the claim that psychology contains parts of "God's truth"
necessary for bringing God's Word up-to-date. The Bible ends
with Christ's promise to "come quickly," preceded by this explicit
and sober warning:

> If any man shall add unto these things, God shall add unto
> him the plagues that are written in this book; and if any
> man shall take away from the words of the book of this
> prophecy, God shall take away his part out of the book of
> life, and out of the holy city, and from the things which
> are written in this book (Revelation 22:18,19).

The Ancient Roots of Cultism/Selfism

Unfortunately, the tendency to disregard God's clearly stated
commands lurks in every heart and lies at the root of most human
problems. It began in the Garden of Eden. Adam and Eve were

the first to take liberties with God's Word. They had no written Scriptures, but God had spoken to them personally and apparently audibly: "They heard the voice of the Lord God. . . . I heard thy voice in the garden" (Genesis 3:8,10). We know nothing of the marvelous insights which God must have shared with this pair, but we do know that He commanded them not to eat of one particular tree in the Garden. God considered this of such great importance that the penalty for disobedience was death.

"That old serpent called the Devil and Satan, which deceiveth the whole world" (Revelation 12:9), was immediately at work in the Garden of Eden providing what has ever since been the most effective rationale for legitimizing disobedience: the *reinterpretation* of what God has said to bring it into line with human desire. Questioning God's command, Satan perverted its meaning, turned the death penalty into a promise of godhood, and persuaded Eve to accept his innovative and appealing interpretation of God's Word.

Eve had found a "prophet" whose twisted but appealing perversion of truth was irresistible. The Bible warns that the time will come when the church will be full of such teachers who "shall turn away their [the people's] ears from the truth. . ." (2 Timothy 4:4). The people, however, are equally guilty, for it is they who "heap to themselves" such false teachers by supporting and following them. Personal accountability cannot be escaped, and certainly God held Eve accountable.

Every cult has its origins in the same deception, voiced by a guru or prophet who pretends to have a new or exclusive insight into what God has *really* said. And the most seductive false prophets serve up on a different platter the same lie which Eve believed and which we each want to hear: that we can escape God's judgment and its consequent suffering, sickness, and death. Through being initiated into an esoteric knowledge that opens the door to our own godhood we can control our own destiny. Somehow we can be like God.

The Evil Origins of Selfism

Satan's seduction of Eve was the original appeal to *self*. "*You* can be like the gods" (or "like God," depending upon the translation) was the seductive promise. Something inside Eve responded to that. It was then that "self had its awful birth, and established its throne,"[1] said William Law. "It is man's dreadful fall from the life of God in his soul that has given birth to self and the deceit of pride."[2] Calling sinful self "one of the greatest curses in life," Lloyd-Jones said, "It is a result of the Fall."[3] Eve succumbed to the same temptation by which her seducer had earlier deceived himself, to his own destruction. Of this once beautiful, wise, and good being, the Scripture declares:

> Thou sealest up the sum, full of wisdom and perfect in beauty. Thou hast been in Eden the garden of God.... Thou art the anointed cherub that covereth...perfect in thy ways from the day that thou wast created, till iniquity was found in thee (Ezekiel 28:12-15).
> How art thou fallen from heaven, O Lucifer, son of the morning.... Thou hast said in thine heart, I will ascend into heaven, I will exalt my throne above the stars of God... I will be like the Most High. Yet thou shalt be brought down to hell, to the sides of the pit (Isaiah 14:12-15).

Here was the birth of the first new theology and the forerunner of all the false theologies that have followed. Each one has been inspired by the same evil genius who is the "god of this world" (2 Corinthians 4:4). Satan's boast, "I will be like the Most High!" was a rejection of monotheism (belief in one God) and the assertion of polytheism (belief in many gods). Satan cannot be accused of atheism. He didn't deny God's *existence*, but challenged God's *uniqueness* by his self-exalting ambition to be *like* Him. Let us not accuse Lucifer of desiring to be *greater* than God; he only aspired to become a god himself, in God's class, with all power at his disposal.

Lucifer's fall presents some solemn lessons. It was the very wisdom and power which God had given him that corrupted Satan: He began to look upon it as his own, something that *he* possessed intrinsically. This secret pride was instantly known to the Most High, and in that moment the wisest and most beautiful and powerful being ever created lost his position in heaven and became the archenemy of God and the epitome of evil. Let every man take warning! The moment we think we are or have something intrinsically good in and of ourselves we have become partners with Satan in his pride. If it was pride in his beauty ("thine heart was lifted up because of thy beauty"— Ezekiel 28:17) that corrupted Lucifer's great wisdom, how much more easily would we of lesser wisdom be corrupted by finding beauty—moral, physical, or intellectual—within ourselves. It was certainly not a "negative self-image" that was Satan's downfall, but a very "positive" one. William Law declared:

> Self-love, self-esteem, and self-seeking are the essence and the life of pride; and the Devil, the father of pride, is never absent from these passions, nor without an influence in them. . . .
>
> Every son of Adam is in the service of self, regardless of education or position in life, until a humility that comes solely from heaven has become his redemption through the indwelling Christ.[4]

The Cosmic Conspiracy

Satan seems to have seen in the human race a means of furthering his claim to equality with God. Judging from the dispute between God and Satan over Job's loyalty to God and the reason behind it, mankind apparently plays a peculiar role in this battle. Satan must have decided that Eve would be easier than Adam to deceive with the promise of godhood. Of course, he didn't tell her that she would be a counterfeit god, nor did Eve realize that the elite club of "gods" she was joining were demonic beings who were already under the judgment of the Most High.

Although Adam was not deceived (1 Timothy 2:14), he joined in the rebellion, apparently in order not to lose his wife. In shame they were banished from God's presence and paradise and from the tree of life, whose fruit otherwise would have kept them alive forever. God would not perpetuate man in his fallen condition. He did, however, promise that one day "the seed of the woman" (i.e. the virgin-born Messiah) would "bruise the serpent's head" and thus provide a just means of forgiveness for rebels who were willing to receive it.

This brief scenario introduced in the Bible's first few pages sets the stage for everything else that Scripture has to say and presents a plot so intriguing that it far surpasses the most ingenious novel ever written by man. Not confined to earth, the breathtaking drama sweeps across the galaxies to the very throne of God in a gigantic battle for control of the universe. What makes this classic story more than fascinating is the fact that this same cosmic struggle rages in every human heart and involves the eternal destiny of each one of us. We have all fallen victim to the proud delusion that destroyed Lucifer and by means of which he has attempted to drag the entire universe with him into the lake of fire, thereby hoping to thwart God's plans and love. Francis Schaeffer attempted to awaken Christians to the reality of this battle and the vital role they must play:

> Do we really believe that we are engaged in this cosmic battle? Do we really believe that there are "powers of this dark world" which rule our age? . . .
>
> The primary battle is a spiritual battle in the heavenlies . . . but it is equally a battle here on earth . . . in the visible world, in the minds of men and women, and in every area of human culture . . . .
>
> But if we are to win the battle on the stage of human history, it will take . . . a life committed to Christ, founded in truth, lived in righteousness and grounded in the gospel.[5]

Our only hope is to stand in the victory that Christ has already won on the cross. Nor is our battle with "flesh and blood, but against principalities, against powers, against the rulers of the darkness of this world, against spiritual wickedness in high places" (Ephesians 6:12). It is equally important, however, to recognize the horrible truth that Satan and his minions have an ally within our own hearts, which will betray us into their hands unless our sinful self is put to death through our identification with Christ in His death on our behalf upon the cross. Giving the secret of victory, John wrote:

> The great dragon was cast out, that old serpent called the Devil and Satan, which deceiveth the whole world . . . . And they [the saints] overcame him by the blood of the Lamb, and by the word of their testimony; and they loved not their lives unto death (Revelation 12:9,11).

What Is Self?

"The whole trouble in life," declared Lloyd-Jones, "is ultimately a concern about self."[6] Taking a different view, one of the all-time best-selling Christian authors has long portrayed Christianity as an "adventure of self-discovery" that helps believers to "become aware of [their] innate goodness."[7] This kind of teaching has become so popular that many Christians have forgotten that self is their biggest enemy. Unfortunately, the influence of psychology in the church has led to a preoccupation with and glorification of self.

Logically we ought to define self before discussing it further. That is not so easily done. The Bible gives no definition of self, and a dictionary says something like "one's own person as distinct from all others," which isn't very helpful. It tells us nothing *about* self, except that it is an exclusionary term—*my*self refers exclusively to me in distinction to all other beings. Thus, to be selfish is to put *my*self ahead of *your*self. One can easily see that Eve put *her*self ahead of God and Adam. Yet such an attitude, due to the influence of humanistic psychology, is commended today not only in the secular world but in the church as well. One evangelical leader declared:

> I hope my wife will never divorce me, because I love her with all my heart. But if one day she feels that I am minimizing her or making her feel inferior or in any way standing in the light that she needs to become the person that God meant her to be, I hope she'll feel free to throw me out even if she's one hundred.
>
> There is something more important than our staying married, and it has to do with integrity, personhood, and purpose.[8]

Such false "integrity" dishonors God, His Word, and the marriage vows in order to be "true to oneself." This is the very self-centeredness that began in Eden and has been recognized since then as the root of evil, but is now being glorified as the answer to our problems due to the influence of psychology.

Humanistic psychologist Carl Rogers's selfism has heavily influenced Christian psychology. Explaining why he was not able to give his wife of many years the attention she needed and should have expected from him in the last months of her terminal illness, Rogers writes:

I realized that it was necessary for my survival to live *my* life, and that this must come first, even though Helen was so ill.[9]

What Satan seduced Eve into was one big self-trip. She was tempted with the thought of how delicious the forbidden fruit would taste to *her*, how wise it would make *her*, and how glorious was the godhood *she* would achieve. She never thought she was doing *evil*. As McCandlish Phillips has so well said, "One of Satan's tactics is to persuade men to disobey God on the promise that they shall obtain good by it."[10] Eve was simply learning the great importance of *looking out for number one*. Her motivation was *self*-interest and *self*-satisfaction, and it took a lot of *self*-assertion, all qualities that are honored today as essential for "getting ahead" and being one's "own person."

Totally absorbed in what *she* would get out of eating this wonderful fruit, Eve stifled any concern for what she *ought* to do. There was no *ought* at all: no regard for duty, moral commitment, or restraint upon her desires—no real concern for anyone but herself. Eve threw out honor and obedience as though she owed nothing to the One who had created and lovingly placed her in this beautiful garden. Eve trampled loyalty and love and trust in her selfish stampede toward what would today be called self-realization or self-actualization. The end was so *good* that surely the means of achieving it could not be wrong. Her decision was totally *self*-centered and therefore doomed her to guilt and sorrow and death.

From that tragic moment her life became a living death in which we all share—the frustrating daily attempt to deny the obvious truth that fulfillment is not found in self but in God, not in what *I* want and think is best, but in what *He* has so lovingly and wisely ordained. The tragic consequences of this choice remain with us all today. Cut off by his own self-will from his Creator, man is like a fish out of water, gasping for air, struggling for life, writhing, dying—and madly grasping at any straw that promises an escape from God's just judgment and the finding of a *self*-satisfied life instead.

Denying a "Hateful" Idol

There is no need to speculate what kind of fruit Eve ate or how beautiful and tempting it looked. The details are immaterial. To Eve it held the key to realizing her full potential, but it was an act of deliberate disobedience. And disobedience, as we all know, is an act of *self*-assertion in *self*-interest. Satan had seduced Eve into the first *selfish* act in human history. Nor is it an overstatement to say that *self* is the root of *sin*. J. Gregory Mantle calls self a "hateful idol" and speaks of those who are obsessed with self-esteem and self-love and "love to worship at the shrine of self."[11]

The seventeenth-century Scottish preacher Samuel Rutherford, so well-known for his inspiring letters, wrote:

> But alas! that idol, that whorish creature *myself* is the master-idol we all bow to. What hurried Eve headlong upon the forbidden fruit, but that wretched thing *herself*? What drew that brother-murderer to kill Abel? That untamed *himself*....
>
> Every man blames the devil for his sins; but the great devil, the house-devil of every man, the house-devil that eateth and lieth in every man's bosom, is that idol that killeth all, *himself*.
>
> Oh! blessed are they who can deny themselves, and put Christ in the room of themselves! O sweet word: "I live no more, but Christ liveth in me!"[12]

Although we cannot define self any more than we can define soul or being or beauty, we can clearly see where self was first manifested, how it happened, and the eternal result. We can also see that self not only defines one person as distinct from all others, but it also defines man as distinct from God. What the Bible seems to mean by self is man cut off from God, acting and possessing independently. This is why Christ made the denial of self a condition to becoming His disciple and why there is a fatal flaw in the theology of self-esteem.

We must also distinguish between a humanistic self-denial and a biblical denial of self. The first is self still on the throne but denying itself certain pleasures; the second is the death of self through our identification with Christ in His death for our sin. If self is not put to death, it will deify itself. "Pride," said

Chambers, "is the deification of self."[13] See the contrast in Christ, the perfect Man, who said:

> My meat is to do the will of him that sent me, and to finish his work (John 4:34).
>
> Verily, verily, I say unto you, The Son can do nothing of himself, but what he seeth the Father do.... I can of mine own self do nothing.... For I came down from heaven not to do my own will but the will of him that sent me (John 5:19,30; 6:38).
>
> The words that I speak unto you I speak not of myself; but the Father that dwelleth in me, he doeth the works (John 14:10).

Unfortunately, the glorification of self that has entered into the church through the influence of Christian psychologists has turned Christian values upside down. One Christian leader tells how involvement in a therapy group allowed him to "deal with"—psychologically but not biblically—long-buried anger against "God, the church, his father, himself and his wife...." His wife went through the same experience, "got in touch with her own anger," and, he confesses, "it was the beginning of the end for us as a couple...." They were divorced, but with the new selfist views firmly implanted, they decided that it was in fact "a healthy new beginning for each of [them]."[14] Decrying such folly, one writer has commented:

> The striking thing is that [he] discerns in this a principle for Christian living.
>
> [He] describes himself as an Abraham, called by faith to leave the security of marriage to embark on a spiritual pilgrimage.
>
> [He] consciously values an undefined search for individual, emotional authenticity over the Christian call to commitment, faithfulness, and perseverance in marriage.[15]

It is saddening that increasing numbers of Christians, through believing that psychology is scientific, are embracing beliefs which even non-Christians recognize to be fallacious and dangerous and warn against. One recent book resulting from five years of study by a team of researchers from a variety of universities warns that "the American 'cult of the individual' is destroying our ability to remain connected" with family and friends and moral values. The study indicates that "Americans in therapy frequently 'give birth to the self,' " causing them to "lack a larger moral fiber on which to base decisions, other than 'present whim.' " The authors go on to say:

> One begins to develop values on the basis of wishes and wants, what things he's willing to give to get it and what he's not willing to give to get it, establishing a perception of the world that has more to do with how things work than how they ought to work....
>
> The question, "Is this right or wrong?" becomes "Is this going to work for me now?"[16]

Exonerating Self

In the footsteps of his ancestors, modern man still conspires to recreate the Eden that self lost: by legislation, technology, and psychotherapy (and its many self-help offshoots) as well as through the revival of mystical and occult practices. If, consequently, anything goes wrong in our schemes (and it inevitably does), the moral culpability is not the individual's. It is the fault of "society," or circumstances, or the abuse that one suffered as a child. Such arguments attempt to deny the loss of Eden and the sin that caused it. It is a mad scheme to shift the blame from ourselves, to deny the obvious—that we are the ones who have destroyed our world—and if all else fails, to find the defendant (ourselves) "not guilty by reason of insanity."

Psychiatrist Thomas Szasz searched all of the reports and findings generated by the murder/suicide of 900 people in Guyana and found that the politicians, journalists, lawyers, psychiatrists, and other experts had universally concluded that Jim Jones was insane. Commenting upon this conclusion, Herbert Schlossberg writes:

> New York columnist James Reston seemed to speak for everyone when he said that Jones was an obviously demented man. Yet Szasz could find no evidence that anyone had doubted Jones's sanity before the incident. In fact, a gala fund-raising dinner in his honor, endorsed by 75 prominent leaders, was scheduled in San Francisco for December 2, 1978, and had to be cancelled after the massacre.

Szasz's explanation makes more sense...."I think he was an evil man.''....

The significant point is that so many people concluded that a monstrous act like Jones's had to be an act of insanity; they no longer believed, if they ever had, that evil acts are done by evil people.[17]

David G. Meyers, himself a professor of psychology, points out that "research psychologists have not said much about evil. In *Psychological Abstracts* the word evil is not an index term and, of the nearly 300,000 titles cited between 1967 and 1978, it appears in only seventeen."[18] Such blatant and blind bias has even infected Christians and affected the proclamation of the gospel, which now must be "positivized" because man is basically good and only needs to be awakened to that fact. As one critic of the New Reformation has written, "He [Schuller] says we convert people not by telling them what they truly are (sinners), but 'By telling them they *are* what we wish they would become.' "[19] One of today's most widely heard Christian leaders attacks what he calls a "basic defect in much of modern Christianity":

> What is that basic flaw? I believe it is the failure to proclaim the gospel in a way that can satisfy every person's deepest need— one's spiritual hunger for glory. Rather than glorify God's highest creation—the human being—Christian liturgies, hymns, prayers, and scriptural interpretations have often insensitively and destructively offended the dignity of the person....[20]

We can only wonder what "Christ" the new gospel wins men to, when instead of telling them that "Christ Jesus came into the world to save *sinners*" (1 Timothy 1:15), its goal is to preserve their dignity. How different the approach found in Joseph Alleine's *Alarm To The Unconverted*. His success at winning souls was considered exceptional even among the outstanding Puritans of his day. Consider the following earnest appeal from Alleine, who died in 1662 at the age of 34 after being twice imprisoned for his faith:

> I am not baiting my hook with rhetoric, nor fishing for your applause, but for your souls. My work is not to please you, but to save you....

If I were to please your ears, I would sing another song....
But how much better are the wounds of a friend than the fair
speeches of the harlot....

I know, if we succeed not with you, you are lost; if we cannot
get your consent to arise and come away, you will perish forever.
No conversion—no salvation![21]

Because he is made in the image of God, man can never be
happy, try what he will, unless he is holy in Christ. Christianity
stands in stark contrast to the empty psychological solutions being
offered today, and we dishonor our Lord and mislead the world
when we lower the gospel to a level that caters to ungodly tastes.

Paradise Lost, Heaven Gained

It was Eve's "spiritual hunger for glory" that got her into
trouble, and God was apparently unconcerned about "offending
the dignity" of Adam and Eve and under no illusion about the
need to restore their shattered self-esteem. In expelling the guilty
pair from the Garden, God was acting both justly and in love.
He kept man from the tree of life because it would not have been
an act of love but a capitulation to man's self-indulgence to
perpetuate him in his fallen condition. One of the marks of those
who have truly met Christ is their willingness to see good in what
they otherwise would have complained against. A young man
recently wrote from prison:

I have been saved and Spirit-filled for a little over a
year...[and] have had such a hunger for spiritual teaching as only
a fellow Spirit-filled Christian can appreciate....

I've been locked up nearly twenty months, and believe it or not,
I thank God for it, because otherwise I'd never have stood still
long enough to hear the Gospel and respond to it.[22]

It is popular today to speak of "unconditional love," often
interpreted to mean "Love me but don't correct me." Yet love
does not operate in a vacuum; true love disciplines and corrects:
"Whom the Lord loveth he chasteneth" (Hebrews 12:6). Love
speaks and applies the truth. Anything less than this is not love
at all, but mere sentimentality. If love fails to act according to
truth and justice it has lost its virtue and has sunk to the level

of lust or insanity or blind indulgence. In God's response to the rebellion of Adam and Eve we see real love in action. God's love does not violate truth or justice, and for God to provide the pardon that His love desires to dispense, man must confess his sin, repent, and receive the remedy that God has provided in Jesus Christ.

The final hell in which all unrepentant rebels will one day find themselves is the state of independence from divine standards that they demanded and the freedom that they insisted upon to do their "own thing." Too late they will realize fully the insatiable loneliness of self cut off completely from its Creator and thus from the source of life, love, joy, and all that is worthwhile. Engulfed in hopeless despair, man will discover at last that he is a false god who has betrayed himself and is now alone and unable to climb out of the eternal grave that he himself has dug.

Heaven is man's return to paradise, which is essentially the return to God. It must therefore be on God's terms or not at all. Those terms are spelled out quite clearly in the opening chapters of Genesis. Sin put the flaming sword of God's judgment between man and the tree of life:

> So he drove out the man; and he placed at the east of the garden of Eden cherubim, and a flaming sword which turned every way, to keep the way of the tree of life (Genesis 3:24).

God was not vindictively barring man's access to eternal life, for in the last chapter of the Bible we see redeemed man in paradise once again and now eating freely of "the tree of life" (Revelation 22:2). What happened to that sword of judgment, from which all men have fled in fear and against whose harsh and final stroke all men have complained so bitterly? In contrast to all others, one Man, the only one who could, one day walked up to that sword and took its fatal stroke for all the rest of us.

Judgment's sword was sheathed in His heart and its flame was quenched in His blood. He had no sin of His own, so He could die for ours. This is why Christ alone, in contrast to Buddha, Krishna, Confucius, and all the founders of the world's great religions, could say without contradiction: "I am the way, the truth, and the life; no man cometh to the Father but by me."

To become the way for us back to the tree of life, He had to take the judgment we deserved.

Paradise regained, however, is much better than the paradise that had been lost. It would be no solution at all simply to restore what Adam and Eve had forfeited. We would lose paradise again just as they did. Something more was needed. The new paradise has a new Adam in charge—the virgin-born "seed of the woman" who is also the Son of God. Jesus Christ is called the "last Adam" and also the "second man" (1 Corinthians 15:45,47). There was no other human being who walked this earth since Adam who deserved to be called a "man" until, as the *first* had been formed from the ground by the hand of God, the *second* was formed in the womb of a virgin. Though He is the *second* Adam, He is called the *last*, because there will never be a *third*, much less a *fourth*. Paradise restored will never be lost again. The new Adam, the second and last, will personally see to that.

Jesus Christ is the progenitor of the new race of those who have been "born again" through faith in Him and who are destined to inhabit God's new universe. Sin will never enter into that new paradise, which will forever be under His direction, having been bought with His blood poured out at Calvary for our sins. The responsibility for keeping paradise restored will no longer rest upon mere human beings but upon Him who is both God and man. Redeemed man will never be banished from God's presence. Forever Christ will maintain the perfect union between God and man in His own person—a union that He brings into every heart that opens to Him as Lord and Savior. In contrast to the pompous rule of self over its false kingdom, the true King who will reign forever said concerning himself: "Take my yoke upon you and learn of me; for I am meek and lowly in heart, and ye shall find rest unto your souls" (Matthew 11:29).

"The way of the cross," says Dave Wilkerson, "is surrender of all that is dear to us in this life."[23] We must follow Christ in that path to the new paradise. As the old hymn said (the new songs usually avoid the cross), "I must needs go home by the way of the cross; there's no other way but this. I can ne'er get sight of the gates of light if the way of the cross I miss." This is not popular teaching, now that the new theology has gained such a strong foothold. As Tozer said:

> Among the plastic saints of our times, Christ has to do all the dying and all we want is to hear another sermon about His dying....
>
> No cross for us, no dethronement, no dying. We remain king within the little kingdom of Mansoul and wear our tinsel crown with all the pride of a Caesar; but we doom ourselves to shadows and weakness and spiritual sterility.[24]

Conflicting Views of Self

Unfortunately, human history is one long tale of man's rejection of God's solution and his hapless persistence in beating the dead horse of his own doomed efforts to restore paradise his own way. Selfisms of every kind are being promoted as desirable not only in the secular world but in the church as well. J. I. Packer has well said:

> ...modern Christians...spread a thin layer of Bible teaching over the mixture of popular psychology and common sense they offer, but their overall approach clearly reflects the narcissism— the "selfism" or "meism" as it is sometimes called—that is the way of the world in the modern West.[25]

As a result of the church giving psychological "truth" an equal status with the Bible, a new view of self has arisen that is in diametric opposition to the long-established one. The Christian Association for Psychological Studies would have us believe: "Humility and positive self-esteem are not based upon self-negation or the 'emptying of oneself.' They are based upon affirmation of God's regard toward us...."[26] Robert Schuller declares, "Self-affirmation then is the pathway to self-denial."[27] So Christ's command to deny self is interpreted to mean affirmation of self. As Jay Adams has said:

> Certainly this older, standard evangelical view of man and his problem, and the New Reformation, self-esteem views are at odds.
>
> There is a new wind blowing through the church today. It demands change—a change of viewpoint, belief, and approach.

Is it true or false? You must decide...man's problem cannot be at the same time too little and too much self-esteem.[28]

What a debt self owes psychology! Instead of being denied, self is now loved, esteemed, and promoted. Indeed, we are being told repeatedly from pulpit, radio, television, books, and magazines that the greatest need facing the church is for Christians to develop their self-love, self-esteem, self-worth, and positive self-image.

One Christian leader calls self-esteem "the single greatest need facing the human race today,"[29] and many others use similar language. Obviously there is a serious conflict between what Jesus said (and what the church has historically believed on the subject of self) and the new view now being popularly accepted: that self-esteem is "the universal hope."[30] Consider, for example, the following from John Calvin in his classic *Institutes of the Christian Religion*:

> Accordingly, in every age, he who is most forward in extolling the excellence of human nature is received with the loudest applause. But be this heralding of human excellence what it may, by teaching man to rest in himself it does nothing more than fascinate by its sweetness and, at the same time, so delude as to drown in perdition all who assent to it. Whosoever, therefore, gives heed to those teachers who merely employ us in contemplating our good qualities, so far from making progress in self-knowledge, will be plunged into the most pernicious ignorance.[31]

Thankfully, there are still dissenting voices calling us back to biblical Christianity. J. Gregory Mantle reminds us that "self-centeredness [is] man's most persistent problem."[32] Humanism, of course, has much in common with the new self-centered gospel, particularly with its emphasis on self-esteem. California State Assemblyman John Vasconcellos, who believes that restoration of self-esteem is the great need, has been in the forefront of the move to push the religion of humanism upon society because he sincerely believes it is our only hope. He explains:

> The issue is *always* whether or not we believe that we humans are inherently good, trustworthy and responsible. This issue is

becoming *the* central social and political challenge of our times: to transform all our relationships and institutions (personal and political) to fit our new-found faithful sense of ourselves.... It is the only way to life!...

We seek means to...open ourselves to our innate potential for goodness; to reclaim our individual self-esteem....[33]

Similar ideas are being promoted by Christian leaders who argue that the primary goal of the gospel must be to meet "every person's deepest need—his hunger for self-esteem, self-worth, and personal dignity."[34] Many others, however, are equally convinced that man's true hunger is for *God*, and that it is God's glory and not man's dignity and self-worth that is at stake.

There is a legitimate desire placed by God within all people to find the purpose and meaning of their existence. The error of humanism and psychology is in looking to self for what only God can provide. "O Lord, I know that the way of man is not in himself," said Jeremiah; "it is not in man that walketh to direct his steps" (Jeremiah 10:23). Augustine said, "Thou has made us for thyself, O God, and we are restless until we find our rest in thee." The selfist attempts to find this rest not through confidence in God but in the self-confidence that comes from a positive self-image. Pascal spoke of the God-shaped vacuum within that only God could fill. But today this inner emptiness is explained as a lack of self-worth and self-esteem; selfist solutions are offered which do not satisfy that spiritual thirst for God Himself.

We are back to a major error that we have already dealt with in slightly different form: seeing God, in effect, as little more than a means to self-fulfillment and viewing all that He has done, including the cross of Christ, primarily from the selfish perspective of what we get out of it. It is the same old rebellion, but now justified by the theories of psychology. In turning the focus from God to man, the selfist gospel does away with grace, which can have no part in self-esteem or self-worth. As Jay Adams points out:

> Many proponents among the self-worth movement are tampering with the precious doctrine of grace in order to support a non-Christian humanistic theory....[35]

Is Self-Esteem Necessary?

Confessing that it "was appropriate for Calvin and Luther to think theocentrically,"[36] the chief apostle of the new reformation argues that a *God-centered* theology is now outdated and must be replaced by a *man-centered* theology that "incorporates psychology."[37] "It is blasphemy," counters Jimmy Swaggart, "to say that we need some kind of man-centered theology to replace the traditional God-centered theology."[38] Were Andrew Murray alive today, he also would vehemently disagree with the new self-centered gospel. "To be nothing before God and men," wrote Murray, "to wait on God alone; to delight in, to imitate, to learn of Christ, the meek and lowly One—this is the very key to the School of Christ, the only key to the true knowledge of Scripture."[39] Defending the new theology (in a book that was sent free to about 250,000 pastors, seminary and Christian college teachers, and other church leaders through funds provided by the president of the Napoleon Hill Foundation), its chief promoter writes:

> Where the sixteenth-century Reformation returned our focus to sacred Scriptures as the only infallible rule for faith and practice, the new reformation will return our focus to the sacred right of every person to self-esteem![40]

The selfist enthusiasts claim that man cannot be happy without a sense of *self*-worth, a "positive" *self*-image, plus *self*-esteem and a host of other *self*-isms. But why is that? We speak of selfless love because that is the only kind of love there is. We speak of selfless service, of self-sacrifice for the good of others. The "what's-in-it-for-me-gospel" is not biblical. Even the rank worldling recognizes this and despises it, though he may not be willing to take the way of the cross. Donald Grey Barnhouse put it all in biblical perspective:

> If you exalt man in any way, God is thereby debased. But if you exalt God as He should be exalted, man thereby takes his true position of utter nothingness, and only then can he find his real exaltation, for it will come to him through the grace of God in Christ.

Man can thus reach the heights by taking the proper place of depth. It is, once more, the divine principle that "every one that exalteth himself shall be abased; and he that humbleth himself shall be exalted" (Luke 18:14).[41]

The redeemed should have no thought of themselves but only of pleasing and glorifying their Redeemer. In heaven all of the attention will be upon our Lord and none upon ourselves. Nor will we want any, because turning to ourselves would destroy heaven. It is true that we will be there in glorified bodies and will be given crowns and rewards and will hear from our Lord's lips, "Well done, thou good and faithful servant...enter thou into the joy of thy Lord" (Matthew 25:21). But will that give us a positive self-image, a sense of self-worth and self-esteem, and cause us to feel good about ourselves? C. S. Lewis answers:

> The child who is patted on the back for doing a lesson well, the woman whose beauty is praised by her lover, the saved soul to whom Christ says, "Well done," are pleased and ought to be.
> For here the pleasure lies not in what you are but in the fact that you have pleased someone you wanted (and rightly wanted) to please.
> The trouble begins when you pass from thinking, "I have pleased him; all is well," to thinking, "What a fine person I must be to have done it."[42]

What Lewis is saying has been the general consensus of the church since its beginning. Self-esteem theology has only lately come on the scene and is trying desperately to prove that it is in fact the "faith once for all delivered to the saints." We learn much of the established doctrine of the church from hymns that have stood the test of time. Consider these words, which were inspired by the letters of Samuel Rutherford and written by Anne Ross Cousin about 100 years ago, and notice not only how at odds they are with the new self-centered theology, but how much better they are:

> The bride eyes not her garment,
> But her dear Bridegroom's face;
> I will not gaze at glory,
> But on my King of Grace:

Not at the crown He giveth,
But on His pierced hand.
The Lamb is all the glory
In Emmanuel's land.[43]

No thought of self there! One could hardly say that because Christ is "all the glory" we have somehow missed out by not "feeling good about *ourselves*." A man who was truly filled with the love and peace and joy of his Lord, Samuel Rutherford died in 1661 repeating these words triumphantly: "*All the glory* in Immanuel's land! *All the glory!*" We may be certain that Rutherford was not thinking of himself but of his Lord.

Neither self-esteem, self-worth, self-acceptance, self-love, nor any of the other selfisms plays any part in "love, joy, peace, longsuffering, gentleness, goodness, faith, meekness, temperance," that supernatural fruit of the Spirit (Galatians 5:22,23) which is the ultimate expression of Christ's life in the believer. No, self-esteem and the many other selfisms are not necessary. In fact those who propose this new theology, no matter how sincere, have introduced a discordant note that clashes with everything the church has stood for, with its hymns and prose, with the testimony of its greatest saints and martyrs, and with the Bible itself.

Why Is Self-Esteem So Important?

Yet the self-theorists insist that self-esteem is not only *necessary*, but that it is the essential ingredient (the *sine qua non*) of human happiness and fulfillment. They are not willing to let go of self, but are determined somehow to salvage some honor for this false god under the mistaken idea that they are thereby honoring the true God. Many people have unwittingly been deceived by the specious theories of humanistic psychology which have been matched with a seeming proof-text here and there.

The attempt to baptize humanistic psychology into Christianity goes against the whole tone of Scripture. There is *not one* hero or heroine of the faith in the entire Bible who can be pointed to as an example of a person who maintained a positive self-image or high self-esteem or who suffered from the lack of any of today's popular selfisms. And the promotion of "me-ism" is as absent from the writings of the saints down through history as it is from the Bible itself. Among his many "self-affirmations" the great apostle Paul called himself the chief of sinners (1 Timothy 1:15), a "wretched man" (Romans 7:24), and "less than the least of all saints" (Ephesians 3:8).

Paul urged the Philippians (and us also), "In lowliness of mind let each esteem other better than themselves" (Philippians 2:3). He warned the believers in Rome with these words: "I say, through the grace of God given unto me, to every man that is among you, not to think of himself more highly than he ought to think" (Romans 12:3). Nowhere in the Bible are we warned not to think more lowly of ourselves than we ought to, yet there should be many such Scriptures if our problem is lack of self-esteem. Clearly that is *not* our problem, but pride surely is. C. S. Lewis acknowledged that, far from having a lack of self-esteem and self-love, his problem was quite the opposite:

> Do I think well of myself, think myself a nice chap? Well, I am afraid I sometimes do (and those are, no doubt, my worst moments)....
> Go a step further. In my most clear-sighted moments, not only do I not think myself a nice man, but I know that I am a very nasty one. I can look at some of the things I have done with horror and loathing.[44]

This kind of honesty opens one up to the biblical perspective of self. When Dan Denk applied it in counseling, the effect was liberating. "I began to take a long look at the psychology of me-ism," Denk relates, "when counseling as a pastor and later as a teacher at a Christian college. Doug came to talk with me one day (as he had many times before). He was feeling down on himself again, overwhelmed with his own shortcomings.... On previous occasions I had tried to help him improve his self-concept. It would work for a while—then he would be in the pits again." Denk goes on to say:

> This time it struck me how self-absorbed Doug was. He didn't need to be more preoccupied with himself.
> "Doug," I said, "I don't think your problem is one of poor self-concept at all. I think you are actually quite proud. The reason

you *feel* inadequate and wretched at times is that you *are*...just like the rest of us. Why don't you accept who you are and get on with life? Forget yourself for a while and get interested in other people and their concerns.''

The look on Doug's face changed from surprise to horror to unbelief...then to a smile. He had never heard advice like that. He certainly didn't expect to hear it from me. But as we continued to talk, his eyes began to light up and a new freedom came over him—freedom from the slavery of self-concern, freedom that comes from taking an honest look at yourself for the first time.[45]

Not I But Christ

The issue before us is much larger than the pros or cons of selfist psychological theories. If we would take Jesus seriously, the difference between His command that His disciples must deny self and the new gospel's promotion of self-love, self-acceptance, and self-esteem could be the difference between heaven and hell (Matthew 16:24,25). Clearly we are confronted with an issue of the utmost importance. It is staggering to realize that psychology has influenced the church to such an extent that *honoring self* is now a major theme in the church. Dave Wilkerson points out:

> Go to any bookstore and count the number of books dealing with human hurts—such as depression, fear, rejection, divorce, remarriage, loneliness, etc. Attend nearly any seminar or crusade, and you will hear much insight on how to cope with personal pain and distress.
>
> Yet how little is written or taught about sharing the sufferings of Jesus Christ, the Lord.[46]

Georgi Vins, so long a prisoner of the Soviets until that historic exchange brought him to the West, challenges us with the choice that he and other Soviet Christians made in obedience to Christ in 1962: "All over the country, believers were taking a stand against apostasy. The disturbing spiritual condition of our churches caused us to examine our own lives.'' Repentance brought a determination to base "all matters of life and faith'' thereafter solely "on the absolute authority of the Bible.''[47] That was the beginning of revival that continues to this day. Though he has suffered much persecution and is now in prison, catch the joy and victory in this statement from Gennady Kryuchkov, president of the unregistered Baptist churches in the USSR:

> We left everything behind and came out from among them, possessing nothing but our faith and the promises of God, and we entered into the abundance of God's blessing. . . .
>
> May the Lord continue His mighty work among us until He comes, that our song of praise to Him, begun in this vale of tears, may continue for all eternity in His heavenly Kingdom.[48]

Self is so obviously not at issue—neither its esteem nor its love nor its worth nor its acceptance—but only Christ. If we are to remain true to our Lord, then we must begin to practice a purely biblical Christianity. We find such a Christianity described in the letters that Paul the apostle wrote from prison in his day. It is also expressed in the prison letters of many of God's people suffering even now in Communist labor camps around the world. Consider this from Vladimir Kosteniuk, 57-year-old preacher from an unregistered church in the Ukraine, serving his second term in the Gulag and threatened with an extended sentence:

> It is the desire of my heart that the Lord make me an instrument of His peace, that where there is hatred, I may sow love; where there is doubt, faith; where there is despair, hope; where there is sorrow, joy; that in everything He would grant that my life be a good example. . . .
>
> My dear ones, there is so much I wish I could say to you in this letter. . . . Mostly I desire to always be ready for the coming of my Savior! I am so grateful to the Lord that He is leading me along this path and that He will not let me out of His hands.
>
> When we look at the path that Christ and His followers walked, our hardships seem small and insignificant. For the most important issue in the life of a Christian is this: what will we take with us when we stand before God? What will we have to lay at His feet?[49]

9

Self-Exaltation and Humility

Let this mind be in you, which was also in Christ Jesus, who...made himself of no reputation, and took upon him the form of a servant...and humbled himself, and became obedient unto death, even the death of the cross.

Wherefore God also hath highly exalted him, and given him a name above every name, that at the name of Jesus every knee should bow...and that every tongue should confess that Jesus Christ is Lord, to the glory of God the Father (Philippians 2:5-11).

MANY CHRISTIANS LIVING under persecution in Communist countries are confused when they hear how socially acceptable Christianity seems to be in the West. Since Paul's statement that "all that will live godly in Christ Jesus shall suffer persecution" (2 Timothy 3:12) has proved true for Russian or Polish or Chinese believers, they wonder why the same is not true for Christians in the West. And they pray that God will help us not to compromise under the pressures of popularity and success, just as they have refused to be corrupted by Communism. These believers would find it astonishing that Christians in the West spend months and even years in "therapy" to overcome the damage to their psyches allegedly caused by "rejection." Those who grow up under totalitarian regimes hostile to the gospel expect to be rejected, despised, ridiculed, and even imprisoned or killed for their faith, and would not understand the importance that Christians in the West place upon self-esteem, self-acceptance, and self-fulfillment.

It would be even more incomprehensible to such suffering

Christians, many of whom have never owned a Bible (and who long for the day when they will receive one smuggled in from the West), to be told that the church in the West considers the Bible to be inadequate and the Holy Spirit insufficient to provide complete spiritual guidance and power for living the Christian life. Indeed, they would find it astonishing that the Western church would so enthusiastically open its arms to embrace new theologies that are founded upon the theories of psychology. One such Western Christian leader, who is devoted to serving the Lord and who has been used of God for much good, has built his ministry around one particular psychological theory: the need for self-esteem. With great concern he declares, "An epidemic of inferiority is raging throughout our society!"[1] Even though many other psychologists, both Christian and non-Christian, disagree, he states further that the "inner pain of inferiority...[is] *the* most dominant force in life, even exceeding the power of sex in its influence."[2] "Lack of self-esteem," he declares, "produces more symptoms of psychiatric disorders than any other factor yet identified."[3]

Part of the problem in such thinking is caused by confusing inferiority feelings with lack of self-esteem. The former involves *performance* or *ability* while the latter pertains to one's feelings of personal *worth.* Clearly the greater a person's self-esteem and self-love, the more disappointment there will be if abilities and performance are not comparable. No one hates *himself,* but he may hate his circumstances or appearance or lack of ability. The very fact that we dislike our appearance or lament our inability or become upset when people or circumstances abuse us is proof that we love and esteem ourselves, for if we did not esteem ourselves we would not care, and if we hated ourselves we would be glad when things go against us.

It is simply not true that lack of self-esteem is the great cause of human failings. In his fascinating book *Inside the Criminal Mind*, clinical psychologist Stanton E. Samenow documents from years of intimate research with criminals that the "positive" self-image that even the worst criminals consistently maintain remains intact, even while planning a crime.[4] In *The Inflated Self*, psychologist David G. Meyers cites numerous psychological studies demonstrating the pervasiveness of self-esteem, pride, and self-serving bias. "People tend to attribute positive behaviors to themselves and negative behaviors to external factors, enabling them to take credit for their good acts and to deny responsibility for their bad acts."[5] The average person also tends "to take credit for success and deny blame for failure." Moreover, laboratory experiments demonstrate that human beings persistently rationalize their own evil behavior in order to justify themselves even at the dishonest expense of others "so as to maintain one's self-image." In spite of all else, "self-esteem remains resilient."[6]

God's Remedy for Inferiority

To feel inferior to others or to feel inadequate for the task at hand is not a defect that must be remedied before one can be useful. On the contrary, recognizing one's inability is the prerequisite for genuine victory, for it is when we are delivered from *self*-confidence that God can use us to *His* glory. Jonathan's lame son, Mephibosheth, called himself a "dead dog," but King David insisted that he eat with him daily at the royal table (2 Samuel 9:6-13). Gideon considered himself incapable, his family poor, and himself "least in my father's house" (Judges 6:15), yet he learned to trust God and became one of Israel's greatest deliverers.

Isaiah shrank from God's call, considering his "unclean lips" unworthy to speak for his Lord (Isaiah 6:5). Amos was no prophet but a mere herdsman (Amos 7:14) whom God used to pronounce judgment upon nations. The turning point in Job's life came when he finally hated himself (Job 42:6): Then and only then could God restore him. When called by God, Moses responded, "Who am I that I should go unto Pharaoh?" (Exodus 3:11) and he insisted that he was "slow of speech" and incapable (Exodus 4:10-13). God's answer to Moses should bring courage to everyone who feels inferior: *"I will be with thee!"*

Far from dealing with Moses' inferiority and building up his "poor self-image," God promised His presence and power. In fact He chose Moses, the meekest man on the earth (Numbers 12:3), to confront the world's mightiest emperor in his palace and deliver His people so that God and not man would have the glory. So it can be with everyone who admits his own inability and unworthiness and then, instead of either groveling in self-deprecation or seeking to overcome his inferiority through humanistic methods, turns from himself to God and in *his* weakness relies upon *God's* strength. Instead of bemoaning his handicap, Paul gloried in his weakness:

> And he said unto me, My grace is sufficient for thee, for my strength is made perfect in weakness. Most gladly therefore will I rather glory in my infirmities, that the power of Christ may rest upon me. Therefore I take pleasure in infirmities, in reproaches, in necessities, in persecutions, in distresses for Christ's sake, for when I am weak, then am I strong (2 Corinthians 12:9,10).

What Is the Basis for These Selfisms?

Of course those who brought selfism into the church (even though they acknowledge that the idea first came from humanistic psychology) attempt to support it from Scripture. One leading Christian psychologist quotes Psalm 139 and suggests that the "wonderful pattern for growth, fulfillment and development" that "God built into our genes...is the ultimate basis for self-esteem."[7] Surely the genius of the genetic code should cause me to bow in wonder and worship at the wisdom and power of God—but *self*-esteem? Seeing the marvels of God's creative power in my genes is no more cause for *self*-exaltation than seeing God's creative power in genes in general or in a sunset or in a beautiful flower—*I* had nothing to do with creating any of it.

Standing awestruck before the beauties and marvels of creation doesn't boost my *self*-esteem or cause me to feel good about *myself*, but it does move me to *worship the Creator*. "The heavens declare the glory of *God*," not *my* glory. If what God has done in creating the universe is to *His* glory, should not what He has done in me and for me as a new creation in Christ be only to His glory as well? It should be evident that self-esteem plays no part in God's grand design either for me or for the rest of creation.

Even if I were physically or mentally or socially better endowed than anyone else in the world, that would be no basis for boasting, according to Paul: "For who maketh thee to differ from another?" he asked. The answer, obviously, is God, though I can't blame Him for defects I have inherited from sinful ancestors. But as to his talents and opportunities, and any goodness that was manifested through his life (and particularly his apostleship), Paul declared, "By the grace of God I am what I am" (1 Corinthians 15:10). No basis for self-esteem there! He goes on to say, "What hast thou that thou didst not receive? Now if thou didst receive it, why dost thou glory, as if thou hadst not received it?" (1 Corinthians 4:7). The hymnology of the church tells us what the consensus has been. This one was written by James M. Gray nearly 100 years ago:

> Naught have I gotten but what I received;
> Grace hath bestowed it since I have believed.
> Boasting excluded, pride I abase;
> I'm only a sinner saved by grace.
> This is my story: to God be the glory,
> I'm only a sinner saved by grace.

No one but saved sinners will be in heaven. Nor will we ever get beyond that glorious fact. Christ will forever bear the marks of Calvary. The scars of what He suffered for our sins will never be erased.

Dare we think that we will ever be able to erase from our memories the fact that we are sinners saved by grace? Who would wish to forget the debt that we owe to the One who redeemed us? The throne of God will be forever known also as the throne of the Lamb (Revelation 22:3). Our glorified Lord and Savior in His resurrection body will appear throughout eternity as the newly slain Lamb, and our song will be forever "unto Him who loved us and loosed us from our sins in His own blood!" The crucified and risen Savior bearing the marks of Calvary will be the glory of heaven. Lloyd-Jones expressed it well:

> Pride is ever the cause of the trouble, and there is nothing that so hurts the natural man's pride as the cross of Christ.
> How does the cross do that? What has happened that there should ever have been a cross? It is because we are failures,

because we are sinners, because we are lost.[8]

The Christian is not a good man. He is a vile wretch who has been saved by the grace of God.[9]

What About Self-Worth?

But God loves us, so doesn't that prove our *self*-worth? That is the Hollywood kind of love that loves the lovely and lovable. It is one thing to ascribe worth to self because of God's love and another thing entirely to realize that God loves not because of who *we* are but because of who *He* is (God is love). Therein lies security for eternity. If He loved us because we were worthy of it, then we could lose that love if our value depreciated sufficiently. But if He loves because *He* is love, then that love can never be lost, since God never changes.

But doesn't the fact that Jesus told His disciples they were "of more value than many sparrows" (Luke 12:7) establish self-worth? Does it really build self-esteem to be told that we are worth more than such insignificant birds? Would that make us worthy of God's love? Jesus made this comparison not to establish that man is worth enough for God to love him, but to assure His disciples that, since God took care of sparrows, surely He would also take care of them. But such gracious assurance doesn't mean that He *needs* us, as some teach,[10] or that because of our great value to Him we can be sure that He will treat us well. For our assurance we look to God's promises and to His character that backs them, not to our worth.

Yes, but didn't Jesus say that "one human life is worth more than the whole world," as the selfists tell us?[11] Again, this is not what the Bible says but another example of twisting Scripture to make it seem to support selfist psychology. Jesus asked His disciples to consider whether it would have been worth it for a man to gain the whole world and "lose his own soul" (Matthew 16:26). Far from stating the value of a soul to God or anyone else, Jesus was comparing the suffering of eternity in the lake of fire, or the loss of eternal joy in heaven, to the fleeting pleasure of having possessed the entire world for one brief lifetime. It was in this context, moreover, that He told them that they must "deny self" or they could not be His disciples. There is no basis here for self-worth; quite the opposite. It may help us, when we are tempted with thoughts of our worth, to remember these words of John the Baptist spoken to prevent the Jews from finding self-esteem or self-worth in their ancestry:

> Think not to say within yourselves, We have Abraham
> to our father; for I say unto you that God is able of these
> stones to raise up children unto Abraham (Matthew 3:9).

Is There a Difference Between Self-Esteem and Pride?

The proponents of self-esteem go to great lengths in their attempts to distinguish what they call "positive self-esteem" from pride. One writer equates self-esteem with "pride in being a human being," but then tries to distinguish between what he calls "positive pride and negative pride."[12] It is his own invention. Such a concept was unknown to either the church or secular society in the past, and certainly cannot be found in the Bible, which condemns pride repeatedly and never once hints at a "positive pride" which is commendable. Yet this popular writer insists:

> Real self-esteem is real humility. Healthy pride and honest
> humility are the same human qualities—just different sides of the
> same coin. We all welcome affirmation and resent being insulted.[13]

Though we do not question this man's sincerity, we can surely question his concepts, which are not biblical and seem to depend upon his own peculiar definitions of words. *Healthy* pride, again, is his own invention. God told Israel that He led them through the wilderness in order to *humble* them (Deuteronomy 8:2), and the entire testimony of Scripture shows the great difficulty of eradicating pride from mankind. Yet this writer insists that exactly the opposite is the case:

> A neurotic fear of pride has motivated the church too long. . . .
> In my lectures to thousands of ordained clergy of the widest cross
> section of historic Christianity, I have found it necessary to tell
> my colleagues:
>
>> Dare to be a possibility thinker! Do not fear pride; the
>> easiest job God has is to humble us. God's almost
>> impossible task is to keep us believing every hour of the
>> day how great we are as his sons and daughters on planet
>> earth.
>
> Don't worry about humility. The easiest job God has to do is

to keep you and me humble. God's biggest job is to get us to believe that we *are* somebody and that we really can *do* something. . . .

Remember, "If your pride is rooted in your divine call, your humility is assured. The Cross will sanctify your ego trip." . . . For the Cross protected our Lord's perfect self-esteem from turning into sinful pride.[14]

This new theology can be confusing, with its apparent new definitions for words that have long had established meanings. We are told that humility and self-esteem are one and the same and that humility is nothing to "worry about." It is puzzling, then, why self-esteem is of such concern if it truly is the same thing as humility, which comes so easily. Despite its obvious contradictions the new theology is even beginning to affect our hymnology. For example, the otherwise-beautiful song *They'll Know We Are Christians* contains the pledge to "guard each man's dignity and save each man's pride." In contrast, John Calvin warned that those who urge a man "not [to] be ignorant of his own excellence and dignity" thereby "fill him with vain confidence and inflate him with pride."[15] F. B. Meyer declared:

> Earthly thrones are generally built with steps up to them; the remarkable thing about the thrones of the eternal kingdom is that the steps are all down to them.
>
> We must descend if we would reign, stoop if we would rise, gird ourselves to wash the feet of the disciples as a common slave in order to share the royalty of our Divine Master.[16]

A. W. Tozer calls self "one of the toughest plants that grows in the garden of life."[17] Andrew Murray says it was "pride that made redemption needful," describes it as a "power that Satan brought from hell,"[18] and warns that we are most in danger of pride when we think we are the humblest.[19] "If you think you are not conceited," warns Lewis, "it means you are very conceited indeed."[20] In *The Screwtape Letters*, Lewis has Screwtape, a senior devil, advising his nephew Wormwood:

> Your patient has become humble; have you drawn his attention to the fact? . . . Catch him at the moment when he is really poor in spirit and smuggle into his mind the gratifying reflection,

"By golly! I'm being humble," and almost immediately pride—pride at his own humility—will appear.

If he awakes to the danger and tries to smother this new form of pride, make him proud of his attempt and so on through as many stages as you please.[21]

New Definitions—or God's Solution

Flying in the face not only of Scripture but of secular literature and of conscience as well, the self theorists in the church protest their humility and insist that the self-esteem they advocate has nothing to do with pride. The Christian Association for Psychological Studies declares, "From what we know of the components of positive self-esteem, humility is the Biblical counterpart, not pride...."[22] One can only wonder, though, why *high* self-esteem is equated with *humility*—and whether *low* self-esteem, its opposite, is therefore the same as pride.

The contradictions become embarrassing. It is argued that positive "self-esteem" comes from recognizing "who we are in Christ." All that we are or have in Christ, however, comes by *grace*, which is of necessity by inability and unworthiness and thus ought to lower one's self-esteem rather than raise it. No matter how one manipulates Scripture or logic, neither supports selfist psychology. Humanistic psychological theories have found their only possible support in new definitions. What we used to label pride is now called positive self-esteem. Boasting has been redefined as "positive self-talk," and one Christian psychologist has written a complete book promoting it.[23] Let the psychologists, Christian and non-Christian, produce their new names and definitions if they will, but in our hearts we all know the truth, whether we admit it or not. A lack of self-esteem is not our problem—and self-esteem cannot be confused for the humility that the Bible declares is more desirable than honor (Proverbs 15:33; 18:12) and with which the true Christian is to be clothed at all times (1 Peter 5:5).

Perhaps, it may be conceded, apostles and mature Christians don't have any need for self-esteem or self-worth, but what about that teenage son or daughter who sobs in front of the mirror and sees reflected there the seeming reason for the ridicule and

rejection faced at school: the homeliness, the ineptitude, the lack
of style? Isn't this a case where the parent needs to build a good
positive self-image in the child? The Bible doesn't propose any
such solution.

Instead of turning the child to himself in order to find some
worth, to feel some personal good, or to "compensate" by
developing what special talent he might possess, shouldn't one
rather turn him to the Lord? The Bible is all about people who
were small and weak and untalented in their own eyes and the
eyes of others, but through whom God was pleased to do great
things. How much better to build a solid confidence in the One
whose love and strength and enabling will not fail, and to aspire
to His "well-done," than to build confidence in one's frail and
failing "self" in order to gain the approval of one's peers.

Pride, A Persistent Human Problem

In the list of seven deadly sins that God says are an "abomina-
tion unto him" (Proverbs 6:16-19), the first one is "a proud
look." God hates all that pertains to pride, and the Bible indicates
that this predominant characteristic of man persists in the face
of even the most humiliating circumstances.

God did His best to humble the children of Israel for their own
good (Deuteronomy 8:1-5), and they above all other peoples (in
view of their miserable failure and the frequent judgments of God
that came upon them as a result) should have been humble in
character. Yet their pride persisted even in the most impossible
circumstances. At the foot of Mount Sinai they had sinned griev-
ously, crediting a golden calf with being the god that had brought
them out of Egypt (Exodus 32:1-6), and God's judgment had
fallen heavily. Yet only a few days later they were strutting about,
preening and decking themselves with ornaments.

It seems impossible that puny man could flaunt himself so
brazenly before Almighty God. If ever the Israelites should
rightfully have suffered from a poor self-image and needed help
from God to restore it, that was the time—but, far from lacking
in self-esteem, it was in fact their perpetual problem. This fits
precisely with the fact that even the worst of criminals see
themselves as basically good people. How much more odious it

must be to God for Christians, who ought to know better, to insist that we are all so naturally humble that God's biggest problem is getting us to realize how great we are!

If ever a band of men ought to have presented an example of humility for all posterity to follow, it was the disciples. Having misunderstood and failed their Lord so many times, they should have been plagued with very low self-esteem. Moreover, after three years in private training by the meek and humble Lamb of God, who continually both taught and set the example of perfect humility, pride should have been eradicated. Not so. Pride not only persisted, but manifested itself under the most humbling circumstances.

After failing to cast out a demon and being rebuked by Jesus for their unbelief, the disciples have a heated discussion among themselves. Reluctant to tell Jesus when He inquires, they finally admit that "they had disputed among themselves who should be the *greatest*" (Mark 9:34). Certainly they were not plagued with low self-esteem!

Come to the Last Supper. Troubled in spirit, Jesus has told His disciples with great sadness, "Verily, verily, I say unto you that one of you shall betray me" (John 13:21). Such a staggering declaration should have brought self-doubt and shattered their self-esteem, but it didn't; there was merely a momentary flurry of concern: "Lord, is it I?" (Matthew 26:21-25).

What sorrow should have gripped them! What a time of self-examination and of examining one another to expose and hopefully resolve this great evil in their midst! Instead, however, their thoughts and conversation quickly returned to what seemed to be a perpetual subject: "which of them should be accounted the greatest" (Luke 22:24).

Perversion of the Virtues

The Holy Spirit reveals the sordid truth in order to help us see the same pride in our own hearts—indeed that pride is the besetting sin of the human race. Yet Christian leaders insist that both Christendom and the secular world are plagued with an epidemic of "poor self-concept," for which the desperately needed remedy is the promotion of a high level of self-esteem!

It is a humanistic approach. After remarking that pride "comes direct from Hell," C. S. Lewis points out how closely it is related to self-respect or self-esteem and a sense of dignity:

> Pride can often be used to beat down the simpler vices. Teachers, in fact, often appeal to a boy's self-respect to make him behave decently: many a man has overcome cowardice, or lust, or ill-temper by learning to think that they are beneath his dignity—that is, by Pride.
>
> The devil...is perfectly content to see you becoming chaste and brave and self-controlled provided, all the time, he is setting up in you the Dictatorship of Pride....[24]

Even love and goodness and every other virtue have been perverted by the self-centeredness that had its birth in Eden. The young man sitting in the car who says passionately to the young lady, "I love you!" may not even realize that what he really means is "I love me and I want you!" And the young lady may discover the truth too late. Perhaps neither will ever realize why the ideal they are both searching for always seems to slip through their grasp. As W. H. Mallock said of the early Fabians more than 100 years ago, modern influences have destroyed the faith they once had, and their "hearts are aching for the God they no longer believe in"[25] and whom they have foolishly replaced with the idol self.

Many a husband or wife has found his or her mate no longer "attractive" and has burned with passion for someone else, convinced in the heat of that selfish lust that happiness can be found in no other way except to be rid of the one and to have the other. It is the same seduction to which Eve succumbed.

A New View of Happiness

Selfish lust robs us of the very happiness we seek. The passion for *our* will blinds us to the fact that true happiness is found only in doing *God's* will. The "happiness" which an adulterer or a person who has divorced one spouse to marry another hoped to find is eroded and eventually destroyed by the guilt that comes from having trampled honor and commitment and true love underfoot. How can one be happy, no matter how much wealth is acquired or pleasure enjoyed (sexual or other), knowing that he or she has stolen it from another person and has mocked God? Such "joy" will eventually turn to "gravel in the mouth" (Proverbs 20:17) and will be replaced by eternal remorse in all those who have not found repentance and forgiveness in Christ.

Whether we yield to temptation or not depends a great deal upon our perspective. Lust is called both "deceitful" (Ephesians 4:22) and "hurtful" (1 Timothy 6:9) because it entices us with pleasure that is brief and involves disobedience to God and thus leads to pain in the long run. Those whose focus is upon themselves think of God's commandments in terms of pleasures being denied them. But those who have denied self find true and lasting pleasure in obedience. There is a joy that comes from pleasing God that is so far beyond any pleasure of this world that temptation loses its power in comparison.

The new theology denies us this path of victory. Its joy is totally selfish. The desire to please God can hardly be one's honest motivation without the denial of self: One cannot deny self and at the same time love, esteem, and accept self. Yet the new "positive gospel," we are told, "is God's pathway to human dignity."[26] Putting man at the center turns everything upside down. Self-denial amazingly becomes self-fulfillment:

> Are we to believe that self-denial means the denial of personal pleasure, desire, fulfillment, prosperity? For too long religious leaders have suggested this with tragic results....
>
> Such attitudes are dangerous distortions and destructive misinterpretations of scattered Bible verses grossly misread by negative-thinking Bible readers who project their own negative self-image onto the pages of Holy Scripture....
>
> By self-denial Christ does not mean the rejection of that positive emotion we call self-esteem—the joy of experiencing my self-worth....[27]

The "joy of experiencing my self-worth" is a poor substitute for the much greater joy of knowing that God loves me in spite of my unworthiness. The experience of Christ's redeeming and eternal love—the wondrous intimacy of knowing Him—is far beyond any joy that could ever come from esteeming myself. Indeed, to be filled with Christ is to be emptied of self.

The Perversion of the Cross

"The death of Christ on the cross," declares a best-selling author, "is God's price tag on a human soul. . . .[28] [it means] we really are Somebodies!"[29] On the contrary, Christ didn't die for *somebodies* but for *sinners*. The price He paid on the cross does not establish my personal worth, but met the claims of divine justice. In fact, the greater the price the costlier my *sin*, not my *worth*! That the sinless Son of God had to die upon the cross to redeem me is not anything that should make me feel good about myself, but ashamed, for it was my sins that nailed Him there. How could that fact build up my self-esteem? Yet the selfist psychologists insist:

> What a foundation for self-esteem! The purchase price tells us the value of an object. . . .
> Of man alone it is said, "You were bought at a price" (1 Cor. 6:20). We are the objects of His redemption (Matt. 20:28; 1 Tim. 2:6; Rev. 5:9).
> What a sense of worth and value this imparts. The Son of God considers us of such value that He gave His life for us.[30]

In a sincere attempt to build up our self-worth, another author writes, "Surely God would not give His Son for creatures He considered to be of little worth!"[31] And another: "I must be of infinite value in God's sight. . . ."[32] "In his crucifixion, Christ has placed unlimited value on the human soul."[33] Such ideas were not derived from the Bible but from psychology, and then imposed upon the Bible. The *Bible Science Newsletter* gives the scriptural view:

> God desires an intimate relationship with each of us which is not based on anything of worth within us. Rather, God's desire for a relationship with us is based on God's love for us. This love led Him to *make* us worthy in Christ. But that worthiness, which is given us from Christ not based on any goodness within us, is a *result* of His love for us, not a cause for it.[34]

Yet the new litany goes on: "If the deepest curse of sin is what it does to our self-esteem," it is argued, "then the atoning power of the Cross is what it does to redeem our discarded self-worth."[35]

The horrors of sin and of hell are reduced to a loss of self-esteem, and the whole purpose of redemption is to restore it! What pride! Self has stolen the glory once again. Much more was at stake than "redeem[ing] our discarded self-worth" and "restoring self-respect, self-esteem, self-worth, and a noble pride in persons."[36]

What of the claims of divine justice? What of God's honor and the vindication of His holy name—and the purifying of heaven itself with the blood of Christ (Hebrews 9:23,24)? And what of the glory to God through having the redeemed around His throne praising Him forever? All of that, if not forgotten, takes second place as soon as we establish *our worth* on the basis of what Christ in love did upon the cross.

Though most of its proponents have no such intent, Christian psychology has robbed "the old rugged cross" of both its shame and its glory. The cross is now viewed purely from the selfish perspective of what it did for *me* and what *I* get out of it. Commenting on the perversion of biblical truth that psychology has brought into the church, Jay Adams writes:

> Here not only redemption but *all* that God promises and does for us is said to be a response on His part to our significance rather than an act of His love, free mercy, goodness, and grace!... Not so! The cross magnifies Christ and His marvelous grace—not us and our supposed worth. Let us cease from magnifying man; let us once again magnify the Lord together and bless *His* holy name![37]

Christ not only endured the cross (Hebrews 12:2) because of His love for us, but also because of His love for His Father. It will indeed bring our Lord great joy to have us with Him forever—but much more was involved. There was the defeat of Satan that was accomplished, ridding heaven of his unholy presence for eternity; and there was the obedience of the Son to the Father's will without swerving. God's righteous claims were also met. Do we not think that much of Christ's joy will forever be because He finished the work which His Father had given Him to do? That is the joy He wants us to share through our fellowship in His suffering (Colossians 1:24-29).

The Testimony of Favorite Old Hymns

How far the new psychologized, self-centered view of the cross is from what the church has understood down through history can be seen most easily by reference to some of the great hymns that have been sung and loved. In the 1700's Charles Wesley wrote in wonder and worship: "Died He for me, who caused His pain? For me, who Him to death pursued? Amazing love! How can it be that Thou, my God, shouldst die for me?" Earlier in that same century Isaac Watts wrote his classic: "When I survey the wondrous cross, on which the Lord of Glory died, my richest gain I count but loss, and pour contempt on all my pride."

About the same time John Newton wrote his *Amazing Grace*, containing the phrase that some choirs today find too "negative"—"that saved a *wretch* like me." Self-worth and self-esteem are not compatible with these songs. Ernst C. Homburg, who went to be with the Lord he loved in 1681, penned these words that can do nothing but turn us from self to Him:

> Jesus! Source of life eternal!
> Jesus, Author of our breath!
> Thou, O Son of God, wert bearing
> Cruel mockings, hatred, scorn;
> Thou, the King of glory, wearing,
> For our sake, the crown of thorn.
> Thousand, thousand praises be,
> Precious Savior, unto Thee!

The great hymns of the faith bear witness to the fact that, consistently down through its history, contemplating the cross has caused Christians to think little of themselves and much of their Savior. Think of the *King of glory* wearing for our sakes the *crown of thorn*! We are to follow Him in His humility: "Let this mind be in you, which was also in Christ Jesus, who...humbled himself...even [to] the death of the cross" (Philippians 2:5-8). The old hymns were filled with that glorious theme so foreign to self-esteem—that out of humility came triumph. Early in this century H. D'A. Champney wrote:

> Verily God, yet become truly human—
> Lower than angels—to die in our stead;

How hast Thou, long-promised "Seed of the woman,"
Trod on the serpent, and bruised his head!
Lord, Thou art worthy: Lord, Thou art worthy;
Lord, Thou art worthy, and worthy alone!

The doctrines of psychology have turned the focus from God to self. Now it is *we* who are worthy, and our great need is to realize it! Whatever God does is now interpreted to be primarily for our benefit, thus proving our infinite worth. Forgotten is God's honor, glory, and holiness. Subtly we have stolen His glory. We are taught to boast, "I may not deserve it [salvation] but I am worth it so don't say I am unworthy."[38]

Unworthy Sinners—Or Worthy?

Have we forgotten that "God so *loved* the world that he gave his only begotten Son" (John 3:16)? Love is not bestowed on the basis of the worth of the one loved. And what about *grace*? It is not grace to pay the value of an object, but to give much more. In fact the price paid had nothing to do with my *worth*, but with the depths of my *sin* and the demands made by God's *justice* and His eternal glory! It is not that I am *worth* the blood of Jesus at all, but that God's righteousness demanded it: "Without shedding of blood is no remission [of sin]" (Hebrews 9:22). Yet the new gospel, influenced by the theories of godless psychologists, declares:

> The most serious sin is the one that causes me to say, "I am unworthy. I may have no claim to divine sonship if you examine me at my worst."
>
> For once a person believes he is an "unworthy sinner," it is doubtful if he can really honestly accept the saving grace God offers in Jesus Christ.[39]

Strange, then, that these were the very words which Jesus put into the mouth of the repentant prodigal son: "Father, I have sinned against heaven and in thy sight, and am *no more worthy* to be called thy son" (Luke 15:21). There was no comment from Jesus that the prodigal thereby erred and would be unable to accept his father's forgiveness: It was his sin that had made him unworthy, and had he not felt it keenly there would have been no repentance, and without that confession he could not have been forgiven. It destroys the true gospel to suggest that although we cannot merit salvation by our *works*, yet we merit it by our *worth*. On the contrary, grace has no more part to play in a gospel of self-*worth* than in a gospel of self-*works*.

The fact that John the Baptist considered himself unworthy even to untie Christ's sandals (Luke 3:16) is certainly never presented in Scripture as a hindrance or as a wrong self-evaluation. Nor did Christ rebuke the centurion for declaring his own unworthiness to have Christ visit his home, but commended him for his great faith (Luke 7:1-10). If we accept the definition of worthiness given by one of the most highly regarded Christian psychologists—"*Worthiness* is a feeling of 'I am good' "[40]—then what do we do with Christ's statement "There is none good but one, that is God"?

One would think that what Jesus had to say to Simon the Pharisee would have forever laid to rest this delusion of self-worth and self-love. In his heart Simon was judging Jesus for allowing a sinful woman to touch him. Knowing this, Jesus told the story of the creditor who forgave two debtors, one who owed him a vast sum and the other who owed almost nothing. Then He asked the Pharisee, "Tell me therefore, which of them will love him [the creditor] most?" Simon replied, "I suppose he to whom he forgave most." Jesus said, "Thou has rightly judged." He rebuked Simon for not having given him any water or a towel to wash His feet, and in contrast pointed out that this sinful woman had been washing His feet with her tears and wiping them with her hair. Then Jesus said:

> Her sins, which are many, are forgiven, for she loved much; but to whom little is forgiven, the same loveth little (Luke 7:36-47).

Is not Jesus telling us that our love for Him and our appreciation of His love and forgiveness will be in proportion to our own sense of sin and unworthiness? There will be no thought that we were worthy of what He did. We will not strut about heaven declaring for all eternity that although Christ died for our sins and is to be praised for that, nevertheless He did it because we were worthy of it. The glory will be His alone, and our joy will spring from gratitude for the fact that He redeemed us at such a cost—but we will never consider this to be the measure of our worth. Jesus declares that the more conscious we are of our sin and unworthiness, the more grateful we will be that He has stooped so low to bring us to Himself.

Decline of the Knowledge of the Holy

The present delusion arising from preoccupation with self would be quickly dispelled if we would spend time in the presence of God. One finds it difficult to imagine that the effect upon Moses of being in God's holy and fearful presence on the summit of Mount Sinai was an awakening to his great self-worth! Nor can we imagine Isaiah, when he "saw the Lord sitting upon a throne, high and lifted up," instead of crying, "Woe is me!" (Isaiah 6:1-5), exclaiming, "How worthy am I!" As the redeemed forever sing in heaven, "Thou art worthy! Worthy is the Lamb that was slain!" (Revelation 5:9-12), will God or the angelic host sing back to them, "But don't forget, *you* are worthy too!"? Such folly would be unthinkable in the presence of God!

The church is presently on a collision course with disaster due to the accelerating rise of selfism. Nothing can stop this trend except a fresh revelation of God. We need a revival of the fear of God and a passion to know Him as He really is, not as we fantasize Him in our imagination. A. W. Tozer declared:

> The decline of the knowledge of the holy has brought on our troubles. A rediscovery of the majesty of God will go a long way toward curing them.
>
> It is impossible to keep our moral practices sound and our inward attitudes right while our idea of God is erroneous or inadequate. If we would bring back spiritual power to our lives, we must begin to think of God more nearly as He is.[41]

Oswald J. Smith wrote that God "will never be satisfied with you until like a slave, a willing slave, you place yourself entirely at His disposal. Then He can use you for His glory."[42] Only those who truly know God are willing to make this surrender. "The heaviest obligation lying upon the Christian Church today," declared Tozer prophetically, "is to purify and elevate her concept of God until it is once more worthy of Him."[43] All of this is impossible until self is denied as Christ commanded. Surely self has been forgotten by those who see Christ as Spurgeon described Him:

> You may look, and study, and weigh, but Jesus is a greater Saviour than you think Him to be when your thoughts are at the greatest. My Lord is more ready to pardon than you to sin, more able to forgive than you to transgress. My Master is more willing to supply your wants than you are to confess them. Never tolerate low thoughts of my Lord Jesus.[44]

When Man Meets God

The inevitable result of a high view of self is a lower view of God. From every biblical instance of those who were taken into the presence of God or to whom God revealed Himself, we learn that two things inevitably happen: 1) God becomes awesomely wonderful to that person, resulting in worship, praise, wonder, fear, and trembling; and 2) the person becomes nothing in his own sight in comparison. Never do we read that being in the presence of God bestows a "positive self-image," much less "positive pride" or a sense of "self-worth." No, the presence of God has the very opposite effect.

It is impossible to know the true God in His splendor without seeing ourselves as very small indeed. There is no surer way to lose one's inflated sense of self-importance. "When viewing our miserable condition since Adam's fall," wrote John Calvin, "all confidence and boasting are overthrown, we blush for shame and feel truly humble."[45] "One of the best tests of whether we are truly Christian or not," said Lloyd-Jones, "is just this: Do I hate my natural self?"[46] C. S. Lewis drove the point home: "The real test of being in the presence of God is that you either forget about yourself altogether or you see yourself as a small, dirty object. It is better to forget about yourself altogether."[47] That is not the message of the gospel of self-esteem. You cannot forget yourself while you are trying to get a positive self-image and build up your sense of self-worth. Tim Stafford points out:

> Part of the difficulty, too, lies in our own sinful natures. If

we don't enjoy the full fellowship with God that we want, it is often because we want to see Him only on our terms, as a possible addition to the good life we have made for ourselves.

But we cannot see Him that way. It is an absurd impossibility—like wanting to see the Grand Canyon on a small scale. Either we see God in grandeur and are transformed, or we do not see Him at all.[48]

So long as we hold a high self-esteem as the ultimate sign of mental health or spirituality, we will not know God as we should. True humility means to esteem others better than ourselves (Philippians 2:3). What the Bible says about pride and humility is put very succinctly by C. S. Lewis:

We must not think Pride is something God forbids because He is offended at it, or that Humility is something He demands as due to His own dignity—as if God Himself was proud.

He is not in the least worried about His dignity. The point is, He wants you to know Him; wants to give you Himself.

And He and you are two things of such a kind that if you really get into any kind of touch with Him you will, in fact, be humble—delightedly humble, feeling the infinite relief of having for once got rid of all the silly nonsense about your own dignity which has made you restless and unhappy all your life.

He is trying to make you humble in order to make this moment possible.[49]

10
Is Seeing Really Believing?

Faith is the substance of things hoped for, the evidence of things not seen (Hebrews 11:1).

Jesus saith unto him, Thomas, because thou hast seen me, thou hast believed; blessed are they that have not seen, and yet have believed (John 20:29).

IN PAST AGES men wrote of their passion to know God. Today the major emphasis is upon knowing oneself. This is a direct result of the influence of psychology, which attempts to look into the depths of man's being in order to understand how he functions, as though the answer lies there. We have moved on from the exploration of outer space to the even more fascinating universe of inner space, the depths of our own psyches. That very process produces delusion, because "the heart is deceitful above all things and desperately wicked" (Jeremiah 17:9).

It is not easy for God to reveal Himself to man and communicate His will to him. Jesus said to His critics: "He that is of God heareth God's words; ye therefore hear them not because ye are not of God" (John 8:47). By *hear* He meant *understand and heed.* Even though God spoke to Eve audibly, it was the serpent's voice that won her attention and obedience. Did she more readily submit to the serpent because she *saw* him but not God? If God had appeared in some visible form to Eve, would that have kept her from being deceived? Is *seeing* really *believing*? Quite obviously not.

There were disciples to whom Jesus "showed himself alive" after His resurrection "by many infallible proofs" (Acts 1:3) and yet they doubted (Matthew 28:17). While seeing Jesus for himself seemed to convince doubting Thomas, he was ashamed at having demanded this special proof. Jesus added these words of encouragement for those of us who were not there: "Blessed are they that have not seen and yet have believed" (John 20:29). Commenting upon this, Boice says:

> He [Jesus] is speaking of faith that is satisfied with what God provides and is therefore not yearning for visions, miracles, esoteric experiences or various forms of success as evidence of God's favor.
>
> More than that, He is saying that a faith without these things is not inferior to but is actually superior to a faith based upon them.[1]

The Enigma of Faith and Unbelief

True faith does not depend upon seeing, but unbelief persists in spite of overwhelming tangible evidence. In the parable of the sower, Jesus emphasized the importance of *understanding* and equated "good ground" with "an honest and good heart" (Matthew 13:19,23; Luke 8:15). Solomon counseled us, "Keep thine heart with all diligence, for out of it are the issues of life." The only way our hearts can be kept honest is to surrender ourselves completely into His hands. We are spiritually blind, and only Christ can give us sight. No blind man is in such danger as the one who is convinced that the fantasies of his mind are real and that he can therefore see.

Most of those who saw Jesus did not recognize Him for who He was. As God become man, Jesus had flawless features and physique and must have been the ultimate example of humanity. Moreover, His perfection was not only physical but spiritual. His face and eyes were aglow with a moral beauty beyond description, for He is "the brightness of his [God's] glory and the express image of his person" (Hebrews 1:3) and "altogether lovely" (Song of Solomon 5:16). Jesus said of Himself, "He that hath seen me hath seen the Father" (John 14:9). Yet Isaiah wrote, "When we shall see him, there is no beauty that we should desire him. He is despised and rejected of men...we hid as it were our faces from him...we esteemed him not" (Isaiah 53:2,3).

Jesus said to the Jews of His day, "Having eyes, see ye not? and having ears, hear ye not?" (Mark 8:18). There is a "seeing" and "hearing" that comes by faith alone. It is neither physical nor mental and goes beyond ordinary comprehension because it involves the revelation of God Himself and His will to man. Those without the faith that perceives the invisible and hears the inaudible will not believe even when confronted with abundant visible and audible proof. The revelation of God must come from *Himself*, and man must be very careful that his own imagination does not enter the process and thereby deceive him. Yet we are now being told that imagination is the key element in meditation, prayer, and knowing God.

How can we be certain we are not being deceived by what we imagine is God's guidance? The Bible provides no "techniques for getting in touch with God," and all such should be avoided. God speaks through *His Word*, and any personal direction or assurance of the Holy Spirit is always in agreement with this Word. But we can no more explain how to receive daily guidance from God than explain how His "Spirit itself beareth witness with our spirit that we are the children of God" (Romans 8:16). To hear God's voice even through the written Word, we must belong to Him and sincerely desire His will instead of our own. Growing in this personal relationship comes through obedience and maturity in the faith under the guidance of the Holy Spirit. Jesus promised:

> When he [the shepherd] putteth forth his own sheep, he goeth before them, and the sheep follow him, for they know his voice. And a stranger will they not follow, but will flee from him, for they know not the voice of strangers,
> I am the good shepherd: the good shepherd giveth his life for the sheep (John 10:4,5,11).

Far from helping God reveal Himself and His will, imagination pollutes with our own thoughts the pure communication of the Spirit. Idolatry down through history has been an attempt to represent God in an imagined form, and *all* such attempts are explicitly forbidden. John Calvin wrote:

> God makes no comparison between images, as if one were more

and another less befitting; he rejects, without exception, all shapes and pictures, and other symbols by which the superstitious imagine they can bring him near to them. . . .

We see how plainly God declares against all figures, to make us aware that all longing after such visible shapes is rebellion against Him.[2]

"If God would only speak to me with an audible voice so I could really hear Him, then I would believe!" has been stated repeatedly with seeming sincerity. Usually there is a sense of self-righteous resentment at God's failure to cooperate and a feeling that one's unbelief is therefore thoroughly justified. However, let us suppose that God does speak from heaven with a loud voice to a large gathering. "I am God, worship me!" sounds the command, clearly understood by all.

The skeptic would remain convinced that what he had heard was not the voice of God, but a billion-to-one coincidence that caused converging sound waves to produce what only sounded like words but really wasn't. A psychologist might suggest that the sound emanating from the atmosphere was in fact not coherent at all, but everyone had merely *imagined* they had heard these words. An occultist present at the time might insist that each had heard the voice of his spirit guide. Those present would tend to believe what they *wanted* to believe; and their imaginations, being the servants of their desires, would help them convince themselves that they were sincere and correct. Only those who sincerely desired God's will would know the truth.

Even if all present were convinced that God had spoken, how many would *understand and obey*? Hearing God speak involves something other than sound waves and eardrums. All Israel heard Him declare the Ten Commandments audibly from Mount Sinai, yet before Moses could come down from the Mount they had broken the law they had solemnly promised to obey. This is why Moses in anger smashed the tables of stone (Exodus 32:19).

The Hearing and Seeing of Faith

We begin to understand better why Jesus ended each letter to the seven churches in the book of Revelation with these words: "He that hath an ear, let him hear what the Spirit saith unto the churches" (Revelation 2:7,11,17,29; 3:6,13,22). Clearly the *hearing* referred to does not depend upon an audible sound and would not necessarily be aroused by a thundering voice from heaven, though proven to be from God Himself. When God did in fact speak with an audible voice to pronounce His approval upon the ministry of Jesus, we are told:

> The people therefore that stood by and heard it [the voice] said that it thundered; others said, An angel spoke to him (John 12:29).

There is a moral quality to faith that enables the blind to see that which is invisible to those with perfect eyesight. That incomparable hymnwriter, Fanny J. Crosby, though blind from birth, wrote prolifically of her Savior's love and presence in such lines as: "Take the world but give me Jesus; let me view His constant smile; then throughout my pilgrim journey light will cheer me all the while.... In His cross my trust shall be, till, with clearer, brighter vision, face to face my Lord I see."[3] God is "invisible...whom no man hath seen nor can see" (Colossians 1:15; 1 Timothy 1:17; 6:16). Moses, we are told, "endured, as seeing him who is invisible" (Hebrews 11:27). Jesus said, "Blessed are the pure in heart, for they shall see God" (Matthew 5:8).

That this seeing does not involve either a mental or a physical image is clear. In fact, Israel was warned that any attempt at imagery would corrupt them: "Take ye therefore good heed unto yourselves, for ye saw no manner of similitude [no form] on the day that the Lord spake unto you in Horeb [Sinai] out of the midst of the fire, lest ye corrupt yourselves and make you a graven image, the similitude of any figure" (Deuteronomy 4:15,16). John MacArthur comments:

> In other words, when God revealed Himself to the Israelites, He was not represented in any visible form. There was no tangible representation of God—and that is true of God throughout the Scriptures. Why? Because God does not wish to be reduced to any image....
> Idolatry does not begin with a sculptor's hammer, it begins with the mind. When we think of God, what should we visualize?

Absolutely nothing. No visual conception of God could properly
represent His eternal glory.[4]

It should be clear that the statement "God created man in his
own image" (Genesis 1:27) is not referring to man's *physical body*
but to his moral and spiritual qualities. Likewise, when Scripture says that Jesus is "the brightness of his [God's] glory and
the express image of his person" (Hebrews 1:3) it is not referring
to anything physical. Moreover, Christ's moral and spiritual
qualities, which were so contrary to this world, seemed to outshine
his physical qualities. This is the only reasonable explanation as
to why His contemporaries saw no beauty in Jesus, who was of
all men the most beautiful. They were blinded by their own
perversion, and instead of loving Him they hated Him "without
a cause" (Psalm 35:19; 69:4; John 15:25). Those who did recognize Jesus were attracted to something deeper than the physical:

> We beheld his glory, the glory as of the only begotten of
> the Father, full of grace and truth (John 1:14).

"He came unto his own," reported John, "and his own
received him not" (John 1:11). Such blindness is moral and
spiritual. God must be seen and heard in the *heart*, and only the
heart that desires His will can hear (John 7:17), no matter how
loudly God's voice sounds upon the ears or what wonders are
seen with the eyes. The truth that God speaks comes neither by
wind, though it be so strong that it breaks rocks, nor earthquake
nor fire, as Elijah learned, but in "a still small voice" (1 Kings
19:11,12) that only His own can hear. Jesus explained it like this:

> My sheep hear my voice, and I know them, and they
> follow me; and I give unto them eternal life, and they shall
> never perish, neither shall any man pluck them out of my
> hand... (John 10:27,28).

An Ancient But Powerful Lie

The history of religion is the tragic tale of those who are morally
and spiritually blind and deaf, yet who devise rituals and symbols
in an attempt to "see" God and "hear" His voice and benefit
from His power through means that the Bible condemns as

idolatry and divination. Witch doctors, medicine men, and other shamans learned long ago that in the imagination one can "see" and "hear" whatever one desires, and that if the scene created in the imagination is vivid enough, contact will be made with a mysterious spirit world that seems just as real as the physical one. Those who attempt to contact God in this manner open themselves to the possibility of demonic delusion from seducing spirits, who are only too happy to pose as "God" or "Christ" or whatever deity is being visualized. In a publication devoted to sharing "guidance and wisdom from the loving beings of the Spirit Plane," a seducing spirit that calls itself "Soli" declares:

> However you perceive of us in the spirit dimension, that is how we shall appear to you.[5]

Experimenting with this "ancient wisdom," psychologists have become convinced that "our minds can't tell the difference between the real experience and one that is vividly and repeatedly imagined."[6] Calling this blessed delusion "The Second Best-Kept Secret of Total Success,"[7] a leading Christian motivationalist writes: "Understanding this secret of the power of the imagined experience is the fundamental key to understanding human behavior."[8] Rather than being cause for concern, the fact that we can be thoroughly deceived by our imagination is actually to our great advantage, so the theory goes, for it means that we can feed any ambition or dream, no matter how outrageous, into the subconscious and it will turn fantasy into reality because it doesn't know the difference. Another leading Christian motivationalist explains:

> ...your subconscious mind...will do exactly as commanded regardless of whether the instruction is positive or negative....
> It accepts, without question, what it is told and doesn't analyze or reject any information....
> The deliberate use of the subconscious mind is an exciting possibility for you, and the benefits are almost unlimited.[9]

Psychology "scientifically" turns occultism into an "exploration of the inner world of the psyche," purges it of demons and real evil by the expedient of new definitions, and turns spiritualism into a purely mental trip, beneficial and now prescribed for numerous forms of psychotherapy and self-improvement. The theories of Carl Jung provide an alleged scientific interpretation which in effect demythologizes occultism so that those practicing it are assured that, rather than dealing with actual spirit beings, they are instead making contact with archetypal images in the collective unconscious. This allows the Jungian analyst to engage in old-fashioned witchcraft under psychological labels. Leading humanistic psychologist Robert Ellis criticizes transpersonal psychology for including the following premises:

> By tapping into transcendental and higher consciousness sources we can create miracles and magical results....
> We all have a God within us who enables us to be perfect, to ward off harm, and to miraculously cure ourselves.[10]

Christianized versions of this psychologized shamanism are now being practiced in the church by inner healers and Christian psychologists who attempt through "active imagination" to "see" and "hear" the things of God. They have fallen for a very ancient but powerful lie—and one that "works." As a result, an extremely dangerous teaching is spreading throughout the church. It suggests that *seeing* is actually the key to faith, and that it can all be done in the mind. Indeed, the exercise of the *imagination* (and especially of visualization as its most powerful form) is being hailed as the secret to spiritual growth and answered prayer, and even to contact with God or Christ.

In the rational world, imagination has always been contrasted to reality. "It didn't really happen," we say; "you just *imagined* it." Moreover, the Bible presents imagination as dangerous and evil. In the first mention of imagination we read, "And God saw that the wickedness of man was great in the earth, and that every imagination of the thoughts of his heart was only evil continually" (Genesis 6:5). By equating imagination with reality we destroy the meaning of both words. And by making imagination the vehicle for a relationship with Christ and the means of obtaining answers to prayer we lower Christianity to the level of a mere fantasy. Charles Finney warned of what he called "The Religion of Imagination":

Individuals shut out from the world of reality and living in worlds of imagination become perfect creatures of imagination. . . .

In every age men have fallen in love with fictions of their own imaginations over which they have stumbled into hell.[11]

The Power of the Imagination

Of course the legitimate uses of imagination and visualization are too numerous to mention. It should be clear that remembering a person, place, or event from the past involves mental imagery—and it is just as harmless (and beneficial) to use the imagination to plan something in the future such as a house one hopes to build. Nor is there anything wrong with mentally rehearsing the delivering of a speech or practicing one's golf or tennis swing in the mind. As soon, however, as we think that visualization somehow creates or influences exterior reality (i.e. visualizing the golf ball dropping into the cup will make it happen) or that contact can be made with Jesus or God, we have opened ourselves to possible demonic influences.

Moreover, while it is true that imagination is a normal part of every person's life, even without occult involvement it can be extremely dangerous if not used with restraint. In its mildest but still problematic forms, mental imagery is a means of escaping the unpleasant real world by retreating into an inner universe of fantasy where one reigns as a god over the creations of one's own mind. Here in this secret kingdom anyone can be seduced with the same dream of godhood that caused Eve to eat the forbidden fruit. As its creators, we can make this imaginary fantasy world within our minds (and its cast of characters, including ourselves as hero or heroine) into whatever we desire. Our fondest ambitions can be realized as we visualize ourselves playing out in fantasy the heroic adventures and triumphs that elude us in real life. Thus we become the "creators" of our own self-deception.

While flights of the imagination can be normal and sometimes even helpful for young children, it is a serious symptom if, as one grows older, one continues to engage in the same childish fantasies but now in an attempt to escape the real world. Nevertheless, psychologists use fantasy for adults as a technique for overcoming fears and phobias; inner healers use it for changing one's attitude toward painful memories; and success/motivation experts use it for developing a "positive mental attitude" and for setting goals. The rationale for the latter is that a goal firmly visualized and implanted in the subconscious mind will cause one to take the steps necessary to reach it.

"We can actively visualize and create our own futures, in advance," declares a leading Christian "behavioral scientist."[12] He goes on to state: "What you 'see' is what you'll get. We perform and behave in life not in accordance with reality, but in accordance with our perception of reality."[13] Thus we can change everything by fantasizing our own reality. In a popular "success" book, a Christian author suggests:

> Form a mental picture of what you desire to achieve. Place yourself in the picture. Experience the emotions of the moment. Bring to bear the use of the five senses. Feel, see, taste, smell, and hear it.
>
> Say it's a new home. Draw all the details in your mind's eye.... That's you in the yard standing by the Mercedes Benz. Whose Cadillac, your wife's?...
>
> It's yours the minute you visualize it, and remember, the joy of the pursuit of earning it may be greater than living in it....
>
> Think about it several times each day. Soon all your powers will be concentrated on its achievement.[14]

While there may be some "motivational" truth involved, fantasy is not the doorway to reality, and cultivating mental images is not a harmless exercise. Even aside from possible occult involvement, in order for a person to practice this technique, the dream of success must become an obsession that constantly occupies the heart and mind of the Christian with materialistic goals. And one easily slips into believing that he is actually *creating* what he visualizes. In an editorial in his *Possibilities* magazine, Robert Schuller writes:

> As I travel around the world and meet successful, dynamic people, I constantly rediscover the one thing they all have in common. The truly successful people attain their goals with the help of visualizing success. They actually picture, often in detail,

the material, physical, or spiritual goal they want to attain....

"The me I see is the me I'll be." Picturing ourselves as the successful people we want to be is the first step towards realizing that goal!... Positive imaging is the first step.[15]

Christianizing Occultism?

As though it were both biblical and scientific, a Christian leader writes of "the projected image as a basic law of mind" and claims that "this technique is effective in just about all the important areas of living."[16] The fact that something produces seemingly good results is no reason for Christians to accept or practice it. Overweight Christians attempt to take off unwanted pounds by visualizing themselves as that slim person they hope to become. Our eyes are turned from Christ to ourselves. Instead of being transformed into His image by the Spirit of God, we now seek to transform ourselves by the power of visualization into the new self-image we have fantasized. Visualization and other occult techniques for activating powerful forces have been practiced secretly and consistently for thousands of years. Today they are out in the open as part of the New Age movement and are widely accepted even by sincere Christians who are not aware of the origins or dangers involved in the practices they are adopting. Typical of what many congregations are hearing these days is the following exhortation from a popular Southern California pastor:

> Last month [a guest speaker]...asked a question which pierced my soul. His question was:
>
> > "What is the greatest thing you can imagine you could ever accomplish for God?... Dream real big! Visualize in your heart something that might seem absolutely impossible...the Lord wants you to know that *that's the dream* he wants you to believe for and work toward."...
>
> I want you to have my four-part teaching on faith and visions. I know it will revolutionize your life! These exciting messages include:
>
> > "*The Power of Positive Believing*" (Part 1)
> > "*The Power of Positive Believing*" (Part 2)

"The Creative Power of Visions and Dreams"
"Spiritual Birthing through Visions and Dreams."[17]

Once again the danger is in confusing our own conjured-up dreams of success with God's will for our lives, developing techniques for fulfilling our desires, and confusing an *imaginative* process that we initiate for *inspiration* that God alone can give.

Unfortunately, the practice of visualization, though begun as an aid to motivation, not only promotes an unhealthy absorption in success but almost inevitably leads to the next step: believing that one's mind somehow exercises or triggers a mysterious force that causes to occur in the real world what has been visualized in the imaginary one. This basic witchcraft belief is the foundation of the Mind Science cults (Science of Mind, Religious Science, Christian Science, Unity, etc.) and of the PMA success/motivation world, and is the common denominator in thousands of self-help groups today. Take for example Concept Therapy, known also as Conceptology, which has "changed the lives" of multitudes through its brand of psychotherapy blended with Eastern mysticism and occultism:

What Concept Therapy does is to present in simple, understandable language the *Wisdom of the Ages*...[such as] the ancient Hermetic law that deals with the relation between things of the physical plane, the thoughts we think, and the acts we perform....

In auto-suggestion or self-hypnosis, you lodge your own images in your subconscious without interfering doubt-thoughts...the subconscious doesn't become impressed with words but rather by feelings....

We get what we *image*...if you can hold one image—to the exclusion of all other thoughts—for thirty-three and a third seconds, it will succeed in "sinking" into the subconscious and in due time it will manifest in your life.

...it is valuable to learn how we can make our wishes come true, not for selfish, mundane reasons, but so that we can finally create and manifest...the MASTER IMAGE...so that you can at last be ONE WITH ALL OF LIFE...[part of] a mighty international organization dedicated to the Truth, *that Truth that makes men Free* [emphasis in original].[18]

Psychologized "White Magic"

Tragically, much that passes for Christianity even within evangelical circles sounds increasingly like the psychologized "white magic" being peddled by a thousand such self-help groups. A highly respected Christian author writes, "Anything you can think of and believe in you can achieve."[19] He claims that Jesus used this "power of belief to heal the sick, to change water into wine" and that it is a universal "powerful force" available to anyone.[20] Very subtly faith ceases to be in God and becomes a power of the mind activated and directed by one's own imagination. One of America's most highly honored ministers tells how he and his wife filled their church one rainy night by visualizing people "streaming into the church...."[21] He attributes this "miracle" to "...the power that He [God] put into our unconscious mind through imaging, the power that turns wishes into realities when the wishes are strong enough."[22] Recently he has advocated even more blatant occultism:

> Marilyn Helleberg suggests a meditation in which you visualize a white mist filled with myriads of little points of energy that gleam like diamonds. Scientists say this is the life substance, the life force....
> Visualize this mist high above you, around you, and at your feet, cascading down like a waterfall of scintillating light.
> Then breathe in the white mist, and visualize it as proceeding upward into your throat, into your nasal passages, into your brain, vitalizing, sharpening and quickening your mind, making it alive with a new power....
> I have been practicing this type of meditation for several days and I can report that after using it only a half dozen times one begins to feel different. It induces a sense of vital energy; an awareness of God's presence.
> Who is God? Some theological being? He is so much greater than theology. God is vitality. God is life. God is energy. As you breathe God in, as you visualize His energy, you will be reenergized![23]

It is incomprehensible that such blatant white magic could be taught by a church leader and accepted by Christians. It is even more unbelievable that other Christian leaders continue to praise such teachers. Recently the "foremost Christian analyst" wrote a full-page tribute to the man, in spite of such teachings as above.[24] The great tragedy is that genuine seekers who want to know God are deluded into believing that this can be accomplished through breathing in an imaginary "white mist"! By such techniques sincere people are being robbed of the very contact with God which they seek.

Christian leaders who should be guarding the church from error are now openly embracing occult methodologies, and some are even suggesting that Jesus Himself was a shaman. Consider the following news release made early in 1986:

> Dr. Doran C. McCarty, professor of ministry at Golden Gate Baptist Theological Seminary, proposed a "new shaman" in his faculty inaugural address....
>
> "The Making of the New Shaman"...was presented as part of the first chapel service of the spring semester.... The New Testament picture of Jesus was that of a shaman, McCarty related.[25]

Such a characterization of Jesus Christ from a Southern Baptist seminary would have been shocking a few years ago, but not today. Prolific writer Morton Kelsey, whose many books have widely influenced the church beyond his own Episcopal and charismatic circles, has probably done more than anyone else to promote the view that Jesus followed a long shamanic tradition and that Christians today should also pursue the "psychic" powers practiced in this tradition. Even though Kelsey advocates all forms of ESP,[26] the use of divination devices such as Ouija boards,[27] and communication with the dead,[28] his books are studied in evangelical seminaries and he has been called by one church leader "[one] of the most significant spiritual leaders in the Church today"[29] and even "the prophet raised up by God for this age."[30]

The Biblical Contrast

Much of the problem results from the gradual acceptance by the church of a new meaning for "meditation." In the Western world, until very recently, to *meditate* meant to rationally *contemplate* (or ponder or think deeply about something). The influence of Eastern mysticism, however, has brought a new type of "meditation" to the West which involves the very antithesis of contemplation—indeed, rational thought is declared to be a hindrance. This kind of "meditation" involves states of consciousness and subjective impressions in which one's own mind is no longer guiding the process; but something else has taken over, and one is swept along in the mystical flow of images and feelings.

Such a practice is in direct conflict with Scripture. Biblical meditation involves God's truth, not feelings or fantasy, and results in a deepened understanding and appreciation of God and His Word and a closer walk with Him. Joshua was told by God that he was to meditate upon the Scriptures "day and night" (Joshua 1:8). David said that he meditated upon God (that would include His person, character, power, love, works, will, etc.) in his bed "in the night watches" (Psalm 63:6). The longest Psalm contains numerous references to meditating upon God's Word, law, testimonies, statutes, and precepts (Psalm 119:15,23,97,99,148, etc.). After presenting much sound doctrine and instruction to him, Paul urged Timothy, "Meditate upon these things; give thyself wholly to them" (1 Timothy 4:15).

There is *not one* verse in all of Scripture that associates imagination or visualization with meditation. Instead of subjective experiences and elusive feelings, biblical meditation is solid and sure. It leads to understanding (Psalm 49:3) and great joy (Psalm 104:34). Jeremiah likened meditation to eating God's Word. His experience should also be ours:

> Thy words were found, and I did eat them; and thy word was unto me the joy and rejoicing of mine heart, for I am called by thy name, O Lord God of hosts (Jeremiah 15:16).

Christian Misuse of Visualization

The attempt to integrate psychology and Christianity has spawned numerous new techniques for prayer and healing unknown to the historic church and not to be found in the Bible. Among the most popular is "inner healing" or "healing of memories," which its current practitioners agree "began with the healing ministry of Mrs. Agnes Sanford in the decade after

World War II.''[31] One of its leading advocates has said, ''A central technique of almost all inner healing is visualization. . . .''[32] In a book comprised of critical responses to *The Seduction of Christianity* by Robert Wise, Paul Yonggi Cho, Dennis and Rita Bennett, and several others, one finds repeated references to such previously unknown terms as ''visualization prayer. . .new forms of prayer,''[33] ''prayer technique,'' ''visualization added force to her spoken prayers,''[34] ''Christian visualization,''[35] ''the role of visualization and imagination in prayers for healing of memories,''[36] ''meditational prayers that use symbols, images and visualization,''[37] ''prayers using imagery,''[38] and other such terminology.

A Christian psychologist who is known as ''one of the pioneers of this method of counseling. . .[using] prayer, imagery, identification and clarification of past hurts and positive visualization. . .''[39] explains that the imagination is used 1) to ''recreate the painful memory. . .visualize it as it once took place''[40] and 2) to visualize Christ present at the time of the painful incident. This is justified, he reasons, because Christ ''is the Lord of time—past, present, and future. . .He transcends all time and space.''[41] To support such ideas, it is declared that ''Francis MacNutt, in his classic book *Healing*, also related the omnipresence of Jesus to healing the inner man''[42] and that through visualization ''we allow Jesus, Lord of history, to walk down the path to where our wounds lie.''[43] However, neither author gives any clear support from Scripture for visualizing Jesus, nor do they explain how it is that MacNutt and other Catholics obtain equally good ''inner healing'' results through the visualization of Mary, who is clearly *not* the ''Lord of time'' nor able to ''walk down the path to where our wounds lie.'' Moreover, assorted occultists obtain equal results through visualizing all manner of ''inner guides.''

The Way of Forgiveness

That we must forgive those who have caused us pain is clear, and the consequences for not doing so are very grave: ''If ye forgive not men their trespasses, neither will your Father forgive your trespasses'' (Matthew 6:15; Mark 11:26). And that no special or lengthy "inner healing" process or "psychological counseling" is necessary in order for us to forgive others is equally clear. Christ said, "When ye stand praying, forgive, if ye have aught against any, that your heavenly Father also which is in heaven may forgive you your trespasses" (Mark 11:25). No real Christian should ever carry a grudge against anyone, no matter how horribly that person may have wronged or harmed him. We can know whether we hold such an attitude and can be delivered from it in a moment by an act of our will based upon the love and forgiveness that we have received from God. Since God has forgiven me, I cannot begrudge Him extending the same love and mercy and forgiveness to others—and how can I not forgive those whom He has forgiven? Do I find it difficult to get along with someone? If I will earnestly pray God's blessing upon that person, my attitude will be changed, for I can hardly be hostile toward or jealous of a person whom I desire God to bless!

The entire "inner healing" process is both unnecessary and a denial of what Christ has accomplished on the cross. For the true Christian the past no longer has any power, but has been done away with through the redemption in Christ's blood. The Scripture says, "Old things are passed away; behold, all things are become new" (2 Corinthians 5:17). This was not theory to Paul, but glorious truth that had transformed his life and caused him to say in triumph:

> ...forgetting those things which are behind, and reaching forth unto those things which are before, I press toward the mark for the prize of the high calling of God in Christ Jesus (Philippians 3:13,14).

Walking by Faith

With this heavenly goal before him, Paul declared, "We walk by faith, not by sight" (2 Corinthians 5:7). Visualization is an attempt to walk by sight and not by faith. Yet justification is offered for visualizing what one is praying for with the argument, "The use of symbols and images in prayer can help people move from possibility to reality...many people need the help that such prayer can offer."[44] Christianized visualization thus becomes a technique for creating faith: "The imagination is used to help God's promises become more real to us."[45] One highly respected church leader suggests, "If a person consciously visualizes being with Jesus, that is the best guarantee I know for keeping the faith."[46] This new theory cannot be supported by Scripture. On the contrary, as W. H. Griffith Thomas states:

> Surely we must trust our heavenly Father! Two Christians were once speaking of their experiences and one said, "It is terribly hard to trust God and realize His hand in the dark passages of life."
>
> "Well, brother," said the other, "if you cannot trust a man out of your sight, he is not worth much; and if you cannot trust God in the dark, it shows you do not trust Him at all."
>
> Psalm 91 does not say, "Under his wings thou shalt see," but "under his wings thou shalt trust."[47]

Those who "visualize" Christ and even God believe that they are somehow touching a deep level of reality made possible through a mysterious power of the mind. Advocates usually link "imaging" with "positive thinking and faith."[48] Commenting favorably upon a best-selling book that presents this concept, one of today's most respected Christian psychologists, an evangelical leader who likewise advocates imaging oneself with Jesus,[49] writes:

> Norman Vincent Peale described it in this way: "...imaging is a kind of laser beam of imagination, a shaft of mental energy...[which] releases powerful internal forces that can bring about astonishing changes in the life of the person who is doing the imaging."
>
> He [Jesus Christ] was the first to teach the power of imaging.[50]

Searching the New Testament in vain to discover when Jesus taught "the power of imaging," one wonders what a visualized mental image created in the imagination has to do with reality and the moral content of faith. And since neither Jesus nor any of the apostles or prophets either taught or practiced "creative imaging," why do so many of today's church leaders consider it to be the "best guarantee" for "keeping the faith"? Again it is psychology, by its sanctioning of visualization as "scientific," which has made this occult technique acceptable both to modern Western society and to the church.

Psychologized/Christianized Visualization

Much of the growing use (both in today's society and in the church) of the imagination, guided imagery, and visualization in order to transform reality, relive the past, and make contact with "inner guides" (including "Jesus," "Mary," and "God") is due to the influence of one man—Swiss psychiatrist Carl Gustav Jung. Agnes Sanford, who brought inner healing and visualization into the church, was heavily influenced by Jung's teachings. Sanford is now dead, but her close friend Morton T. Kelsey continues to promote within the church the theories which Jung received from demonic sources. Jung's "active imagination" and "archetypal images" play a vital role for Kelsey in encountering the world of the spirit:

> There are many ways to enter the strange, beautiful—and sometimes terrifying—territory of the inner world. The methods mentioned here are well-tried ways of using imagination for religious purposes.[51]
> Only through the use of images in our meditation can we actually open the door to the inner world and walk through it to experience the riches available in spiritual reality....[52]

Morton T. Kelsey was Agnes Sanford's pastor for a time in Monrovia, California. He and Agnes's son "Jack" (John Sanford) went to Zurich, Switzerland, to study at the C. G. Jung Institute and returned thoroughgoing Jungians. Their numerous books since then have expanded upon Jung's teachings, dressing them up in Christian terms and passing them off to an unsuspecting church.

The references to Carl Jung in *The Seduction of Christianity* caused a pastor in Flushing, New York, to undertake an intensive six-month investigation of Jung, Sanford, and Kelsey and their influence upon the church. In a letter to a leader in the charismatic movement, in which he acknowledged his own 15-year involvement and leadership, this pastor wrote: "I have arrived at the conclusion that...there is a *massive* seduction and deception in the church today...predominantly involv[ing] the theories and methodology of one *Carl Gustav Jung*...[who] tells us that the antecedents for his work are to be found in heretical Gnosticism and medieval occult alchemy.''[53] To two well-known Christian leaders he wrote:

> Those involved in the healing of memories techniques have to "come clean" and recognize the Jungian root in Agnes Sanford. If you do not, you are practicing deceit. You also *have to explain to the church* why you feel it is permissible to bring Jungian occult theory into Christianity....[54]
>
> [Jung] strongly attributes his insights to...his "ghostly guru" Philemon, as he calls him, who was his "spirit guide."...
>
> In my opinion...the theories of Carl Jung provide us with a deception of the highest order. It was no ordinary demon who put this one together....
>
> How does it make you feel that a book which you called a classic of this generation contains material attributable to Carl Jung's spirit-guide?[55]

The Insidious Influence of Carl Jung

That Jung was a heavily demonized occultist from childhood through adulthood is impossible to deny,[56] and his connection to "inner healing" and "visualization" practices within the church is too clear to require further comment.

When the two great masters Freud and Jung met, in 1909 and again in 1912, Jung deliberately caused "poltergeist activity" that so frightened Freud that he fainted dead away. After the second episode, Freud accused Jung of harboring a death wish against him (Freud had an obsessive fear of death), which Jung came to believe when in a dream he killed the Wagnerian hero Siegfried. In his demented state, Jung interpreted Siegfried to mean "Sig" Freud and became overwhelmed with fear.[57] For six years thereafter Jung teetered on the brink of insanity.

At first in dreams, then in visions, and finally in fully wakened consciousness (when he became so psychotic that the distinction between reality and delusion blurred almost completely), Carl Jung had repeated "visitations and revelations" from the spirit world, even including experiences with "God" and the "Holy Ghost" descending upon him "in the shape of a dove."[58] Jung's wide variety of occult experiences[59] included alleged conversations and even travel with the dead.[60] It was the "revelations" he received out of this milieu of spiritism and near-insane occultism, especially from his spirit guide Philemon, that became the basis for the psychological theories that Jung developed over the remainder of his life.[61]

This is not supposition; Jung freely admits it. And it is upon these "doctrines of devils," and not Scripture, that much of the practice of "inner healing" and other "meditation" and "visualization" techniques now accepted in the church are based.

Using Jung Discerningly?

Are Christian leaders who promote Jung's theories aware of their actual source? Some perhaps realize, as Leanne Payne acknowledges, that Jung's "presuppositions are not Christian—they are gnostic [which] he freely confesses...."[62] Nevertheless, like so many other Christian leaders, Payne finds Jung's insights "helpful." Abbot David Geraets of the Benedictine abbey at Pecos, New Mexico (a Catholic charismatic retreat center that has heavily influenced the entire inner-healing movement, both Catholic and Protestant), states, "You have to read Jung discerningly...he did make some mistakes."[63] Yet the Pecos abbey is known for having "incorporated the Jungian approach into teachings on charismatic renewal and spiritual growth."[64] Are demonic dealings merely "mistakes"? And is "discerningly" really the way to deal with the doctrines of devils taught by seducing spirits? Nick Cavnar, executive editor of *New Covenant*, explains the Jungian concepts that he feels have been helpful:

- Jung identified certain unconscious images or forces [which] he called "archetypes"...[such as] the *anima* and *animus*.

  Jung believed that the unconscious mind...was the realm of the spiritual and the mystical. Those who felt that the modern church had become too rationalistic found in Jung support for a more mystical, experiential religion.

  The charismatic renewal, with its emphasis on spiritual experience and inner healing, has been a natural field for interest in Jung.

  Truth is truth wherever it is found; whatever is true in Jungian psychology can be adapted and used by Christians.[65]

One can only wonder whether Christians who advocate using Jung "discerningly" have really faced the fact that they are adapting into Christianity "revelations" which Jung received from demons! While denying that he is influenced at all by Carl Jung, leading inner-healer John Sandford admits to "borrowing" the term "archetypes" from Jung. However, the similarity between his usage and Jung's is undeniable.[66] Sandford claims that God revealed to him from Genesis 1:27 that the male embodies also a "female nature" and the female a "male nature," which he called the female and male "poles."[67] The fact that Jesus explained this verse in an entirely different manner (Matthew 19:4-6) and the undeniable similarity between Sandford's "poles" and Jung's *anima* and *animus* raises a question about the source of Sandford's "inspiration." Sandford further declares that God told him to visualize "the poles reversed as I have shown you, and then stand and see as I reach in to disentangle those poles and set them in order."[68] The Sandfords tell how a Christian head of the psychology department at a Washington college tried this technique on homosexuals and found that it worked:

> He bound the archetype, traced down psychological causes, and prayed accordingly, and then prayed by vision [visualization] and authority concerning the male and female poles as the Lord had instructed. . . .
>
> "I don't know what it is, John" [the psychologist reported], "but I know it works. Hallelujah!"[69]

Biblical Support for Visualization?

The entire concept of Christian visualization is built upon the fallacy that *seeing* is *believing*, that a visual image is the key, and that to create one's own image in the imagination will therefore produce faith and healing. One of today's most highly regarded and prolific Christian authors suggests that "the Bible writers" such as Moses, David, Isaiah, and Jeremiah created differing images of God in their minds "block by imaginary block" and that the "mental image" which each held was the key to his spiritual life.[70] This growing belief that visual images created in the imagination open the door to a closer walk with God is part of an epidemic of extrabiblical teaching that is being accepted in the church today. The door is being opened to demonic delusion, and it is astounding how many Christians are walking through it.

The practice of visualization has taken such firm root in the church that those who question it are accused of misinterpreting the Bible. In an extremely critical CAPS (Christian Association for Psychological Studies) *Journal* review that accused the authors of *Seduction* of being "unbiblical, anti-Christian, irrational, inaccurate...extremely biased" and dishonest, as well as "encouraging the power of demons while pretending to discourage it," the following biblical support for the use of visualization was claimed:

> The authors [of *Seduction*] many times make the point that visualization is not taught in the Bible. The Bible clearly does teach visualization: Philippians 4:8; Romans 6:11; II Corinthians 4:18; I John 5:15; Colossians 3:2; Joshua 1:8; Mark 11:24; Hebrews 11:1; II Corinthians 3:18, etc.[71]

These verses represent the best biblical "proof" for visualization that the reviewer can muster, yet none of them even hints at visualization, much less teaches it. Philippians 4:8 says, "*Think* on these things"; Romans 6:11 says, "*Reckon* ye also yourselves to be dead indeed unto sin"; 1 John 5:15 says, "We *know* that we have the petitions that we desired of him"; Colossians 3:2 says, "*Set your affection* on things above"; Joshua 1:8 says, "This book of the law shall not depart out of thy mouth, but thou shalt *meditate* therein day and night, that thou mayest observe to do according to all that is written therein"; Mark 11:24 says, "*Believe* that ye receive them, and ye shall have them"; Hebrews 11:1 says, "Faith is...the evidence of things *not seen*." Trying through visualization to "see" the things "not seen" would seem specifically to contradict the last reference as well as everything else the Bible teaches about faith.

While 2 Corinthians 3:18 and 4:18 refer to "*beholding* as in a glass the glory of the Lord" and *looking* "at the things which are not seen," there is no basis for saying that these verses "teach visualization." Such words are commonly used in a nonvisual sense. The Scriptures often speak of *seeing* or *beholding* or *looking* at God, but at the same time we are repeatedly told that God is invisible, that no one has ever seen Him nor ever can. When we are told that Moses by faith "endured, as seeing him who is *invisible*" (Hebrews 11:27), it is referring to the *seeing* of faith, not that of physical eyes. Nor is there any hint that he conjured up a mental image of God, which is both impossible and absolutely forbidden.

A Deadly Departure from Scripture

It is staggering to see that beliefs and practices which the Bible specifically warns against are being taught by Christian leaders. One of the most blatant examples is a new Christian book written for youth ministers. After explaining a Yoga-related relaxation technique that one is to practice each day, the author states:

> Repeat this breathing exercise several times. Next, try to imagine God; keep searching in your mind (for however long it takes) to form an image of God. When the image is there, you will know it.
>
> Do not worry if this first exercise takes a long time. After the image is clear, focus on it for as long as you can.
>
> You may have to fine-tune it by focusing on each part of the image and visualizing yourself with that image.
>
> Eventually it will speak to you....
>
> Incorporate sounds or visuals into your mental image. Allow the sights and sounds to fade as you continue keeping God's image at the center of your picture.[72]

This is Christianized spiritualism. That the image *speaks* does not guarantee that one has made contact with God. In fact, that could not be the case, since the true God has specifically forbidden the use of images for contacting or worshiping Him. Therefore, one has been deceived by one's own imagination or, worse yet, contact has been made with a masquerading demon that has been given the ultimate disguise by the unsuspecting idolater. In numerous transmissions from the spirit world through mediums, the demons have boasted of their ability to take on whatever form the visualizer will accept. An entity that claims to be an angel named Raphael boasts:

> We work with all who are vibrationally sympathetic; simple

and sincere people who feel our spirit moving, but for the most part, only within the context of their current belief system.[73]

In a witchcraft network newspaper a practicing witch explains that the breathing exercises being adopted by Christians are "the most important part of relaxing," and that this is the way children especially are to be led into "chakra work, meditation, trance work" and all "other craft [i.e. witchcraft] work."[74] In the same issue the essential role of visualization in occult healing rituals is mentioned; then the author explains how easily those who "do not follow our way" can be led into witchcraft. Even Christians, she says, "do not see the rite as a threat to their religious beliefs" because the visualization "allows them to put their own 'names' and 'labels' on the deities."[75]

It should be clear how deadly a departure visualization of "God" or "Christ" is from the teaching of Scripture. Christians involved in such techniques are either self-deluded by their own fantasy or they are naively trafficking with demons, imagining that they are in contact with God or Christ.

Beware the Imaginary Jesus

The Bible assures us that one glad day—and not until then—we will at last be like Christ, and John gives this thrilling reason: "For we shall see him as he is" (1 John 3:2). That indescribably wonderful sight is reserved for those who have already seen Him by faith and have made Him Lord of their lives. Those who love Him "love his appearing" (2 Timothy 4:8) and long for that future day. Until then all attempts that we initiate in order to see Him are unbiblical. Those who have a passion to know the *true* God and Jesus Christ will not attempt to make contact through conjuring up fantasy images. Referring to the "trial of your faith" that would bring glory to God "at the appearing of Jesus Christ," Peter wrote:

> Whom *having not seen*, ye love; in whom, though *now ye see him not*, yet believing, ye rejoice with joy unspeakable and full of glory; receiving the end of your faith, even the salvation of your souls" (1 Peter 1:8,9).

Visualization of a fantasized Jesus is an attempt to manufacture "his appearing" before God's time. The consequences of this practice, now sweeping the church and deceiving naive Christians, are too serious to be brushed aside. The real Jesus will never stoop to become the servant of our imaginations. Paul warned of those who preach "another Jesus" (2 Corinthians 11:4) and expressed his concern lest, "as the serpent beguiled Eve," the Corinthian believers should also "be corrupted from the simplicity that is in Christ."

Even without occult involvement, visualization of "Jesus" can result in spiritual disaster. It is the perfect technique for deceiving those who do not know Christ into imagining that they have made contact with Him. The more real the "fantasy Jesus" conjured up in the mind, the less likely that one would seek and come to know the real Jesus by faith. Tozer left this solemn reminder:

> There are a great many bogus Christs among us these days. John Owen, the old Puritan, warned people in his day: "You have an imaginary Christ, and if you are satisfied with an imaginary Christ you must be satisfied with an imaginary salvation."[76]

11
Imagination or Revelation?

JOHN OWEN'S INCISIVE rebuke of those who are content with an "imaginary Jesus" pierced the hearts of his contemporaries. Today, however, the meaning of what he said has been completely subverted through the subtle intrusion of psychology. In Owen's day those who were not able to tell the difference between what they imagined and what was real were to be pitied. In our day such delusion is deliberately cultivated as one of the benefits of the "subconscious mind." Common sense, however, would tell us that if a visualized feast, no matter how sumptuous, will not nourish the body, neither will a visualized Christ nourish the spirit.

The growing use of visual imagery is closely related to the Hindu belief in *maya* (that everything is an illusion created by mind), and its endorsement by psychology has given it respectability within modern Western culture and thus in the church. A *Course In Miracles*, which is being taught in churches around the world, is a perfect example. The *Course*, dictated to atheist psychologist Helen Shucman[1] by a spirit "voice" that claimed to be "Jesus," is described by psychologist Kenneth Wapnick, President of the Foundation for "A Course In Miracles," as "a rich and unusual blend of New Age Christianity and Freudian psychology." Basically the *Course* purports to correct the many errors that allegedly crept into the Bible, explaining, for example, that we are each the son of God, that evil does not exist ("Death is the central dream from which all illusions stem"), and that forgiveness is simply recognizing that there is no sin and thus nothing to forgive.[2] Giving a clear view of a major delusion that is spreading throughout the church today in various forms, and which he endorses, Wapnick explains that, "as in Eastern philosophy," in the *Course* "the world is viewed as a dream, a collective illusion," and thus the solution to all problems is to change "people's perceptions about themselves and the world."[3] But in fact God's Word should change our perception to conform to His truth, which is altogether different from this teaching that we create our own "truth" by changing our perceptions through the use of imagination.

A Growing Popular Delusion

Imagination is increasingly being equated with *revelation* and *visualization* with *inspiration* even though the former is initiated by man and the latter by God. Great confusion results when these terms are mingled. To justify the growing practice of cultivating mental images as a means of hearing from God, it is being taught that symbols and imagery have a peculiar power and are superior to language for communicating truth. A book written to refute *The Seduction of Christianity* declares:

> The human mind does not think in words, but rather in pictures. When we were children, our parents pointed to the picture of a car, or horse, or airplane, and we began to associate the WORD with the IMAGE or PICTURE. That is simply because GOD programmed the human mind to think in PICTURES. The language of the Holy Spirit is, according to Dr. [Paul Yonggi] Cho, the language of VISION AND DREAM....
> When the Church learns to pray properly, it will learn the biblical use of VISION AND DREAM. VISUALIZATION is not the technique of Eastern mystics; it is intended by God to be the very medium of the communication of our FAITH to HIM, and HIS ideas to US [emphasis in original].[4]

Sincere and enthusiastic though the authors may be, their

conclusions are both illogical and unbiblical. Moreover, this belief that is growing in the church parallels similar developments in the secular world, which in turn are admitted by their chief advocates to be a revival of ancient shamanism. As one article in a professional journal recently stated:

> Can you picture an ancient shaman standing in a hospital ward, clipboard in hand, watching graph paper emerge from a biofeedback machine?
> This image is not as fantastic as it may seem; ancient shamanic practices are currently being adapted for contemporary use in healing illnesses, ranging from cancer to severe burns.
> ...the core of most shamanic practices is the belief that *imagination* links the mind with the body. This imaging capacity is important because the body does not hear words well....[5]

Unfortunately, thousands of Christians, including many reputable leaders, are making the tragic plunge into visual imagery without thinking through the process carefully for themselves. One well-known leader insists that using one's imagination for "visualizing or picturing the Lord" is "one of the most important ways the Lord works." He suggests that "the ability to visualize is much closer to the center of our being than the ability to verbalize." Because so many people "are being healed and blessed by the Lord through it," he considers warnings against the dangers of visualizing Jesus to be "an attempt on Satan's part to cripple the ministry of inner healing." Much of his reasoning is based upon the false assumption that the Holy Spirit can deal with us more effectively through images than through verbal understanding because "pictures are more effective than words."[6]

The Humiliation of the Word

Anyone willing to reflect carefully for a moment will readily see the gross error in the assertion that the human mind does not think in words but in pictures, and that the latter are therefore more effective in communicating God's truth than the former. While the mention of physical objects such as "horse" or "car" or "tree" may evoke a mental image, the same is not true of even the most elementary ideas. For example, consider the words and thoughts in this very paragraph. No image is even possible from a consideration of such words as while, the, mention, may, evoke, same, not, true, even, ideas, consider, thoughts, possible, necessary, or certainly. Not only the simplest concepts but, more important, truth and morals are not visual and cannot be depicted in imagery.

To "think only in pictures" would eliminate all that we understand of goodness, justice, holiness, wisdom, discretion, reverence, love, kindness, and of God Himself. Just as no image can represent God, so no image can represent those unique capacities and concepts that separate humanity from animals and bear witness to the fact that man is made in the moral and spiritual image of the invisible Creator God.

While it pretends to bring deep insight and even to be the avenue of vital inspiration from God, the use of mental imagery in the pursuit of spirituality breeds superficiality in actual fact and is the ideal vehicle for brainwashing and seduction. Yet a major critic of *Seduction* suggests that "visualization and imagery are a normal part of the devotional practices described in the Bible...visualization puts people 'in touch' with God." He also declares that "images are much larger and more powerful symbols than words."[7] In sharp contrast, summing up the message of Jacques Ellul's latest book, *The Humiliation of The Word*, one reviewer has said:

> Our generation has largely given up on language as the primary means of communication, preferring images instead. Whether it is television, computer graphics, or the psychological technique of visualization, images are primary while language and dialogue are eclipsed....
>
> Language is the medium with which we ask and answer the question of truth. With language we are able to formulate our ethics and make judgments.
>
> While the spoken word promotes reasoning, interaction and careful thinking, the image promotes conformity and mass manipulation.
>
> When imagery becomes primary, our very humanity is threatened.[8]

Revival of an Ancient Evil

Although our minds make frequent and valid use of imagery, we don't *think* (reason) in images. The old saying "A picture is worth a thousand words" refers to the fact that pictures, far from communicating something precise, are interpreted differently by nearly everyone who views them. Each person supplies his own "thousand words" from his own imagination, which may differ entirely from what the artist had in mind. To attempt to communicate with pictures would not only be laborious, but the message would necessarily have to be very simple. Even then it could be easily misunderstood.

Far from leading us to a deeper faith and to a fuller understanding of the things of God, cultivating mental images under the mistaken impression that they are the language of the Holy Spirit will prevent us from hearing what God has *said*. The Bible was written not in *pictures*, but in *words* that communicate truth and a depth of understanding that cannot be conveyed by imagery. It is of course normal for the mind to create its own images; but we must remember that these represent how we *imagine* things to be and do not necessarily equate with truth. Knowing God or Jesus Christ involves something much deeper than anything a mental image could provide, even if it were accurate. It is a new form of the idolatry that John Owen rebuked as unable to produce true spirituality:

> For they made crucifixes and images with paintings to represent Him in His sufferings and glory. Their carnal affections being thus excited by their senses, they suppose themselves to be affected with Him and to be like Him.[9]

This new evangelical mental idolatry is a revival of the same error that long ago corrupted Israel and finally brought God's judgment. Much of the book of Jeremiah was written specifically to combat this evil. Repeatedly the prophet links Israel's refusal to hear God's *Word* with her eagerness to follow *imagination*. The following is only a small sample:

> The Lord saith, Because they have...not obeyed my voice...but have walked after the imagination of

their own heart...I will scatter them also among the heathen....

This evil people, which refuse to hear my words, which walk in the imagination of their heart...shall even be... good for nothing (Jeremiah 9:13-16; 13:10).

As it was in Jeremiah's day, so today the imagination is being followed and is even touted as the secret to obtaining miracles. In a book that enthusiastically offers to the church the secret "keys to miracles and blessings," a leading charismatic writes:

I believe miracles begin in the soil of your *imagination*.... Abraham used his IMAGINATION to *strengthen his faith*.... Your imagination can unleash *unexpected energy* [emphasis in original].[10]

A Sign of Maturity?

The current exaltation of imagery above language and the promotion of visualization of Jesus and God is but one more indication that Christians are following the secular world's revolt against reason and reality. It smacks of the teenager's superficial love affairs with the photos pasted on his or her bedroom walls. Christians have something infinitely more real—an intimate, personal relationship with God Himself through the indwelling Holy Spirit. Visualization techniques do not promote faith but cater to the very unbelief which Jesus condemned in what He called "an evil and adulterous generation [that] seeketh after a sign" (Matthew 12:39).

Even so, a highly honored Christian author in a book that has gained great popularity among evangelicals urges his readers to "accent the creative gifts of fantasy and imagination." He approvingly quotes liberal Harvard theologian Harvey Cox, who has embraced Eastern mysticism: "...man's celebrative and imaginative faculties have atrophied...fantasy is viewed with distrust in our time."[11] And it ought to be!

Somehow this sincere enthusiast manages to interpret a propensity for childish fantasy as a sign of maturity by suggesting that those who don't engage in it "are insecure about their own maturity."[12] In contrast, Herbert Schlossberg laments the blatant superficiality of the present generation. It seeks reality by appealing to imagination rather than truth. Exposing what he calls the "irrationalities that today are increasingly celebrated," Schlossberg remarks:

> Marshall McLuhan's popularity shows that he has struck a responsive chord with his teaching that decisions are made not by thinking seriously about evidence but by responding to sensations.
> And here is [Harvard theologian Harvey] Cox, reveling in the rebirth of fantasy and feeling rather than intellect.[13]

Faith: The Evidence of Things Not Seen

The appealing and widely-accepted fallacy that the imagination is the doorway to reality cannot be shrugged off as though it matters little. Increasing numbers of today's Christian leaders are echoing the dangerous and fallacious claim that "we simply must become convinced of the importance of thinking and experiencing in images."[14] Those who teach this concept are not content to wait for God in His own time and way to give visions and dreams to whom He will. They are promoting techniques for creating their own visions through mental imagery under the assumption that God will dutifully "sanctify" their fantasies if they only ask Him to.

There is a growing number of books promoting such techniques. In its most dangerous form, contact is made with a spirit entity that one believes to be Jesus or God and that actually speaks to the visualizer. The Association of Church-centered Bible Schools, which is establishing many schools in churches across America and Canada, includes in its curriculum a course that is designed to teach "Spirit-to-spirit encounters with Almighty God" whereby students are able to establish "two-way dialogue with God in their prayer lives."[15] The Dean of Students and Director of Curriculum for the ACBS explains how he first made this encounter:

> As I peered intently into the [visualized] picture and looked to see what might happen, it came alive through the Holy Spirit. Jesus moved and gestured...[and] there came into my

heart His words and directives for my life. . . .

I found as I repeated this experiment in subsequent days that God continued to move through these "self-initiated scenes," causing them to come alive with his own life and become supernatural visions direct from the throne of grace.

At this point I want to stop to answer some of the questions you may be asking. First, "Don't you limit God by forcing Him to fit into the scene you have set for Him to fill?" The answer is, "Absolutely yes!"

Of course, God has some variance as He takes over the scene you have set.[16]

To avoid being charged with idolatry, this man argues: "According to Webster a graven image is 'An object of worship carved usually from wood or stone.' Obviously, the scene we set in our minds is not carved or worshiped. It serves simply as a stepping-stone to this living flow of divine images."[17] However, every idol formed of wood, clay, or stone was first of all visualized in the mind. It is the act of forming the image of deity—mental or physical—that constitutes idolatry.

It is not wrong if a pastor on his knees, because this is the passion of his heart, sees in his mind his church filled to overflowing and people going forward to repent, and cries out to God in prayer for this to become a reality. It is wrong, however, if he thinks that by concentrating on this imaginary scene until it becomes vivid in his mind he will thereby help it to occur, and he then practices this technique in order to make what he visualizes come to pass. Mental imagery is a normal function of the human mind, and the use of mental pictures can be helpful in such areas as memorization, planning, recalling, gaining insight, or helping to explain a complex concept. But to attempt to visualize God or Jesus, or to change or create reality by visualization, is to step into the occult.

We have already noted that faith, according to the Bible, is "the evidence of things *not seen*" (Hebrews 11:1). It would therefore be destructive of genuine faith to make it dependent upon one's ability to "see" either the God and Christ to whom we pray or the answer we seek in prayer by visualizing a mental image. This is an attempt to walk not by *faith* but by *sight* and is in direct conflict with everything the Bible teaches concerning faith. Nevertheless, a popular evangelical author writes:

> As with meditation, the imagination is a powerful tool in the work of prayer....
>
> Imagination opens the door to faith. If we can "see" in our mind's eye a shattered marriage whole or a sick person well, it is only a short step to believing that it will be so....[18]

"Believing" on what basis? Surely faith that depends upon our ability to visualize what we desire rather than upon our relationship to God, our trust in Him, and our submission to His will is not genuine faith at all. Instead of faith in God, this is faith in the visual image we have created in our minds. Again it is psychology that has undermined Scripture and given credibility to what would otherwise be recognized as blatant shamanism but is now confused with Christianity. For example, the Institute for Transpersonal Psychology in Menlo Park, California, now encourages "spiritual experiences" that include the following, all of which are considered to be equally valid:

> Seeing visions. Speaking in tongues. Walking and talking with Jesus. Blissed out on Buddha. Wrestling with Satan. Sighting UFOs.[19]

The Secret to Answered Prayer?

Prayer is the communion of the loving, trusting, worshiping, and obedient (or repentant) heart with God. Very subtly, however, the focus has been shifted from God as the One we worship and trust to *techniques* that have as their primary goal not obedience and His glory but getting what we think we should have. Arguments for visualization and imagination are presented so convincingly by those who seem to be so well-qualified and so sincere that the average Christian is completely disarmed. There are a variety of enticing ways in which well-meaning Christians are led in seemingly innocent steps to believe that visualization is a doorway to truth, special spiritual benefits, and answered prayer. In a newsletter to his supporters, one of the leaders in the Positive Confession movement writes:

> Well, I'm excited to tell you I'm going back to my prayer cabin
> to get alone with God once again...interceding for you....
>   I wish I could have you and my other dear Partners there with
> me. Since that is not possible, I want you to do the next best thing
> so that you'll be there in spirit and experience the miracle power
> of God flowing through me.
>   There will be moments during those three days and nights when
> the anointing on me will be greater than any need you have. So
> here's what I'm led of God to have you do....
>   1. FIRST, take the photo I've enclosed of me standing in front
> of my prayer cabin and place it in a place where you can see it.
> See yourself with me while I'm in there praying for you. This is
> very important...as you visualize yourself there with me, remem-
> ber there is no time nor distance in the realm of the Spirit....
>   Your seed-faith offering will also be in your envelope...when
> you release your FAITH WORDS.[20]

This man presents himself as a channel of God's power flowing through him to his supporters. Their relationship to *him* is
their means of obtaining miracles and answered prayer.

The prayer letter contains no challenge to holiness or obedience
or submission to God's will. Instead, three specific things are listed
as "very important" in getting "results": 1) visualizing themselves there with him; 2) filling out and returning to him a
" 'Covenant of Agreement' prayer form" together with the
essential "seed-faith" offering to his ministry which he describes
as "good soil"; and 3) "The very moment your letter leaves your
hand to be mailed back to me SAY WITH YOUR MOUTH (OUT
LOUD)—'Lord Jesus, my miracle has started! It's working for me
now!' " (Emphasis in the original.) The focus is self-centered,
and faith is placed in man and ritual. It is a far cry from John's
assuring and challenging declaration:

> This is the confidence that we have in him, that, if
> we ask anything according to his will, he heareth us (1 John
> 5:14).
>   Whatsoever we ask, we receive of him, because we keep
> his commandments, and do those things that are pleasing
> in his sight (1 John 3:22).

Taking us away from the simplicity of Scripture, methodologies for guaranteeing answers to prayer are gaining in popularity. It is not easy to resist the earnest advice of a highly respected and successful Christian leader when he states authoritatively: "You must see your [prayer] objective so vividly and graphically that you can really feel it in your emotions. If you do not exercise this law of faith, you can never really get an answer to everything you request."[21] He explained to a woman why her prayers for her daughter's salvation were not being answered:

> In your mind you were always submitting just the picture of a prostitute, weren't you?
> But if you want to see her changed, then you must submit another mental blueprint. You must clean the canvas of your imagination, and you must start drawing a new picture.[22]

There is nothing in all of Scripture from which such a teaching can be drawn. In fact, this pastor does not even claim that he learned it from the Bible, but that it came to him as a new "revelation" from God when he was praying for a bicycle, desk, and chair. "God" told him that He could not answer vague prayers. It was necessary to let God know exactly what bicycle, desk, and chair he wanted.[23] This was to be accomplished by visualizing clearly in his mind the precise thing he was praying for. He practiced this and it worked.[24] This is now the heart of what he teaches, and it seems to produce answers to prayer and apparent miracles not only for him but also for many others.

Although this "revelation from God" was a turning point in this man's life,[25] it denies God's omniscience, which is so clearly taught in Psalm 139 and many other Scriptures. Rather than using visualization in order to get what we want from God (even if it worked), would it not be better, since God is infinite in wisdom and knowledge, to leave room in our prayers for Him to fill in the details as He knows best and according to His will? This has been the practice of men and women of God down through the centuries. Christ Himself declared, "Your Father knoweth what things ye have need of before ye ask him" (Matthew 6:7,8).

Christ's Pattern for Prayer

What a contrast to today's proliferating techniques is found in the simple yet glorious prayer pattern given by Christ to His disciples: "After this manner therefore pray ye..." (Matthew 6:5-15). Each true Christian can come "boldly unto the throne of grace" (Hebrews 4:16) in Christ's name (John 16:23,24), without any intermediary except Him (1 Timothy 2:5), as a child of God (John 1:12,13), confident of his Father's love and care (John 16:26,27). This great privilege and responsibility is to be exercised by each individual personally and privately (Matthew 6:6) in the full assurance that it is not our "much speaking" (Matthew 6:7)—and thus no other technique—but God's love and wisdom that we rely upon to meet our needs.

The entrance by faith into God's staggeringly majestic presence brings first of all a sense of wonder, awe, and worship as we consider how great is the One to whom we pray: "Our Father which art in heaven, Hallowed be thy name!" The immediate result is surrender of one's will to His will in a fervent desire that God would be known and loved and worshiped and honored as He ought to be: "Thy kingdom come. Thy will be done in earth, as it is in heaven." The realization that all else must be subservient to the coming of His kingdom brings simplicity of desire and recognition of one's complete dependence upon God even for "life, and breath, and all things" (Acts 17:25): "Give us this day our daily bread."

Prayer is only possible because Christ has satisfied the holy claims of God's righteousness so that we could be forgiven. That being the case, no one can expect God to hear his prayer if he has not forgiven others as God has forgiven him: "And forgive us our debts [sins], as we forgive our debtors...for if ye forgive not men their trespasses [sins against you], neither will your Father forgive your trespasses." Each time we pray is a fresh reminder of the fact that God has forgiven us and is a renewal of the joy and freedom we experience through no longer holding a grudge, resentment, or unforgiving thought against anyone for even a moment.

"Lead us not into temptation" does not imply that God would

do such a thing, "for God cannot be tempted with evil, neither tempteth he any man" (James 1:13). It is, however, the acknowledgment of our weakness and complete inability to live a Christian life in our own strength. As Paul reminds us, "Let him that thinketh he standeth take heed lest he fall" (1 Corinthians 10:12). We "resist the devil" and he flees from us (James 4:7), but we do not boast of our ability to do so nor ask for confrontations with temptation, but rest in the victory Christ has won.

"For thine is the kingdom, and the power, and the glory, for ever. Amen." Prayer produces worship. Its primary focus is upon God's kingdom and will, not upon our needs, much less our selfish desires. Through prayer our desire becomes a longing for His glory. What deliverance true prayer brings from the petty complaints and whinings and anxieties that cause such misery for those who are wrapped up in themselves! Following Christ's pattern of prayer, our hearts are filled with joy and gratitude and His love, and we experience the victory Paul knew. Though in prison and faced with suffering and death, Paul could sincerely express the desire:

> That in nothing I shall be ashamed, but that with all boldness, as always, so now also Christ shall be magnified in my body, whether it be by life or by death. For to me to live is Christ, and to die is gain (Philippians 1:20,21).

Pursue God, Not Fantasy Images

Jesus plainly stated that we are to have faith *in God*. Surely fantasizing a mental image of what we are praying for would not help us to know God better, which is the only way to increase our faith in Him. On the contrary, it represents an occultic method for mentally producing a result that has nothing to do with God's will or our relationship to Him. The more proficient we become at this divination technique, the deeper we may be drawn into occultism and the farther we will be led away from a right relationship with the true God. Tozer offered this wise counsel:

> True faith is not the intellectual ability to visualize unseen things

to the satisfaction of our imperfect minds; it is rather the moral power to trust Christ.

To be contented and unafraid when going on a journey with his father the child need not be able to imagine events; he need but know the father. . . .

The wise Christian will not let his assurance depend upon his powers of imagination.[26]

D. L. Moody, Charles Spurgeon, G. Campbell Morgan, Andrew Murray, A. W. Tozer, and other outstanding Christian leaders of the past, far from advocating visualization, warned against it. Spurgeon wrote, ". . .the Christian is a nobler being than to live and walk by sight. He lives by faith. . . . And truly 'tis better to see Christ by faith than it is to see him by sight."[27] John Owen warned, "An imaginary Christ will effect nothing in the minds of men but imaginary grace."[28] Charles Finney wrote, "Don't try to imagine a God after your own foolish hearts, but take the Bible and learn who God is."[29] John MacArthur reminds us:

God cannot be reduced either to a physical image or a theological abstract. He is a personal spirit, and He must be worshiped in the fullness of the infinity of His eternal being. . . .worship, no matter how beautiful or consistent or well-intentioned it is, is unacceptable if it is directed to a false God.[30]

No longer content to know that Christ dwells in their hearts by faith (Ephesians 3:17), some sincere but misguided Christians must "see" Him in the fantasy scenes of their imagination; and finding His words that are recorded in Scripture insufficient for their daily meditation, they now require a continual flow of fresh words spoken by their own personal visualized Jesus. Such a practice is not only without biblical foundation, but is highly dangerous. Those who dare to speak forth to the church or follow in their own lives what they have "heard from God" through activating their imaginations would do well to heed God's indictment through Jeremiah:

Ye have done worse than your fathers; for, behold, ye walk every one after the imagination of his evil heart, that they may not hearken unto me (Jeremiah 16:12).

Visions, Dreams, and Imagery in the Bible

While it is true that God does speak through visions and dreams, it is equally clear that imagery is not *the language* of the Holy Spirit, as so many Christian leaders are teaching. Take for example Peter's vision of a sheet being let down from heaven "wherein were all manner of fourfooted beasts of the earth, and wild beasts, and creeping things, and fowls of the air" (Acts 10:12). Without the voice accompanying the vision—"Rise, Peter; kill and eat.... What God hath cleansed, that call not thou common [unclean]" (Acts 10:13,15)—Peter would not have understood the vision's meaning. The image he saw was not sufficient. Nor was Peter engaged in *visualization*. The vision was sovereignly given to him by God. The new emphasis today, however, is upon *"developing* dream and vision..." [emphasis added].[31]

There is an obvious difference between *receiving* visions and dreams from God and *developing* them ourselves. God's prophets carefully state that God's words, revelations, and visions *came* to them from the Lord as He willed. Never is there even a hint that they took the initiative and made contact with God through some technique in which the prophets were trained. Repeatedly Jeremiah declares, "The word of the Lord which came to Jeremiah" (Jeremiah 14:1; 18:1; 27:1; 46:1; etc.). Twice in the first chapter Jeremiah uses the expression "The word of the Lord came unto me" (verses 4 and 11). Ezekiel writes "The word of the Lord came unto me" nearly 50 times, and the other prophets use similar expressions. Peter declared that "holy men of God" were inspired to write Scripture not through practicing self-initiated techniques for getting in touch with God but "as they were moved by the Holy Spirit" (2 Peter 1:21).

We dare not tamper with the supernatural process whereby the Holy Spirit communicates with man. As we have already seen, any attempt to do so is denounced as divination and is absolutely forbidden in Scripture. It is a means of making contact in the spirit realm with Satan or his demons posing as angels of light, but not with God. However, techniques are now being taught to "assist Christians in encountering the living God." As one author assures us:

> ...anyone can enter into this experience. It is not reserved for a select few...the techniques presented in this book actually are effective in bringing people into two-way dialogue with Almighty God.[32]

God desires to manifest Himself and communicate His truth to us even more than we desire it. But He has set conditions and guidelines, and visualization and imagination have no place in God's revelation of Himself and His truth to man. By faith in His promise we *know* that Christ is both with us and in us—and to suggest that this can only or better be known through visualization is to deny the faith that believes without seeing. Paul declared, "The Spirit itself beareth witness with our spirit that we are the children of God" (Romans 8:16). It is not our *visualizing* but a witness within our hearts from the Holy Spirit who indwells us that assures us that we are His children: "God hath sent forth the Spirit of his Son into your hearts crying, Abba, Father" (Galatians 4:6). Jesus promised, "At that day ye shall know that I am in my Father, and ye in me, and I in you" (John 14:20). Far from visualization being the means of arriving at this confident knowing of faith, it is *obedience* which brings the glorious manifestation of God and Christ to the believer. As Jesus went on to say:

> He that hath my commandments and keepeth them, he it is that loveth me; and he that loveth me shall be loved of my Father, and I will love him and will manifest myself to him (John 14:21).

What about the language of Scripture? Isn't it highly visual? On the contrary, the language of the Bible provides no detailed descriptions to serve as a basis for visualization. In comparison with the rich, descriptive detail of a novel, biblical language is deliberately sparse. In contrast to the claim that Christ promoted visual imagery as a means of communication, His parables provide the barest skeleton upon which to hang objective truth. It is precisely because a parable does present a "picture" that it needs an interpretation. No symbolism or imagery communicates in itself the full intended meaning.

Even the symbolic language of the Bible is not intended to

inspire visualization. Quite the opposite. John's description of the resurrected Christ in heaven—"Out of his mouth went a sharp two-edged sword" (Revelation 1:16)—is not an encouragement to visualize Jesus with a literal sword emerging from His mouth. That would be absurd. John is trying to convey the piercing power and authority with which Christ speaks. The same is true of all symbolic language appearing in Scripture. For example, Psalm 91:4 says, "He shall cover thee with his feathers, and under his wings shalt thou trust." Are we therefore to visualize God as some kind of giant bird? Obviously not.

Yet the teaching that images are primary grows ever more popular in spite of the lack of biblical support and in spite of logic to the contrary. Some writers even go so far as to say:

> When God wrote His revelation to man, He chose images over analytical thought as a primary mode of communication....
>
> I see the entire process of Bible study, as God has designed it, to involve visualization, and God speaking to us out of the midst of the image (created by the Word) which is set before our eyes.[33]

Dangerous Delusion

Representative of a growing trend today, one well-meaning evangelical writer urges, "Seek to live the [Bible] experience, remembering the encouragement of Ignatius of Loyola to apply all our senses to our task. Smell the sea [of Galilee]. Hear the lap of the water along the shore. See the crowd. Feel the sun on your head and the hunger in your stomach."[34] He has us concentrating on the very things which, had we been there in that crowd around Jesus and done so, would have distracted us from hearing what Jesus was saying. And he would have us believe that if we can only create in our own fantasy the biblical scene as we *imagine* it might have been, we have thereby gained deep insight into what Jesus taught.

In fact, we are subtly being led to substitute feelings and images for truth. As we have already seen, those who seek insight through imagery are actually robbing themselves of the moral content of conceptual thought and the truth that only language can convey. The psalmist exulted, "Thy *word* [not imagery] is a lamp unto my feet and a light unto my path. . . . *It* is my meditation all the day" (Psalm 119:105,97). Jeremiah wrote:

> Thy *words* were found, and I did eat them; and thy *word* was unto me the joy and rejoicing of mine heart. . . .
>
> Is not my *word* like as a fire? saith the Lord, and like a hammer that breaketh the rock in pieces? Therefore, behold, I am against the prophets. . .that steal my *words* every one from his neighbor. . .that prophesy false dreams. . .and cause my people to err by their lies. . . (Jeremiah 15:16; 23:29-32).

The most dangerous delusion is the belief that one has actually come in contact with God or Christ through visualization. The author quoted above who teaches techniques for developing two-way conversation with God writes, "The Lord spoke to me: 'Remember that vision [active imagination/visualization] is more than technique. . . . It *is* an encounter with Me. It is Me, nothing more, nothing less, just Me!' "[35] Another evangelical author declares:

> As you enter the [visualized] story, not as a passive observer but as an active participant, remember that since Jesus lives in the Eternal Now and is not bound by time, this event in the past is a living present-tense experience for Him.
>
> Hence, you can *actually* encounter the living Christ in the event, be addressed by His voice and be touched by His healing power.
>
> It can be more than an exercise of the imagination; it can be a genuine confrontation. Jesus Christ will actually come to you.[36]

Biblical Appearances of Christ

When Jesus said to His disciples, "A little while and ye shall not see me; and again, a little while and ye shall see me, because I go to the Father" (John 16:16), He did not even hint, much less teach, that they could "see" and "encounter" Him and be addressed by His voice and know Him present with them through the marvelous power of visualization. He warned them that they would "be scattered, every man to his own" (verse 32) and would forsake Him, and that deep sorrow and trial would come upon them. Why did He not teach them the technique of visualization whereby they could enjoy His comforting presence? Instead, He promised that the *Holy Spirit* would come to comfort them and that "at that day" they would know that He (Christ) was living in their hearts (John 14:20).

When Jesus appeared to His disciples on the lakeshore after they had fished all night and caught nothing, we are told, "This is now the *third time* that Jesus showed himself to his disciples after he was risen from the dead" (John 21:14). Paul tells us that Christ "was seen of Cephas [Peter], then of the twelve; after that he was seen of above five hundred brethren at once. . . . After that he was seen of James; then of all the apostles. And last of all he was seen of me also. . ." (1 Corinthians 15:5-8). From such language it is clear that His disciples were not visualizing Jesus and thereby causing Him to appear as they pleased; *He* initiated His appearances. It is the same today. To imagine that we can summon from the right hand of the Father the Son of God by visualizing Him is to deceive ourselves. And we give to seducing spirits the ultimate disguise when we offer them the identity of God or Christ.

The Passion for God

One of the chief characteristics of men and women of faith mentioned in the Bible is their love of God and insatiable thirst to know Him better. That was the passion of Moses: "I beseech thee, show me thy glory!" (Exodus 33:18); and of David: "O God. . .my soul thirsteth for thee. . .my soul followeth hard after thee" (Psalm 63:1,8). No less should we be consumed with this same passion. J. I. Packer writes:

> For what higher, more exalted, and more compelling goal can there be than to know God?[37]

The Bible declares that God rewards those who diligently seek *Him*. It makes no promise to those who seek *things* or *success*. If we allow our hearts to adopt this false goal, God soon becomes to us little more than a rich patron whose friendship is cultivated only to the extent necessary for staying in His good graces and keeping the blessings flowing. In a *Moody Monthly* article James Bjornstad reminds us:

At one time, most Christians believed that to have a close relationship with God, a person should magnify God, deny himself and the pleasures of this world, repent and confess his sins, and live a holy and separated life. Their heroes were missionaries who gave up everything to serve God and martyrs who suffered because of their faith.

Today, it's becoming a different story. Many Christians believe that to have a close relationship with God, a person should realize the importance of himself as God intended, pursue his dreams and aspirations, and become affluent and successful. Their heroes are those celebrities and self-made individuals who h.,ppen to be Christians.

Behind this new gospel stands a variety of distinguished teachers, preachers, and evangelists proclaiming a variety of ways to attain prosperity and success. But examining their theological models and points of emphasis reveals one common element—they are simply not biblical.[38]

God must be sought for Himself, and the person who seeks Him for any other reason obviously doesn't really know Him or all else would pale in comparison. Tozer stated it clearly:

God being who He is must always be sought for Himself, never as a means toward something else.... Whoever seeks God as a means toward desired ends will not find God.

The mighty God, the maker of heaven and earth, will not be one of many treasures, not even the chief of all treasures.... God will not be used...He will not aid men in their selfish striving after personal gain....

Yet popular Christianity has as one of its most effective talking points the idea that God exists to help people to get ahead in this world.[39]

Let us beware that our desire to know God does not become perverted into seeking a God who will be our servant. Our hearts are deceitful, and the imagination of our hearts is evil. That is why *techniques* for getting in touch with God are forbidden, and why Satan has been able to use them so effectively to his ends. "Exploring the inner world," which is now being openly advocated by Christian leaders, can be extremely dangerous even for those whose motives are the best, if scriptural principles are violated. The fact that a person sincerely desires to know God is no excuse for attempting to contact God through a Ouija board, for example—and the techniques of visualization and activating the imagination through looking within are just as much divination devices as a crystal ball. "Visualization" is the foremost technique recommended by the "spirit entities" that speak through today's most popular mediums. As one who calls himself "Emmanuel" recently said, "The use of visualization is a most powerful tool for you to use."[40]

Seducing Spirits

Satan and his minions have always used such methodologies to communicate to man while posing as angels of light. Paul warned that the last days would be characterized by an increase in such activity and that even some who professed faith in Christ would "depart from the faith, giving heed to seducing spirits and doctrines of devils" (1 Timothy 4:1). One example is *Jonathan Livingston Seagull*, which dressed basic Hinduism in psychological, success/motivation language. Thousands of copies were sold in Christian bookstores. Unsuspecting purchasers, inspired by this charming tale, did not know that its author, Richard Bach, claimed that it had been dictated to him by a "spirit." So numerous and popular are these seducing spirits today—appearing on popular television talk shows[41] and even writing the script for a miniseries on national television[42]—that they are being discussed in newspapers, magazines, and books. In fact, they even *write* books.[43]

Demonically inspired writings have been deceiving Christians for many years. *God Calling*, long regarded as a Christian classic and a perpetual best-seller in Christian bookstores, is another example. Tim Timmons has pointed out that although *God Calling* is full of good thoughts, "much of what it teaches sounds as though it originated from the angel of light (2 Corinthians 11:14) rather than the living Christ."[44] John Weldon bluntly says of this popular book, "A demon makes the ranks of evangelical best-sellers!"[45] Ed Gruss comments, "Its prominence on the [best-seller] list is indicative of the lack of spiritual discernment in these 'last days.' "[46]

The book came about as two apparently sincere women known as "the anonymous 'two listeners'" started to practice sitting down with pencil and paper, letting their minds go blank and then "writing down whatever flashes across the mind as God's orders for the day...."[47] Unfortunately, similar techniques are being popularized by Christian leaders who are sincerely trying to put people in closer touch with God. "Journal-keeping" is becoming increasingly prevalent among Christians as a new genre of books emphasizes the "inner life" and presents various methodologies for "hearing from God." Certainly, meditating on the Word of God and seeking closer communion with Him and deeper insights into His will ought to be an important part of every Christian's daily life. And to write down for future reference insights or guidance that we believe to be from God can be very helpful.

However, caution must be exercised. Journaling can be dangerous, yet is gaining popular acceptance. It is used by occultists to make contact with the spirit world and by psychologists to contact deep levels of the psyche and thereby tap into the ancient wisdom allegedly contained in the "collective unconscious." Ira Progoff is one of the foremost leaders in this particular application of Carl Jung's depth psychology, known also as Process Meditation.[48] He believes that through journaling "mankind has to renew its sacred Scriptures (including the Bible), which are now outdated."[49] According to Progoff, whose "Intensive" workshops, retreats, and seminars are extremely popular, journaling enables mankind to get in touch with the "underground streams of images and recollections within each of us."[50]

Christian books on journaling, however, seldom warn of the dangers of mistaking one's imagination for communication with God and of spending more time upon one's own inward thoughts than upon God's Word. Whether through a proper use of journaling or other forms of meditation, our focus must always be upon the Scriptures and must never deviate from that Guide. The Psalms remind us:

> His delight is in the law of the Lord, and in his law doth
> he meditate day and night (Psalm 1:2).

O how love I *thy law! It* is my meditation all the day (Psalm 119:97).

I have more understanding than all my teachers, for *thy testimonies* are my meditation (Psalm 119:99).

Thy word is a lamp unto my feet and a light unto my path (Psalm 119:105).

A Time of Testing

The widespread acceptance of occult powers under the guise of the "scientific use of the imagination" could play an important part in separating the true followers of Christ from those who falsely claim to be His. It is disturbing that so many people today are more enamored with "signs and wonders" than with truth and that they more readily follow a popular teacher's pleasing interpretation of the Bible than what God's Word actually says. When Christians are more impressed with "miracles" and "results" than with adherence to sound doctrine, the church is in serious trouble. Out of great concern over developments in his local fellowship, one reader of *The Seduction of Christianity* wrote:

> In early August...a [visiting] pastor from New York gave two teachings at our fellowship.... There were references to concepts such as visualization, sanctified imagination, mind's eye, the unconscious, incubation, synchronization, holograms, Third and Fourth Dimension....
>
> I suspect that the process of discipling our church into these beliefs is already beginning. A prayer group meets every morning [in which]...one sits in silence and is to be sensitive to the images that are seen in the mind.... We are encouraged to verbalize these images regardless of how strange they may seem....
>
> I am writing to you for help.[51]

One of the most telling characteristics of Christianity today is the lack of that awesome reverence and "fear of God" which the Bible declares to be "the beginning of wisdom" (Proverbs 9:10). In the days of old when the Bible was being written by apostles and prophets to whom "the word of the Lord *came*" (Micah 1:1; Haggai 1:1; etc.), the revelation of God did not come "by the will of man" (2 Peter 1:21) or through techniques, but at long intervals of time as God willed. Although Abraham was known as God's special friend (James 2:23), even to him God only occasionally manifested His presence. And when God spoke, His people trembled, for they knew the heavy consequences of disobeying that voice. The contrast between a Moses, an Isaiah, or a John on his face before God and today's Christian routinely conjuring up a mental image that "speaks" (or church leaders teaching other techniques for allegedly carrying on a two-way conversation with God at will) only shows how far we have gotten from biblical Christianity!

It bears repeating that just because something "works" does not mean that it is of God, even though church growth and much that seems to be good may be achieved. When dispensed by a sincere and persuasive leader who seems to be well-qualified by apparent success, false teachings are almost irresistible. The only antidote is to test every doctrine and practice by the Bible. And whether we follow the revealed Word of God or an apparently successful extrabiblical technique will in the final analysis determine whether we pass the test that God is allowing in these last days—or fail it to our everlasting loss. What God spoke through Jeremiah seems an especially applicable warning for our day:

> Thus saith the Lord of hosts, Hearken not unto the words of the prophets...they speak a vision of their own heart, and not out of the mouth of the Lord.
> ...they say unto every one that walketh after the imagination of his own heart, No evil shall come upon you.
> ...they are prophets of the deceit of their own heart, which think to cause my people to forget my name by their dreams.
> ...ye have perverted the words of the living God (Jeremiah 23:16,17,26,27,36).

The unbiblical and delusive penchant for new "revelation knowledge" that comes apart from the words of Scripture has led many Pentecostal/charismatic splinter groups into gross heresy and even into full-blown occultism. This delusion seems to be growing today as part of the last-days apostasy which the Bible warns must come before Christ returns (2 Thessalonians 2:3-12). We cannot be reminded too frequently or too solemnly of the necessity of being certain that we do not believe or practice *anything of a spiritual nature* that cannot be clearly substantiated from God's Word. If we are indeed in the last days prior to Christ's return, then the delusion is going to grow ever more seductive, and we must be ever more vigilant to remain true to our Lord and to His Word.

12
The Better Way

Hath the Lord as great delight in burnt offerings and sacrifices as in obeying the voice of the Lord? Behold, to obey is better than sacrifice, and to hearken than the fat of rams.

For rebellion is as the sin of witchcraft, and stubbornness is as iniquity and idolatry. Because thou hast rejected the word of the Lord, he hath also rejected thee from being king (1 Samuel 15:22,23).

IMPLICIT IN THE CALL for a return to biblical Christianity is the belief that the Bible itself is our only and final authority in all spiritual matters. This means, as Paul said, that we are not to give heed even to "an angel from heaven" who brings a message that contradicts what God has already spoken in His Word (Galatians 1:8). Because the gospel of Jesus Christ presented in the Bible is essential to human life and holds the key to the destiny of mankind, anyone, whether man or angel, who teaches "any other gospel" that contradicts or perverts God's truth is to be "accursed" (Galatians 1:8,9). The Holy Spirit could not have chosen stronger language, and we must therefore take doctrine and truth very seriously.

Satan attempts to undermine God's Word in several ways. Most obvious is the claim that the Bible is not really inspired of God but is merely a compilation of ancient myths and human opinions. But of course there is too much evidence to the contrary for that argument to convince any sincere investigator. More appealing is the suggestion that the Bible is only one of many sacred scriptures. However, it is clear that the Bible contradicts and condemns all other religions, so it must be accepted for what it claims to be, the *only* Word of God to man, or else rejected entirely. Even more seductive is the idea that Scripture embodies *secret and hidden meanings* known only to initiates. Cults and occult groups have long used this ploy to their advantage.

Closely related is the teaching that only an elite few know the true *interpretation*. This fallacy is accepted by the followers not only of false "prophets" such as Joseph Smith, Mary Baker Eddy, Herbert W. Armstrong, and other cult leaders, but also by the many Catholics who are convinced that they dare not interpret the Bible for themselves but must accept whatever the Church hierarchy declares. Many Protestants may be just as guilty of letting a pastor or denomination do their thinking for them. Some do this out of laziness or in an attempt to escape personal accountability to God. Others have been taught that their responsibility is not directly to God but to a "shepherd," who makes their decisions for them and to whom they must submit even when he is wrong, for he alone is accountable to God if he leads them astray. As we have already seen, this is not biblical. There is no way that we can escape our personal responsibility to know for ourselves what the Bible says and to communicate to others in word and deed God's truth without compromise.

Ongoing Prophetic Revelation?

There is an even more subtle and dangerous belief. Previously confined to fringe Pentecostal and charismatic groups, the false teaching concerning "revelation knowledge" is beginning to spread rapidly throughout the church. It is understood in two ways: 1) that a proper understanding of Scripture does not come through *interpretation* but through *revelation* (given only to certain leaders), and 2) that these prophets also receive "ongoing prophetic revelation"[1] that supplements the Bible and must be accepted by the church as the key to a "great move of God" that will establish His kingdom upon earth. For example, the brochure advertising a large conference for pastors and church leaders held near Atlanta, Georgia, in October 1986 stated: "What hinders the release of God's Spirit on earth? Reluctance of [church] leadership to embrace revelation knowledge as God continues to speak to his people."[2]

The new revelations, which the church allegedly needs in order to move on in maturity, come through a class of prophets who are not to be judged.[3] And since "judging is out of order,"[4] only these self-appointed prophets can decide who they are, for no one who is not on their level is competent to make that judgment. Of course one of the chief proponents of this idea considers himself to be one of these prophets.[5] This dangerous and destructive teaching contradicts numerous Scriptures, among them 1 Corinthians 14:29, which states that prophets must be judged. Otherwise, the church would become a follow-the-leader-blindly cult. All Christians should be "Bereans" who "search the Scriptures daily" (Acts 17:11) for their own edification and to prevent being taken in by false doctrine. If even the apostle Paul's teaching was to be judged in this manner, then so also must the teaching of any "prophet" or church leader today, no matter who he may be. Those who fail to do so will not be able to plead ignorance for embracing false doctrine but will be held accountable by God.

Manifest Sons of God and Positive Confession

The acceptance of "new revelation" has spawned a growing movement within the church that is usually associated with the words kingdom, dominion, restoration, and/or reconstruction. Although similar ideas can be traced back at least to the eighteenth century, the current explosion of the kingdom/dominion emphasis began with the "Latter Rain" movement, which came out of apparent revival in Canada in 1948 and was declared heretical by the Assemblies of God in 1950.[6] It became known as The Manifest Sons of God movement because of its teaching that an elite group of "overcomers" manifesting immortality would conquer the world and establish the kingdom of God. Only then could Christ return, not to rapture His own but to reign over the kingdom they had presented to Him. An important part of this scenario is the restoration of the "five-fold" ministry that would include apostles and prophets working great signs and wonders.

This is a logical extension of Positive Confession teaching, though most of its adherents may not have understood that fact as yet. If Christians can "operate on the same level of faith as God"[7] and in fact "have all the capabilities of God,"[8] and if we can indeed "write our own ticket with God"[9] and "can have what we say,"[10] then we ought to confess blessing, healing, prosperity, and salvation for the whole world and set up the kingdom of God upon earth right now. Moreover, if it is "never God's will for any Christian to be ill,"[11] then we ought to manifest immortality here and now in these bodies without waiting for the resurrection, and certainly the rapture would be unnecessary. The head of a large charismatic campus ministry writes that "all nations will flow" into the kingdom in the last days because a "ruthless" band of overcomers, without the resurrection, will have become immune from sin and sickness and even death.[12] As another leader says:

> You can study books about going to heaven in a so-called "rapture" if that turns you on. We want to study the Bible to learn to live and to love and to bring heaven to earth.[13]

"The Word of faith shall grip their [the overcomers'] hearts, and they shall reach out and appropriate the Resurrection and the Life even now in this life," we are told in *The Feast of the Tabernacles*. "If they do not, Christ never will return to earth."[14] Although written in 1951, this book continues to be a major manifesto of the movement. A 1986 Manifest Sons publication declares that belief in the rapture among mainline denominational members is waning and that increasing numbers of Christians are discovering "the Bible's New Age principles of ruling and reigning here on earth."[15]

Paradise Restored?

It is the task of Christians, so we are told, to take *dominion* back from Satan and (as the rightful gods of this world, according to some) to restore planet Earth to the beautiful paradise that it once was before Adam and Eve sinned. However, man has not lost the dominion that God gave him "over the fish of the sea, and over the fowl of the air, and over every living thing that moveth upon the earth" (Genesis 1:26,28; Psalm 8:6). To speak of *restoring* dominion to man is therefore meaningless. The problem is not man's *loss* of dominion but his *abuse* of it. Nor was dominion intended to be exercised by some men over other men, but only by man over creatures under him. Showing the contrast between His kingdom and the kingdoms of this world, and indicating that dominion is far from the goal of salvation, Jesus reminded His disciples:

> Ye know that the princes of the Gentiles exercise dominion over them, and they that are great exercise authority upon them. But it shall not be so among you, but whosoever will be great among you, let him be your minister; and whosoever will be chief among you, let him be your servant; even as the Son of man came not to be ministered unto, but to minister, and to give his life a ransom for many (Matthew 20:25-28).

Jesus said to Pilate, "My kingdom is not of this world: if my kingdom were of this world, then would my servants fight...but now is my kingdom not from hence" (John 18:36). To His disciples (and to us today) He declared: "Ye are not of the world, but I have chosen you out of the world" (John 15:19). And to His Father, speaking of His disciples (and of us today), Jesus said: "I have manifested thy name unto the men which thou gavest me out of the world.... I pray not for the world, but for them which thou hast given me.... They are not of the world, even as I am not of the world.... As thou has sent me into the world, even so have I also sent them into the world" (John 17:6,9,16,18). We have been sent by our Lord into all the world to "disciple all nations" (Matthew 28:19). This sending forth has been known as "the Great Commission," and it seems quite clear, from this and many other Scriptures, exactly what Christ meant.

A New Christian Agenda for the World?

A new meaning, however, has now been given to the "Great Commission." It is found in the popular assurances (heard repeatedly on some Christian radio and television programming and presented in some Christian books and magazines) that

Christianity is on its way to conquering the world. It is just a matter of raising enough money to get enough Christian television stations, programs, and satellites to saturate the airwaves, and of organizing enough conservative voters to put sufficient qualified Christians in key political offices. While we ought to use every legal means to influence the moral climate for good and to improve the government, we must also remember that political organization and social action in themselves will never fulfill the "Great Commission." We must beware that "cleaning up society" does not become a substitute for preaching the gospel of Christ.

As for the Christian's role in changing or governing this present world, Christ's total silence toward an evil Caesar and the corrupt and oppressive Roman presence in Palestine contrast sharply with His continual and stinging reproof of Israel's religious leaders. He mentioned Caesar on only one occasion: "Render therefore unto Caesar the things which be Caesar's, and unto God the things which be God's" (Luke 20:25). Both Paul, who testified under oath of his obedience to Roman law ("nor yet against Caesar have I offended anything at all"—Acts 25:8), and Peter urged Christians as "strangers and pilgrims" in this world to "be subject" and "submit to" earthly governments and to set an example of "good works" (Romans 13:1-10; 1 Peter 2:11-20). Obedience, holy and exemplary living, self-sacrifice, loving neighbor as oneself, preaching the gospel of Jesus Christ, using the sword of God's Word, and praying seem to be the weapons of transformation which the Christian is to aim at this world. Paul sums it up:

> I exhort therefore that first of all supplications, prayers, intercessions, and giving of thanks be made for all men: for kings and for all that are in authority, that we may lead a quiet and peaceable life in all godliness and honesty. For this is good and acceptable in the sight of God our Savior, who will have all men to be saved, and to come unto the knowledge of the truth.
>
> I will therefore that men pray every where, lifting up holy hands, without wrath and doubting (1 Timothy 2:1-4,8).

Although Christ assured His disciples that the world would

treat them as it treated Him, it is now being suggested that a "positive approach" using "tested concepts and principles for church growth"[16] will enable Christians to become the dominant force in society. Desirable though that may sound, the Bible sets no such goal and makes no such promise. Although church growth ought to be pursued, it too often becomes an end in itself, with success determined by *quantity* rather than *quality*. And to fill churches with "Christians" whose passion is to become the world's dominant political force rather than to call out of the world disciples who will submit to the truth which sets men free would be destructive of God's real purpose. It is tragic that for growing numbers of "Christians," *rescuing the lost* has somehow metamorphosed into *taking over the world*. Derisively calling the rapture "God's helicopter escape," a recent ad for a series of four books declared:

> A new vision has captured the imaginations of a growing army of registered voters.... It's called *dominion*. For the first time in over 300 years, a growing number of Christians are starting to view themselves as an army on the move. This army will grow. This series [of books] is designed to help it grow. And to grow tougher.
>
> The authors of this series are determined to set the agenda in world affairs for the next few centuries.... We are calling the whole Christian community to debate us, just as Luther called them to debate him when he nailed the 95 theses to the church door, over four and a half centuries ago.
>
> If we're correct about the God-required nature of our agenda, it will attract a dedicated following. It could produce a social transformation that will dwarf the Reformation [emphasis in original].[17]

One gets the impression that *registered voters* effecting *social transformation* are more important than *disciples* preaching the *gospel*. Yet Christ never promised that the *world* would be won even with the gospel of His grace; much less did He intend that the church's weapon would be political/social action. We ought to be sincerely concerned with the feeding and clothing of the poor, but if we follow Christ's example our primary concern will be to present to them (as to all men) the gospel of Jesus Christ. Yet the concern for social justice is now becoming paramount, and Pope John Paul II has declared it to be the rallying point for uniting all of the world's religions.[18] It is a dangerous suggestion, yet a small but growing group of evangelical socialists is advocating a similar ecumenism.

The Gospel of a False Peace

The early Christians went forth "preaching peace by Jesus Christ" (Acts 10:36), not crusading against weapons or demonstrating for a humanistic "peace." Their message was that we have "peace with God through our Lord Jesus Christ" (Romans 5:1) because He "made peace through the blood of his cross" (Colossians 1:20). This simple gospel that brings *peace with God* into individual hearts is the only hope for peace among nations; yet many well-meaning Christians have relegated it to second place in their zeal to join in activist programs to promote world peace—something unknown to Christ or the apostles. Social activism has become "the larger mission of the church" and is expected to bring peace, love, and brotherhood to a world that is still at war with God. It is like offering an aspirin when open-heart surgery is required. We dare not join in the world's clamor for peace on a humanistic basis. Instead, like Jeremiah we ought to rebuke the false prophets who cry, "Peace, peace, when there is no peace" (Jeremiah 6:14; 8:11).

Sincere and well-intentioned Christians are being persuaded to join in activist causes with all who share "common social concerns," whether they be humanists, Moonies, or Mormons. Christians ought to stand for righteousness and oppose abortion, pornography, exploitation of the poor, and other evils. However, they should do so as *Christians*, for biblical reasons, and not join themselves in coalitions with those who, though they oppose the same evils, reject the only real and lasting solution, which is reconciliation to God through the redemptive work of Jesus Christ. As Schlossberg reminds us:

> To link humanitarianism with Christian social action is wholly untenable. They are completely at odds with one another.[19]

We must beware not to encourage the deadly delusion that there is any hope for peace except through transformation of the human heart through Christ. Indeed, if the world were seemingly able to solve all of its problems without embracing the true gospel of our Lord Jesus Christ, that would be the greatest of all deceptions and precisely what Satan will seek to do through the Antichrist, whose world government will be a counterfeit of God's kingdom. Although they may not realize it, those who join, no matter how sincerely, in humanistic efforts to unite the world in a false peace are not furthering the cause of Christ but in the long run the cause of the Antichrist.

If we are to be biblical Christians, God's Word must be our guide in all we say and do, no matter how unpopular that makes us. We dare not compromise the message which Christ called us to proclaim. Only His truth can set men free, and it is this truth which the world does not want to hear that it desperately needs. The gospel was not designed to liberate men from the corrupt Roman Empire but from the far worse bondage of sin and its eternal penalty. Israel misunderstood the mission of the Messiah, thinking that He would free them from the yoke of Rome, when in fact their real enemy was within their own hearts, the *self* that had to be denied. It is no less erroneous to imagine that one's Christian mission is to set up God's kingdom by taking over the world for Christ, when in fact we are to call disciples (out of a world that is doomed by God's judgment) to become citizens of heaven.

A Hopeless Scenario

Today's world faces tremendous problems unknown to past generations. There are urgent social, economic, and political issues of crisis proportions which the church cannot ignore. Although we have not been able to deal with them in detail in this book, biblical parameters have been pointed out. At this critical juncture in history we must be very careful that our understanding of God's Word does not lose its eternal, heavenly perspective and become temporal and earthly in its application. Having lost this perspective, a popular Christian writer declares:

One of the basic themes of Scripture is that *salvation restores man to his original purpose*. In the beginning God created man in His own image in order that man would have *dominion....*

Ultimately, Biblical salvation turns back the Curse, brings back Edenic conditions, repairs personal and social relationships, and blesses the earth in every area. The whole earth will be saved, and remade into the Garden of God...the restoration of Eden is an essential aspect of the salvation that Christ provides.[20]

Such teaching sounds appealing. However, restoration of the Edenic state could hardly be the solution, since that is where mankind fell and sin began. If Adam and Eve failed so miserably in the Garden of Eden (with no one but themselves there and only one law—not to eat from a certain tree), what purpose would there be in "restoring the Edenic state" to billions of people now subject to the Ten Commandments and facing temptations that Adam and Eve never even imagined? This is not God's plan at all, and even if it were, the church could not accomplish it.

The Biblical Hope of the Church

How could the church be expected to establish the kingdom by taking over the world when even God cannot accomplish that without violating man's freedom of choice? During His thousand-year reign, Christ will visibly rule the world in perfect righteousness from Jerusalem and will impose peace upon all nations. Satan will be locked up, robbed of the power to tempt. Justice will be meted out swiftly. The lion will lie down with the lamb and the desert will blossom like a rose. The whole earth will resemble the Garden of Eden before the fall. Yet at the end of the thousand years, when Satan is released, millions of those who have experienced the Edenic state and Christ's perfect reign all their lives will be deceived, just as Eve was. Converging from all over the world to war against Christ and the saints at Jerusalem, these rebels will finally have to be banished from God's presence forever (Revelation 20:7-10).

The millennial reign of Christ upon earth, rather than being the kingdom of God, will in fact be the final proof of the incorrigible nature of the human heart. The true kingdom which "flesh and blood cannot inherit" (1 Corinthians 15:50) pertains to the heart into which Christ has been received as Lord and Savior, and will be fully realized only in the "new heaven and new earth" (Revelation 21:1). Of this "everlasting kingdom" (Psalm 145:13) and the peace it establishes "there shall be no end" (Isaiah 9:6,7); yet the millennium ends, and in a war. A perfect Edenic environment where all ecological, economic, sociological, and political problems are solved fails to perfect mankind. So much for the theories of psychology and sociology and utopian dreams.

Christ declared that it was not the things on the outside but *what man is within his heart* that causes him to do evil (Matthew 15:16-20). Only those who admit this fact and in humility confess their guilt, cry out to God for mercy, and accept His remedy in Christ are cleansed of sin and made into new creations. They alone can dwell in God's new universe. The victorious Christian has enthroned Christ in the place of self, having received Him to dwell in his heart by faith (Ephesians 3:17). Indeed, Christ has become his very life (Colossians 3:3,4). The practical evidence for that fact, so often lacking among those who call themselves Christians, is the power to live for others instead of for self:

> Is not this the fast that I have chosen? to loose the bands of wickedness, to undo the heavy burdens, and to let the oppressed go free, and that ye break every yoke? Is it not to deal thy bread to the hungry, and that thou bring the poor that are cast out to thy house? when thou seest the naked, that thou cover him; and that thou hide not thyself from thine own flesh? (Isaiah 58:6,7).

Far from being restored to Adam's state, by God's grace what we have received in Christ as the last Adam is infinitely better than anything known to the first Adam. Those who are in Christ are part of a new creation for whom "old things are passed away; behold, all things are become new" (2 Corinthians 5:17). Our primary goal is not to "restore earth" but to call mankind to citizenship in a "new heavens and a new earth" (2 Peter 3:13). We know, in fact, that "the heavens and the earth which are now" are doomed, "reserved unto fire against the day of judgment and perdition of ungodly men." "But the day of the Lord will come as a thief in the night, in which the heavens shall pass away with a great noise, and the elements shall melt with fervent heat; the

earth also and the works that are therein shall be burned up"
(2 Peter 3:7,10). This destruction of the present universe must
not be dismissed as "negative" or "gloom and doom." On the
contrary, it ought to motivate the Christian, as it did Peter, to
holy living:

> Seeing then that all these things shall be dissolved, what
> manner of persons ought ye to be in all holy conversation
> and godliness, looking for and hasting unto the coming of
> the day of God, wherein the heavens being on fire shall be
> dissolved, and the elements shall melt with the fervent heat?
> Nevertheless we, according to his promise, look for new
> heavens and a new earth, wherein dwelleth righteousness
> (2 Peter 3:11,12).

The Narrow Gate to Heaven

The fact that the Christian no longer belongs to this earth but
to heaven is a major teaching of the New Testament. Paul wrote
that God has "blessed us with all spiritual blessings in heavenly
places in Christ" (Ephesians 1:3). As our forerunner and representative, Christ has entered into heaven for us (Hebrews 6:19,20).
Indeed, Paul declared that we are already seated "in heavenly
places in Christ Jesus" (Ephesians 2:6), having become by His
grace "fellow citizens with the saints, and of the household of
God" (Ephesians 2:19), and are now "heirs of God and joint-
heirs with Christ" (Romans 8:17). Our citizenship "is in heaven"
(Philippians 3:20). Peter assures us that we have an "inheritance
incorruptible and undefiled" that is "reserved in heaven" for
us (1 Peter 1:4). It is to heaven where Christ has gone to His
Father's right hand, and it is to heaven that we expect at any
moment to be taken in an ecstatic catching-away (rapture):

> In my Father's house are many mansions; if it were not
> so I would have told you. I go to prepare a place for you.
> And if I go and prepare a place for you, I will come again
> and receive you unto myself, that where I am, there ye may
> be also (John 14:2,3).
> The Lord himself shall descend from heaven with a
> shout...and the dead in Christ shall rise first; then we which
> are alive and remain shall be caught up together with them

in the clouds to meet the Lord in the air; and so shall we ever be with the Lord. Wherefore comfort one another with these words (1 Thessalonians 4:16-18).

Far from indicating that the world will be converted, the Bible makes it clear that the overwhelming majority of people will reject Christ. We will be able to persuade only a "chosen few" (John 15:16-19) to enter through the "strait gate" onto the "narrow way" to heaven (Matthew 7:13,14) that Christ Himself claims to be and of which He said, "Few there be that find it." And we are to assure these "few that be saved" (Luke 13:23) that Christ is returning to rapture them out of this world before God's judgment falls upon it. Far from expecting Christianity to become the prevailing belief system in this world, we know that "the preaching of the cross is to them that perish foolishness" (1 Corinthians 1:18) and that those who perish, sadly enough, represent the overwhelming majority:

> Wide is the gate and broad is the way that leadeth to destruction, and many there be which go in thereat; because strait is the gate and narrow the way which leadeth unto life, and few there be that find it (Matthew 7:13,14).

Knowing that most of those he encountered would reject the gospel of Christ did not discourage Paul from preaching this gospel; rather it increased his determination to win as many as he could. The love that caused Christ to die for those who hated and rejected Him (and even for those who crucified Him) "constrained" Paul to carry the message of that love to the world of his day (2 Corinthians 5:14)—and to warn them of the eternal consequences of rejecting Christ. "Knowing therefore the terror of the Lord [in judgment]," Paul wrote, "we persuade men" (2 Corinthians 5:11). Driven by Christ's love and his own passion for the lost, Paul declared:

> I am made all things to all men that I might by all means save some. And this I do for the gospel's sake (1 Corinthians 9:22,23).

We ought to do the same. Although apostasy must come before Christ's return, and deception and seduction will grow worse and false prophets increase in number and influence, that is not an excuse for any true Christian to become discouraged or to lessen his efforts to win the lost. Christ's parable of the ten virgins ("At midnight there was a cry made, Behold, the bridegroom cometh, go ye out to meet him"—Matthew 25:1-13) indicates an awakening even among those who have "slumbered and slept" while "the bridegroom tarried." And his parable of the "man [who] made a great supper, and bade many" (Luke 14:16-24) indicates that alongside the last-days apostasy there will also be perhaps the most fruitful time of evangelism in history:

> Go out quickly into the streets and lanes of the city, and bring in hither the poor, and the maimed, and the halt, and the blind. And the servant said, Lord, it is done as thou hast commanded, and yet there is room. And the Lord said unto the servant, Go out into the highways and hedges, and compel them to come in, that my house may be filled (Luke 14:21-23).

Making an Essential Choice

Heaven was both the great hope that Christ left with His disciples and an integral part of the gospel preached by the early church. Christ told His disciples, "Lay not up for yourselves treasures upon earth...but lay up for yourselves treasures in heaven...for where your treasure is, there will your heart be also" (Matthew 6:19-21). While we ought to demonstrate genuine concern and to work to restore ecological wholeness, we must also remember that every solution to earth's problems which is not founded upon the lordship of Jesus Christ and the forgiveness of sins we have in Him is temporary at best and ultimately doomed to fail. Paul cites as evidence of the Thessalonians' newfound faith not only their "work of faith and labor of love and patience of hope" and the fact that they had "turned to God from idols to serve the living and true God," but also that they were "wait[ing] for his Son from heaven" (1 Thessalonians 1:3-10). John reminds us of the importance of expecting Christ's imminent return: "Every man that hath this hope in him purifieth himself, even as he is pure" (1 John 3:3).

The very heart of the gospel calls people to make a choice

between earth and heaven. Christ made this clear. He told the Jews, "Ye are from beneath, I am from above; ye are of this world, I am not of this world." He warned them, "Except ye believe that I am, ye shall die in your sins, and where I go ye cannot come." Where was He going? To heaven, a place which He referred to as "my Father's house." A well-known Puritan author said, "The most dangerous mistake of our souls is to take the creature for God and earth for heaven."[21] Schlossberg adds this wise comment: "Ironically, those who seek their ultimate value in the next world are the only ones able to do much good in this one."[22]

Making temporary solutions to social problems the overriding concern of Christians blunts the gospel and obscures God's eternal solution. The focus is turned from heaven to this earth, from a new universe that only God can create to a new world that we hope to fashion by our own efforts. It is just one more form of the selfism that plagues society and the church, another way of becoming little gods, of turning from Him to ourselves by assuming a responsibility to do what only He can do. It is easy to be caught up in a "good" cause that isn't biblical. We cannot be reminded too often that we must check against the Word of God what even the most popular and seemingly fruitful Christian leaders teach. It is the responsibility of each Christian to stand firmly for the truth without compromise, heeding the words of Paul:

> Preach the word; be instant in season, out of season; reprove, rebuke, exhort with all longsuffering and doctrine. For the time will come when they will not endure sound doctrine. . .and they shall turn away their ears from the truth (2 Timothy 4:2-4).

Sound Doctrine and Understanding

There are many who call themselves Christians and attend Christian churches but deny Christ with their lives. Of course they need to recognize their self-centeredness and lack of concern and compassion for others. The solution, however, is not for such persons to reform their lives. Such an attempt represents a Christianized form of humanism and can only produce either guilt, frustration, or self-righteousness. Those who practice self-sacrifice and self-abnegation in order to help the poor and oppressed can become pharisees also, looking down upon others who don't live that way and taking pride in their own seeming humility. As we have already noted, Christ did not teach self-denial (self still on the throne but giving up much of what it might enjoy), but *denial of self* (the death of self) through His cross. He didn't say, "Except you deny yourself you cannot be my disciple," but "Except you deny yourself *and take up the cross* and follow me you cannot be my disciple." Without the cross self can never be denied.

No less important than the way we live is what we *believe*. As Schlossberg rightly says: "Action cannot be separated from the belief that gives rise to it."[23] There is no value to the way we live, no matter how exemplary it may seem, unless our lives are founded not upon *pragmatism* but upon God's *truth*. When Paul reminded Timothy of the example of Christian living he had set for the church, he mentioned first of all the *doctrine* that determined his life: "Thou hast fully known my doctrine, manner of life, purpose, faith, longsuffering, charity, patience, persecutions, afflictions. . ." (2 Timothy 3:10,11). We live what we *believe*, not what we profess to believe. Our manner of life betrays our true faith, and faith depends upon our understanding of the One whose promises we believe.

This is why the Bible places much emphasis upon *understanding*. Speaking through Jeremiah, God said, "Let him that glorieth glory in this, that he *understandeth and knoweth me*, that I am the Lord which exercise lovingkindness, judgment, and righteousness in the earth; for in these things I delight, saith the Lord" (Jeremiah 9:24). God wants us to *understand* who He is: infinite in love, yet no less just and righteous. He wants us to *know* Him intimately. And we can know and love God only for who He is, not for what we imagine Him to be. Moreover, we must come to Him on His terms and obey His truth. Explaining the parable of the seed that was carried away by the birds before it could take root, Jesus said:

Hear ye therefore the parable of the sower. When anyone

> heareth the word of the kingdom and *understandeth* it not,
> then cometh the wicked one and catcheth away that which
> was sown in his heart (Matthew 13:18,19).

One of the greatest problems **within** the church today is superficiality. We too often fail to **make** certain that those who are called upon "to decide for Christ" fully understand the decision they are being asked to make. We often build to an emotional climax as a means of persuading people to make a "decision." There is nothing wrong with emotion that accompanies reality, but we must be careful not to encourage a commitment to Christ that is founded upon emotion and not upon an understanding of and commitment to the truth of who He really is, why He came, and what He demands of us.

When our Lord called Saul of Tarsus to preach the gospel, He sent him forth to do three things that we must also do if those to whom we witness for Christ are truly to be saved: "To open their eyes, and to turn them from darkness to light, and from the power of Satan unto God..." (Acts 26:18). Only then, Christ clearly told Paul, could those who hear the message "receive forgiveness of sins and an inheritance among them which are sanctified by faith that is in me." The emphasis throughout Scripture, and to which the church must return today, is clearly placed upon truth and *understanding*. So John writes:

> We *know* that the Son of God is come, and hath given
> us an *understanding*, that we may *know* him that is true;
> and we are in him that is true, even in his Son Jesus Christ.
> This is the true God and eternal life. Little children, keep
> yourselves from idols (1 John 5:20,21).

Faith and Understanding

A lack of this necessary *understanding* was apparently the problem with those of whom we read, "As he spoke these words, many believed on him" (John 8:30). Although they "believed," their "faith" in Christ was not based upon a clear understanding of who He was and what He came to do. In fact, they were resistant to the truth when He tried to present it to them. Christ had to say to "those Jews which believed on him":

> Why do ye not *understand* my speech? Even because ye
> cannot hear my word. Ye are of your father the devil, and
> the lusts of your father ye will do: he was a murderer from
> the beginning, and abode not in the truth, because there is
> no truth in him. When he speaketh a lie, he speaketh of his
> own, for he is a liar, and the father of it. And because I
> tell you the truth, ye believe me not (John 8:43-45).

On another occasion "many believed in his name when they
saw the miracles which he did" (John 2:23). On the surface that
sounds so good, yet "Jesus did not commit himself unto them
because he knew all men, and needed not that any should testify
of man, for he knew what was in man" (John 2:23-25). He knew
that although the miracles had convinced them that He was the
Messiah, yet they did not *understand* the real reason for the
Messiah's coming. They may have been like those in John 6 who
wanted to make Christ their king by force so that He would heal
and feed them, but who were not willing to let Him reign as Lord
of their lives.

In contrast to these men to whom Christ would not commit
Himself, the next verse begins with these words: "There was a
man of the Pharisees named Nicodemus..." (John 3:1). Here
we are given an insight into where the others erred. Like those
who "believed on him," Nicodemus was convinced that Jesus
was "a teacher come from God" who did miracles not "by
Beelzebub the prince of the devils," as the other Pharisees claimed
(Matthew 12:24), but through the power of God (John 3:2). However, that was not enough, and we have the famous passage
concerning being "born again" as Christ helps Nicodemus
understand the truth he must know in order to be saved from
eternal judgment:

> Verily, verily, I say unto thee, Except a man be born
> again, he cannot see the kingdom of God.
> That which is born of the flesh is flesh, and that which
> is born of the Spirit is spirit.
> For God so loved the world that he gave his only be-
> gotten Son, that whosoever believeth in him should not
> perish but have everlasting life. For God sent not his
> Son into the world to condemn the world, but that the

world through him might be saved.

He that believeth on the Son hath everlasting life, and he that believeth not the Son shall not see life, but the wrath of God abideth on him (John 3:3,6,16,17,36).

Being a Christian does not come about through superficial belief in the existence of a historical Person named Jesus of Nazareth who did miracles and taught sublime truths. It involves personally receiving Him into one's heart and life as Savior and Lord and believing that He died for one's sins and rose from the dead. This is the gospel (good news) which, if truly believed, will transform one's life. Genuine faith is based upon *understanding* and results in *obedience*. Acts 6:7 tells us that "a great company of the priests were *obedient* to the faith." Paul preached "*obedience* to the faith among all nations" (Romans 1:5; 16:26) and warned of the judgment that would one day come upon all who "*know* not God and that *obey* not the gospel of our Lord Jesus Christ" (2 Thessalonians 1:8). This is why Jesus said:

If ye continue in my word, then are ye my disciples indeed; and ye shall know the truth, and the truth shall make you free (John 8:31,32).

This freedom is not produced by semantics. The attempt to bring peace to all men by promoting the myth of "universal brotherhood" is doomed by the fact that we are *not* all brothers therefore serious differences exist. It is axiomatic that there is no real brotherhood of man without the Fatherhood of God. And Jesus made it clear that no man is a child of God unless he has been "born again" by the Spirit of God into the family of God. Until then, Jesus said, we are the children of our "father the devil" and reflect his evil character in our attitude and actions toward God and one another.

Faith, Love, and Obedience

Christ declared that in order to be His disciples we must be disciplined by His Word. This will require submission to His lordship in every detail of our lives, even to allowing Him to take us through trials of faith that are intended to mature and strengthen and deepen our understanding and fellowship with Him. Charles Colson reminds us:

> Obedience is the beginning of the Christian life: obedience is essential to truly living as a Christian. . . .
> It takes courage to be obedient, courage found only in total dependence on the Holy Spirit.[24]

There is a tendency in the church today to emphasize unity and love at the expense of truth and to speak disparagingly of those who place great emphasis on doctrine in contending for the faith. Those who put "unity" ahead of truth and fail to rebuke today's false values and superficiality among Christians (and especially the many charismatics who reject the call to repent of false teachings as "negative" and insist that we are now in the greatest revival in history) would do well to take seriously the prophecy spoken during the famous Azusa Street revival in Los Angeles in 1906:

> In the last days three things will happen in the Great Pentecostal Movement: 1) There will be an overemphasis on power, rather than on righteousness; 2) there will be an overemphasis on praise, to a God they no longer pray to; 3) there will be an overemphasis on the gifts of the Spirit—rather than on the lordship of Christ.[25]

Keith Green warned about a "man-made unity [which] is not what God desires" because it is not based on holiness and obedience to God's Word.[25] While we ought not to split hairs in disputing over trivial questions, we must also recognize that our Lord demands *obedience*. We dare not take lightly the call to obey His commandments—and we can hardly obey His Word if we are loose concerning doctrine. It is folly to imagine that we can love our Lord and worship Him without knowing and obeying His Word. Jesus solemnly said:

> If a man love me, he will keep my words; and my Father will love him, and we will come unto him and make our abode with him. He that loveth me not keepeth not my sayings (John 14:23,24).

Seeking promised blessings from God is biblical, but at the same time we must heed God's *commandments*, exhort one another to *obedience*, and contend earnestly for sound *doctrine*. We do well to remember what the prophet Samuel told King Saul: "Rebellion [disobedience] is as the sin of witchcraft!" Disobedience cost Saul his kingdom and his life. Saul had lost his earlier humility and had begun to think he was somebody. He had forgotten that his position as king had been given to him by God. "When thou wast little in thine own sight," Samuel reminded Saul, "the Lord anointed thee king over Israel" (1 Samuel 15:17).

Saul mistakenly thought that offering a large sacrifice to God would take care of everything. We can easily enough understand God's contempt for such an attitude. Is a mother who is neglected and exploited all year pleased when her husband and children "honor" her with a present on Mother's Day? On the contrary, she is grieved and even insulted at such blatant hypocrisy. Nothing we can give God can substitute for *obedience*; and "love" without this vital ingredient is declared by Christ Himself to be unacceptable. We lack stability and strength and joy in our lives if we are not willing to submit to His daily discipline. It is through obedience to His Word that we are shaped and formed into the pattern He has planned so that He can use us for His glory.

It helps to remember that we are being disciplined by love for our good and that the ultimate purpose is that we might know Him who is love. As Hugh Black said: "Life is an education in love, but the education is not complete till we learn the love of the eternal."[26] His love can only effect its purpose in our lives if we submit humbly and obediently and joyfully to His will. An unknown poet put it so beautifully:

> When I stand at the judgment seat of Christ
> And He shows me His plan for me,
> The plan of my life as it might have been
> Had He had His way, and I see
> How I blocked Him here and
> I checked Him there,
> And I would not yield my will,
> Will there be grief in my Savior's eyes,
> Grief though He loves me still?
> He would have me rich but I stand there poor,

Robbed of all but His grace,
While my memory runs like a hunted thing
Down paths I cannot retrace.
Lord of the years that are left to me,
I give them to Thy hand;
Take me and break me and mold me
To the pattern Thou hast planned.

The True Path to Victory

What God can do *in* us is at least as important as what He can do *through* us. That we should be molded to God's will as we bow before His majesty in prayer is far more important than that He should grant our every request. The victory that Christ won over Satan came about through His submission to the Father's will: "Father, if thou be willing, remove this cup from me; nevertheless, not my will but thine be done" (Luke 22:42). When we follow that same path, then His triumph is ours. This way of victory confounds not only Satan but also sincere Christians who mistakenly believe that God's purpose has been frustrated and the church defeated if we do not take over the world and set up His kingdom. They misunderstand true victory. For His own, Jesus conquered sin, death, and hell by allowing His enemies to kill Him (Acts 2:23). " 'Tis mystery all, *the Immortal dies!*" wrote Charles Wesley. Christ destroyed death and Satan by dying: "That through death he might destroy him that had the power of death—that is, the devil—and deliver them who through fear of death were all their lifetime subject to bondage" (Hebrews 2:14,15). As the old classic hymn, so long loved by the church, puts it:

> By weakness and defeat
> He won a glorious crown;
> Trod all our foes beneath His feet
> By being trodden down.
>
> He Satan's power laid low;
> Made sin, He sin o'erthrew.
> Bowed to the grave, destroyed it so,
> And death by dying slew.[27]

It is beyond our comprehension that the wounds inflicted in murderous hatred and contempt by thorns, lash, nails, and spear drew forth the blood that saves those who believe that Christ died for them. Who can fathom such grace and mercy! Prophetically the psalmist declared: *"Mercy* and *truth* are met together; *righteousness* and *peace* have kissed each other" (Psalm 85:10). For evil He returned good; for hatred, love—and not mere sentimentality but a pure and steadfast love that unswervingly obeyed His Father's will and satisfied the claims of divine justice.

It is this path of the cross that we must take if we are to be Christ's disciples. And only as His love is awakened in our hearts is this possible. Contrary to popular thinking, this way of the cross and the denial of self to know His resurrection life is the way of inexpressible joy! Describing the secret of victory over "that old serpent called the Devil and Satan," John writes:

> They overcame him by the blood of the Lamb and by the word of their testimony; and they loved not their lives unto the death (Revelation 12:11).

Victorious Christians are those who have gained such an insight into the cross that it has left its indelible stamp on their hearts and lives. Overwhelmed by the staggering realization that the Creator of the universe would become a man in order to bear the full weight of the eternal judgment that they deserved, they have been captured by His divine love. Gladly confessing that they no longer belong to self but to the One who has purchased them with His blood, they have been freed from that inner tyrant and its self-centered anxieties that blinded them to the joy of surrender. Their lives are not their own, for they now belong to Christ totally and forever. They are securely under His care. He who has given them eternal life will never let them perish.

That divine love which has won their hearts and transformed their lives is to be the unmistakable mark of His true disciples. "By this shall all men know that ye are my disciples," said Christ, "if ye have love one to another" (John 13:35). John added this insight under the inspiration of the Holy Spirit: "Beloved, let us love one another, for love is of God; and everyone that loveth is born of God and knoweth God" (1 John 4:7).

Such love is described as "the fruit of the Spirit" (Galatians 5:22). Christ declared, "I am the vine, ye are the branches. He that abideth in me and I in him, the same bringeth forth much fruit; for without me ye can do nothing" (John 15:5). It is Christ who produces in us the beautiful *fruit* of "love, joy, peace, longsuffering, gentleness, goodness, faith, meekness, temperance" (Galatians 5:22,23). The branch need not be concerned whether it rains or shines; it needs only to remain open to the flow of life and fruitfulness.

Without this simple abiding as branches in Christ "the true vine," the call for a return to biblical Christianity would generate the frustration of ineffective self-effort and a stifling legalism of words without the power of the Spirit. One can spend a lifetime attempting to "master the written Word," when what is needed is to be *mastered by Christ the living Word.* There is a simple faith in God that delivers from the sophisticated foolishness of this ungodly world; there is a love for the truth that deepens as we meditate upon the Word of truth and upon Him who is the truth; and there is a godly prosperity and success that is not temporary but eternal because it is not earthly but heavenly. The psalmist worded so beautifully what we have tried to say in calling the church back to biblical Christianity:

> Blessed is the man that walketh not in the counsel of the ungodly, nor standeth in the way of sinners, nor sitteth in the seat of the scornful. But his delight is in the law of the Lord, and in his law doth he meditate day and night. And he shall be like a tree planted by the rivers of water, that bringeth forth his fruit in his season; his leaf also shall not wither, and whatsoever he doeth shall prosper (Psalm 1:1-3).

NOTES

NOTES

Back to the Source

1. Thomas F. Reid and Mark W. Virkler, *Seduction? A Biblical Response* (Buffalo, NY, 1986), p. 1.
2. D. Martyn Lloyd-Jones, *The Basis of Christian Unity* (Eerdmans, 1983), p. 5.
3. Ibid.
4. Charles Colson, *Who Speaks For God?* (Crossway, 1985), Introduction.
5. Ibid.
6. Michael Harner, *The Way of the Shaman* (Harper and Row, 1980), p. 136, etc.
7. Hunt and McMahon, *The Seduction of Christianity* (Harvest House, 1985), pp. 97-103, 113-35, 139-46, 150-65, etc.
8. Review by Rick Bradford in PRRM *Renewal News*, Mar.-Apr. 1986, p. 14; Robert Wise, "Speaking Out: Welcome To The Inquisition" in *Christianity Today*, May 16, 1986, p. 10; Terry C. Muck, "Open Season" in *Christianity Today*, Nov. 21, 1986, pp. 16-17, etc.
9. James Montgomery Boice, *Foundations of the Christian Faith* (InterVarsity Press, 1986), p. 25.

Chapter 1—A Return to Biblical Christianity

1. Boice, *Foundations*, p. 459.
2. Wilbur M. Smith, *Therefore Stand: Christian Apologetics* (Baker Book House, 1965), p. 423.
3. Professor Thomas Arnold, *Sermons on the Christian Life* (London, 1859), p. 324.
4. Smith, *Stand*, pp. 425, 584; see also Josh McDowell, *Evidence That Demands A Verdict* (Campus Crusade For Christ, 1972), for an excellent treatment of evidence for the Christian faith.
5. Irwin H. Linton, *A Lawyer Examines The Bible* (W. A. Wilde, 1943), pp. 13-25, etc.
6. Simon Greenleaf, *Testimony of the Evangelists* (Baker Book House), Introduction.
7. Tim Stafford, *Knowing the Face of God* (Zondervan, 1986), p. 21.
8. Colson, *Who Speaks?* pp. 20-21.
9. Charles Farah, *From the Pinnacle of the Temple* (Logos International), p. 78.
10. Jay E. Adams, *The Biblical View of Self-Esteem, Self-Love and Self-Image* (Harvest House, 1986), p. 84; citing Robert Pear, *The Washington Star*, Aug. 15, 1976.
11. R. J. Stuart, "How To Get Along With Yourself—You Are Important," a photocopied study guide for young married couples at a particular church.
12. Randy Smith, "Combatting the 'Epidemic' of Low Self-Esteem," in *Human Potential*, Dec. 1985, p. 20.
13. Ibid.
14. Boice, *Foundations*, p. 97.
15. Andrew Murray, *The Inner Life* (Zondervan, 1980), p. 50.
16. John Wesley, *John Wesley's Theology* (Abingdon, 1982), p. 121.
17. C. H. Spurgeon, *All of Grace* (Moody Press), pp. 68-69.

18. Robert Schuller, *Self-Esteem: The New Reformation* (Word, 1982), p. 19.
19. Ibid., p. 4.
20. Wesley, *Theology.*
21. A. W. Tozer, *Gems From Tozer* (Christian Publications, 1969), p. 54.
22. D. Martyn Lloyd-Jones, *The Cross* (Crossway, 1986), p. 49.
23. John Calvin, *Institutes of the Christian Religion* (Eerdmans, 1983), Vol. 1, p. 211.
24. Andrew Murray, *Absolute Surrender* (Moody Press), pp. 26-27.
25. A. W. Tozer, *Man: The Dwelling Place of God* (Christian Publications, 1966), p. 72.
26. C. S. Lewis, *Mere Christianity* (MacMillan, 1952), p. 114.
27. Robert Schuller, *Self-Esteem,* p. 115.
28. A. W. Tozer, *The Divine Conquest* (Christian Publications, 1950), pp. 59-60.
29. C. S. Lewis, *The Grand Miracle and Other Selected Essays on Theology and Ethics From God In The Dock* (Ballantine Books, 1970), p. 67.
30. A. W. Tozer, *The Knowledge of the Holy* (Harper & Row, 1961), pp. 6, 10.
31. Jacques Ellul, *The Humiliation of the Word* (Eerdmans, 1985), Preface, p. vii.
32. Colson, *Who Speaks?* pp. 20-21.
33. Robert Tilton, *God's Laws of Success* (Word of Faith, 1983), p. 3.
34. Gloria Copeland, *God's Will Is Prosperity* (Harrison House, 1978), p. 60.
35. Tozer, *Divine,* p. 51.
36. Ellul, *Humiliation,* from the Preface by Joyce Main Hanks, p. vii.
37. Colson, *Who Speaks?* p. 88.
38. From the undated letter signed by Robert H. Schuller on the letterhead of the Robert H. Schuller Institute For Successful Church Leadership that accompanied the approximately 250,000 copies of his book *Self-Esteem: The New Reformation* mailed to church leaders "through the generosity of an anonymous friend," whom Schuller later identified on an Hour of Power program as W. Clement Stone, member of Schuller's international board and President of the Napoleon Hill Foundation.
39. Franky Schaeffer, *Bad News For Modern Man* (Crossway Books, 1984), p. 68, quoting from a personal letter to him from Herbert Schlossberg dated Oct. 19, 1983.
40. McCandlish Phillips, *The Bible, the Supernatural and the Jews* (Bethany Fellowship, 1970), p. 313.
41. J. I. Packer quoted by Tim Stafford in "Testing The Wine From John Wimber's Vineyard," in *Christianity Today,* Aug. 8, 1986, p. 22.
42. A. W. Tozer, *Keys To The Deeper Life* (Zondervan, 1959), p. 13.
43. John Wimber in an interview in *New Wine,* Jan. 1986, p. 18.
44. Vinson Synan, Chairman of the "ecumenical" General Congress on the Holy Spirit & World Evangelization that is expected to attract about 70,000 Christian leaders to the New Orleans Superdome in July 1987, in a letter promoting the congress.
45. Paul Crouch, TBN, Feb. 5, 1986, P.O. Box A, Santa Ana, CA 92711.
46. The third Congress was held July 2-4, 1986, at the Shoreham Hotel in Washington D.C. Information can be obtained from the founder and director of COR (Coalition on Revival), 89 Pioneer Way, Mountain View, CA 94041.
47. Boice, *Foundations,* p. 25.
48. Tozer, *Keys,* pp. 7-8.
49. Spurgeon, *Grace,* pp. 36-37, 40.

Chapter 2—The Church's Most Desperate Need
1. Paul Yonggi Cho, *The Fourth Dimension, Volume Two* (Bridge Publishing, 1983), pp. 56-57.

2. Kenneth Hagin, Jr., in *The Word of Faith*, Nov. 1984, p. 3.
3. *The Believer and Positive Confession*, published in 1980 by the Assemblies of God, Gospel Publishing House, Springfield, MO 65802.
4. E. W. Kenyon and Don Gossett, *The Positive Confession of the Word of God* (Tulsa: Custom Graphics, 1981), p. 129.
5. J. I. Packer, "Put Holiness First," in *Christian Life*, May 1985, p. 46.
6. J. I. Packer, *Keep in Step with the Spirit* (Revell, 1984), p. 121.
7. Exodus 30:22-33; 37:29; 40:12-16; Numbers 3:3; 1 Samuel 9:16; 10:1; 16:12,13; 2 Samuel 2:4; 5:3; 1 Kings 19:15,16; Isaiah 61:1; Acts 4:27; 10:38; 2 Corinthians 1:21.
8. Andrew Murray, *Humility* (Whitaker House, 1982), pp. 47-48, 86, 52-53.
9. Spurgeon, *Grace*, pp. 35, 40-41.

Chapter 3—Contending for the Faith
1. "Shall We Fear God?" An interview with theologian Carl F.H. Henry in *Cornerstone*, Vol. 12, Issue 69, p. 13.
2. Packer, *Christian Life*, op. cit., p. 47.
3. Charles Capps, *Seedtime And Harvest* (Harrison House, 1986), p. 23.
4. Charles R. Swindoll, *Growing Deep In The Christian Life* (Multnomah Press, 1986), p. 406.
5. David Wilkerson, *Last Days Ministries Tract LD #45*, Lindale, TX.
6. Kenneth Copeland, "Questions and Answers," in *Believer's Voice of Victory*, June 1986, "Questions and Answers," p. 14.
7. Kenneth Copeland in TBN interview with Paul and Jan Crouch, Feb. 5, 1986.
8. Copeland, *Believer's Voice*, op. cit.
9. Tozer, *Gems*, p. 54.
10. Oswald Chambers, *My Utmost for His Highest* (Dodd, Mead & Co., 1935), p. 79.
11. Norman Vincent Peale, *The Power of Positive Thinking* (Fawcett Crest, 1983).
12. Claude Bristol, *The Magic of Believing,* (Prentice-Hall, 1948).
13. Napoleon Hill and W. Clement Stone, *Success Through A Positive Mental Attitude* (Prentice-Hall, 1960).
14. Norman Vincent Peale, "Confident Living," in *Salesman's Opportunity*, May 1974, p. 63.
15. Ibid.
16. Norman Vincent Peale, "What Does It Take To Be a Christian?" in *Plus: The Magazine of Positive Thinking*, Apr. 1986, p. 3.
17. Colson, *Who Speaks?* p. 36.
18. Wilkerson, *Last Days*.
19. Charles Colson, *Who Speaks?* p. 36.
20. *The Believer*, The Assemblies of God, op. cit.
21. Daniel Ray McConnell, *The Kenyon Connection: A Theological and Historical Analysis of the Cultic Origins of the Faith Movement*, a thesis submitted to the Theological Faculty, Oral Roberts University, Tulsa, Oklahoma, May 1982, p. 2.
22. Chuck Smith, *Charisma Vs. Charismania* (Harvest House, 1983).
23. McConnell, *Connection*, p. 1.
24. Charles Farah, Jr., "A Critical Analysis: The 'Roots and Fruits' of Faith-Formula Theology," paper delivered to the Society of Pentecostal Studies, Fall 1980.
25. Kenneth Copeland in TBN interview with Paul and Jan Crouch, Feb. 5, 1986.
26. Charles Capps, *The Tongue—A Creative Force* (Harrison House, 1976), pp. 12, 19, 129; Kenneth Copeland, *The Power of the Tongue* (KCP Publications, 1980), pp. 4-5.

27. Capps, *Tongue*, pp. 131-32.

28. Ibid., pp. 17, 26.

29. Copeland, *Believer's Voice*, op. cit.

30. Capps, *Tongue*, pp. 7, 129.

31. Ibid., p. 135; Copeland, *The Power*, p. 3.

32. Kenneth Hagin, *Having Faith In Your Faith* (Rhema, 1980), pp. 2, 4; *Kenneth Copeland's Reference Bible,* pp. xlvii, lvi; Capps, *Tongue,* pp. 131-32, etc.

33. Capps, *Seedtime*, p. 53.

34. Capps, *Tongue*, p. 30.

35. Ibid., p. 56.

36. Robert Tilton, *God's Laws of Success* (Word of Faith Publishing, 1983), pp. 170-71; Kenneth E. Hagin, *Plead Your Case* (Tulsa, 1985), p. 3; Charles Capps, *God's Image of You* (Harrison House, 1985), p. 34; and many others.

37. Hagin, *Faith*, p. 3.

38. Capps, *Image*, p. 34.

39. Copeland, *The Power*, pp. 5-7.

40. Copeland, TBN interview on Feb. 5, 1986.

41. Copeland, *Believer's Voice,* op. cit.

42. Capps, *Tongue*, p. 130.

43. Hagin, *Faith*, p. 3; Paul Yonggi Cho, *Fourth, Two*, pp. 37-39.

44. Hagin, *Faith*, pp. 3-4.

45. Capps, *Tongue*, p. 132.

46. Ibid., p. 24.

47. Kenneth E. Hagin, *Words* (Faith Library, 1979), p. 12.

48. Hagin, *Words*, p. 10; Don Gossett, *What You Say Is What You Get* (Revell, 1976), pp. 12-13, etc.; Frances Hunter, *How To Develop Your Faith* (Hunter Books, 1979), pp. 17-20; Capps, *Tongue*, pp. 139-43.

49. Cho, *Fourth, Two*, p. 32.

50. Gloria Copeland, *God's Will Is Prosperity* (Harrison House, 1978), p. 85.

51. Tilton, *Laws*, p. 114.

52. Hagin, *Words*, pp. 9-10.

53. Capps, *Tongue*, pp. 128, 141.

54. Cho, *Fourth*, pp. 39-45; *Fourth, Two,* p. 36; Capps, *Tongue*, p. 137.

55. Kenneth E. Hagin, *New Thresholds of Faith* (Kenneth Hagin Ministries, 1974), p. 51; Capps, *Tongue*, p. 55-78, 90-92; Capps, *Seedtime*, pp. 18-21, etc.

56. Capps, *Seedtime*, p. 16.

57. Don Basham, "On The Tip of My Tongue: How your words can curse and destroy, or bless and restore," in *New Wine*, June 1986, p. 6.

58. "The Wisdom of Martyn Lloyd-Jones" (selected by Dick Alderson), in *The Banner of Truth*, Aug./Sep. 1986, p. 7.

59. Kenneth Copeland, TBN "Praise The Lord" program, Feb. 5, 1986.

60. Charles Capps, *God's Image of You* (Tulsa, 1985), pp. 28-34.

61. *New Wine*, June 1986—this entire issue of the magazine was devoted to promoting this error; Capps, *Tongue*, pp. 13-16, etc.

62. Hagin, *Faith In Faith*, pp. 2-3.

63. Capps, *Tongue*.

64. Kenneth E. Hagin, *You Can Have What You Say* (Faith Library Publications, 1980).

65. Letter on file.

66. Cho, *Fourth, Two*, pp. 36-41, 64.

67. Hagin, *Faith In Faith*, pp. 3-4.

68. W. H. Griffith Thomas, *St. Paul's Epistle To The Romans* (Eerdmans, 1974), p. 133.
69. Tozer, *Of God and Men* (Christian Publications, 1960), p. 57.
70. Charles Capps, *How To Have Faith In Your Faith* (Harrison House, 1986), p. 64.
71. Hagin, *Faith In Faith*, p. 5.
72. Letter on file.
73. Capps, *Tongue*, p. 27.
74. Horatio W. Dresser, ed., *The Quimby Manuscripts* (Citadel, 1980), p. 9.
75. Charles S. Braden, *Spirits in Rebellion: The Rise and Development of New Thought* (SMU Press, 1966), p. 20.
76. Edwin Franden Dakin, *Mrs. Eddy: The Biography of a Virginal Mind* (Scribner, 1929-1968 edition), pp. 35-37, 43-44.
77. Dresser, *Quimby*, p. 131.
78. Ibid., pp. 388-91.
79. *Houston Chronicle*, Aug. 2, 1986, Section 6, p. 2.
80. McConnell, *Connection*, p. 95.
81. Frederick Price, *Faith, Foolishness or Presumption?* (Tulsa, 1979), p. 16.
82. Hagin, *Right and Wrong Thinking* (Tulsa, 1966), p. 30.
83. Colson, *Who Speaks?* p. 36.

Chapter 4—Submission to Love
1. Sherry Andrews, "Kenneth Hagin: Keeping the Faith," in *Charisma*, Oct. 1981, pp. 24-30.
2. Taped interviews on file at the Holy Spirit Research Center, Oral Roberts University, cited in McConnell, *Connection*, footnotes on page 9.
3. McConnell, *Connection*, p. 11.
4. Kenyon and Gossett, *Positive*, pp. 133-37, 152-55.
5. Compare: E. W. Kenyon, *The Two Kinds of Faith: Faith's Secrets Revealed* (Kenyon Gospel Publishing Ass'n., 1942), pp. 7, 27, 32; *What Happened from the Cross to the Throne?* (Kenyon, 1945, 5th ed.), p. 109; *Jesus The Healer* (Kenyon, 1943), p. 77; Kenneth Hagin, *What Faith Is* (Faith Library, Tulsa, 1978), pp. 3, 11, 12; *Bible Faith Study Course* (Tulsa, 1980), p. 17; *New Thresholds of Faith* (Tulsa, 1980), p. 11; *The Real Faith* (Tulsa, 1980), pp. 24-25; Frederick Price, *How Faith Works* (Harrison House, 1976), pp. 42, 51.
6. Kenyon, *Two Kinds*, pp. 65-67, 72; Hagin, *Word of Faith*, Nov. 1974, pp. 1-2; *In Him* (Tulsa, 1975), p. 1; *Right and Wrong Thinking* (Tulsa, 1966), pp. 8-9.
7. Kenyon, *The Hidden Man: An Unveiling of the Subconscious Mind* (Kenyon, 1970), p. 98; Kenyon and Gossett, *Positive*, p. 25; Hagin, *Study*, p. 92; Charles Capps, *Releasing the Ability of God Through Prayer* (Harrison, 1978), p. 67.
8. Kenyon, *Hidden Man*, p. 102; Kenyon and Gossett, *Positive*, p. 67; Hagin, *Word of Faith*, Nov. 19, p. 4.
9. Kenyon, *What?* p. 62.
10. Ibid., pp. 173-76.
11. Hagin, *Faith In Faith*, pp. 3-4.
12. Paul Yonggi Cho, *Fourth Dimension*, pp. 39-40; *Fourth, Two*, pp. 35-42; etc.
13. Kenyon, *Hidden*, p. 26; *Two Kinds of Life* (Kenyon, 1971), p. 107.
14. Kenyon, *Two Kinds*, p. 20.
15. Hagin, "The Law of Faith" in *Word of Faith*, Nov. 1974, p. 2; "The Secret of Faith" in *Word of Faith*, Mar. 1968, p. 2; Kenyon, *Two Kinds*, p. 20; Kenneth Copeland, *The Force of Faith* (Copeland), pp. 18-20; Capps, *Tongue*,

271

pp. 7-18, 131-40; Capps, *Releasing,* pp. 7-11.

16. Kenyon and Gossett, *Confession,* pp. 129-36, 152-55, 182-85, etc.
17. McConnell, *Connection,* p. 24.
18. Kenyon and Gossett, *Confession,* p. 206.
19. Charles Farah, "A Critical Analysis," op. cit., cited in McConnell, *Connection,* p. 111; see also p. vii.
20. Kenyon and Gossett, *Confession,* p. 208.
21. John Coffee and Richard L. Wentworth, *A Century of Eloquence: The History of Emerson College, 1880-1980* (Alternative Publications, 1982), p. 68.
22. McConnell, *Connection,* p. 82.
23. Braden, *Spirits,* p. 386.
24. Ibid., p. 380.
25. Hagin, *Authority,* p. 22.
26. Hagin, *Word of Faith,* Nov. 1974, pp. 2-3; Copeland, *Laws of Prosperity,* pp. 18-19.
27. Gloria Copeland, *God's Will,* p. 54.
28. *Media Spotlight,* News, Apr.-June 1986, p. 4.
29. Kenneth Copeland in *Believer's Voice of Victory,* Jan. 1985, p. 3.
30. Kenneth Copeland in *Prayer Partners Newsletter,* undated but issued around Feb. 1986; Oral Roberts et al.
31. Kenneth Copeland, TBN, Feb. 5, 1986.
32. *Time,* Feb. 16, 1986, p. 69, quoting Kenneth Copeland.
33. Copeland in *Voice,* pp. 2-6.
34. Ken L. Sarles, "A Theological Evaluation of the Prosperity Gospel," in *Bibleotheca Sacra,* Oct.-Dec. 1986, p. 338.
35. Gordon Fee, "The 'Gospel' of Prosperity—An Alien Gospel," in *Reformation Today,* Nov./Dec. 1984, p. 39.
36. Kenyon, *What?* p. 48.
37. Ibid., p. 40.
38. Ibid., p. 47.
39. Copeland, *Believer's Voice of Victory,* Apr. 1982, p. 3.
40. Kenyon, *What?* p. 60.
41. Kenyon, *Identification,* op. cit., pp. 8, 18, plus other quotes.
42. Copeland, "Did Jesus Die Spiritually?" Photocopied material mailed out to answer inquiries on this subject, p. 2.
43. Kenyon, *Healer,* p. 44.
44. Ibid., p. 67; Hagin, *Redeemed,* pp. 19, 23.
45. Kenyon and Gossett, *Confession,* p. 149.
46. Rodney Clapp, "Faith Healing: A Look at What's Happening," in *Christianity Today,* Dec. 16, 1983, pp. 16-17.
47. Ibid., p. 15.
48. *Los Angeles Times,* Jan. 18, 1983, Sec. I, p. 3.
49. "Oral Roberts Shares His Heart," in *Charisma,* June 1985, p. 57.
50. Bernhardt J. Hurwood, "Healing and Believing: A special report on faith healing in America," in *Health,* June 1984, p. 16.
51. *Houston Chronicle,* July 5, 1986, Section 5, p. 6.
52. Undated appeal for funds, signed by Oral Roberts "Urgent Reply Requested."
53. Ibid.
54. Promotional material advertising a new book by Oral Roberts titled *Attack Your Lack of money, of health, of good relationships, of joy and peace of mind: 12 Spiritual Tools to help you get your lack FULLY FILLED—from*

the man who has learned to use these tools!.

55. Clapp, *Christianity Today*, p. 14.
56. "Missions & Ministries" in *Charisma*, June 1985, p. 92.
57. *Abundant Life*, Mar./Apr. 1986, pp. 12-13.
58. Ibid., p. 11.
59. Ben Patterson, "Cause for Concern," in *Christianity Today*, Aug. 8, 1986, p. 20.
60. Tozer, *Keys*, p. 25.
61. Clark H. Pinnock, "A Revolutionary Promise," in *Christianity Today*, Aug. 8, 1986, p. 19.
62. Wilkerson, *Last Days*.
63. Ibid.
64. Spurgeon, *Grace*, p. 44.
65. Jimmy Swaggart, *The Evangelist*, Sep. 1986, p. 46.
66. Larry Parker, *We Let Our Son Die* (Harvest House, 1980).
67. Farah, "Roots and Fruits," cited in McConnell, *Connection*, p. 111.
68. McConnell, *Connection*, p. 117.
69. Colson, *Who Speaks?* p. 15.
70. Spurgeon, *The Metropolitan Tabernacle Pulpit*, 1874, Vol. XIX, p. 60.

Chapter 5—Unbelief Has Many Faces

1. Spurgeon, *Grace*, p. 48.
2. Linton, *Lawyer*, introductory chapter.
3. A. W. Tozer, *Gems*, p. 63.
4. John Calvin, *Institutes of the Christian Religion* (Eerdmans, 1983), Vol. 1, p. 470.
5. Ibid., p. 471.
6. Spurgeon, *Grace*, pp. 56-57.
7. Boice, *Foundations*, p. 101.
8. William Law, ed. Dave Hunt, *The Power of the Spirit* (Christian Literature Crusade, 1971), pp. 182-83.
9. Boice, *Foundations*, p. 25.
10. Stafford, *Knowing*, pp. 32-33.
11. Philip Yancey, "God, the Jilted Lover," in *Christianity Today*, May 16, 1986, p. 72.
12. Law, *Spirit*, p. 183.
13. Charles Spurgeon, *The New Park Street Pulpit, Vol. I* (Pilgrim Publications, 1975), p. 27.
14. Linton, *Lawyer*, introductory chapter.
15. C. S. Lewis, *The Abolition of Man* (Macmillan, 1978 ed.), pp. 76-88.
16. Hugh Black, *Friendship* (Revell, 1907), pp. 216-17.
17. Ibid., pp. 217, 219.
18. A. W. Tozer, *Of God and Men* (Christian Publications, 1960), p. 113.
19. B. F. Skinner, *Walden Two* (MacMillan, 1948 ed.), p. 193.
20. C. S. Lewis, *Abolition*, pp. 70-71, 86.
21. Chambers, *Utmost*, p. 210.
22. Ibid., p. 246.
23. Swindoll, *Growing*, p. 89.
24. Denis Waitley, *Seeds of Greatness* (Revell, 1983), p. 148.
25. Ibid., pp. 160-61.
26. Ibid., p. 162.
27. Thomas, *Romans*, p. 133.
28. Oral Roberts, *Attack*, title of chapter seven.

29. Chambers, *Utmost*, p. 118.

Chapter 6—Too Glorious to Be Easy
 1. Schuller, *Self-Esteem*, pp. 21-22.
 2. Ibid., p. 27.
 3. Thomas Szasz, *The Myth of Psychotherapy* (Doubleday, 1978), p. xxiv.
 4. Lawrence Le Shan, *How To Meditate* (Boston, 1974), pp. 150-51.
 5. *Los Angeles Times,* Part V, Dec. 18, 1985, p. 16.
 6. Ibid.
 7. *Time*, Dec. 23, 1985, p. 59.
 8. Ibid.
 9. Ibid.
10. Ibid.
11. John Leo, "A Madness in Their Method," in *Time*, Sep. 30, 1985, p. 78.
12. *Time*, Dec. 23, 1985, p. 59.
13. *Los Angeles Times*, op. cit., p. 17.
14. A. W. Tozer, *Who Put Jesus on the Cross?* (Christian Publications, 1975), pp. 124-25.
15. Elisabeth Elliott, an article in *Christian Life*, Apr. 1986, pp. 26-29.
16. Martin and Deidre Bobgan, *The Psychological Way/The Spiritual Way* (Bethany, 1978), p. 173.
17. Henrietta C. Mears, *What The Bible Is All About* (Gospel Light, 1966, Special Edition for Billy Graham Evangelistic Association), p. 89.
18. Lloyd-Jones, "Wisdom," in *Banner of Truth,* op. cit., p. 12.
19. Chambers, *Utmost*, p. 165.
20. Law, *Spirit*, pp. 20-21.
21. Bernie Zilbergeld, "The Myths of Psychiatry," in *Discover*, May 1983, pp. 66, 71.
22. Chambers, *Utmost*, p. 305.
23. C. S. Lewis, *God In The Dock* (Eerdmans, 1970), p. 99.
24. Geoffrey T. Bull, *When Iron Gates Yield* (London: Hodder and Stoughton, 1955), pp. 241-42.
25. Chambers, *Utmost*, p. 240.
26. Lloyd-Jones, "Wisdom," in *Banner*, p. 8.
27. Richard S. Taylor, "Misrepresenting God's Love," in *Message of the Cross*, Mar./Apr. 1985, p. 25.
28. Boice, *Foundations*, p. 25.
29. Zilbergeld, *Discover*, op. cit., p. 74.
30. Carl Henry, *Cornerstone*, op. cit.
31. Chambers, *Utmost*, p. 165.

Chapter 7—Is All Truth God's Truth?
 1. Adams, *Self-Esteem,* pp. 54-55.
 2. Bruce Narramore, *You're Someone Special* (Zondervan, 1978), p. 22.
 3. Schuller, *Self-Esteem*, p. 115.
 4. Ibid., pp. 22, 117-19.
 5. J. Vernon McGee, personal letter to Martin Bobgan dated Sep. 18, 1986.
 6. Schuller, *Self-Esteem*, p. 47.
 7. Frank B. Minirth and Paul D. Meier, *Counseling and the Nature of Man* (Baker Book House, 1982), p. 51.
 8. Ibid., pp. 56-57, 78.

9. J. Sutherland and P. Poelstra, *Aspects of Integration*, a paper presented to the Western Association of Christians for Psychological Studies, Santa Barbara, CA, June 1976.
10. Schuller, *Self-Esteem*, p. 27.
11. John D. Carter and Bruce Narramore, *The Integration of Psychology and Theology* (Zondervan, 1979), p. 15.
12. Ibid., p. 12.
13. Ibid., p. 37.
14. Martin L. Gross, *The Psychological Society* (Random House, 1978), pp. 56-57.
15. *Los Angeles Times*, Part V, Dec. 18, 1985, p. 16.
16. E. Fuller Torrey, *The Death of Psychiatry* (Penguin, 1974), p. 107.
17. Letter on file dated Sep. 7, 1985.
18. Bernie Zilbergeld, *The Shrinking of America: Myths of Psychological Change* (Little, Brown, 1983), p. 5; quoted by Bobgan in *How To...* (Moody, 1985), p. 11.
19. See Adams, *Self-Esteem*, pp. 29-61. For an example of how this false and humanistic idea becomes the basis for an evangelistic approach to winning the lost, see Joseph C. Aldrich, *Life Style Evangelism* (Multnomah Press, 1981), pp. 93-96.
20. Letter on file dated Jan. 11, 1986.
21. Letter on file dated Sep. 19, 1985.
22. Carl Rogers, *On Becoming A Person* (Houghton, Mifflin, 1961); see also Martin and Deidre Bobgan, *The Psychological Way/The Spiritual Way* (Bethany, 1978), pp. 118-124; Paul Vitz, *Psychology As Religion: The Cult of Self-Worship* (Eerdmans, 1977), pp. 20-23.
23. William Glasser, *Reality Therapy* (Harper & Row, 1965); see also Bobgan, *Psychological*, pp. 124-132.
24. Abraham Maslow, *Motivation and Personality* (Harper, 2nd ed., 1970), Ch. 11 and pp. 169ff; see also Vitz, *Psychology*, pp. 23-24.
25. Arthur Janov, *The Primal Scream* (Dell, 1970), pp. 25, 41-42.
26. Robert H. Schuller, *Self-Love, The Dynamic Force of Success* (Hawthorn, 1969), p. 32.
27. Rita Bennett, *You Can Be Emotionally Free* (Revell, 1982), pp. 41-42.
28. Ibid., pp. 43-47.
29. Gross, *Society*, pp. 43-44.

Chapter 8—The Roots and Fruits of Selfism
1. Law, *Spirit*, p. 143.
2. Ibid., p. 148.
3. Lloyd-Jones, "Wisdom," in *Banner*, p. 10.
4. Law, *Spirit*, pp. 141-42.
5. Francis A. Schaeffer, *The Great Evangelical Disaster* (Crossway Books, 1984), pp. 24-25.
6. Lloyd-Jones, "Wisdom," in *Banner*, p. 11.
7. Peale in Norman Vincent Peale and Smiley Blanton, *Faith is the Answer* (Fawcett Crest, 1950), p. 47.
8. Bruce Larson, *The Relational Revolution*, cited in *Pastoral Renewal*, Nov. 1979, p. 37.
9. Carl Rogers, *A Way of Being* (Houghton, Mifflin, 1980), p. 81.
10. Phillips, *Supernatural*, p. 93.
11. J. Gregory Mantle, *Beyond Humiliation* (Bethany, 1975), pp. 46-47.
12. The Letters of Samuel Rutherford (Moody Press, 1951), p. 277.
13. Chambers, *Utmost*, p. 164.

14. K.F.P., "Feelings as Guide, Goal, and Ground of Being," in *Pastoral Renewal*, Nov. 1979, p. 37.
15. Ibid.
16. Fredrick Brewster, a book review of *Habits of the Heart* (University of California Press), in *Common Boundary*, Mar./Apr. 1986, p. 4.
17. Herbert W. Schlossberg, *Idols for Destruction* (Thomas Nelson, 1983), pp. 265-66.
18. David G. Myers, *The Inflated Self* (Seabury Press, 1981), p. xiii.
19. Richard P. Belcher, *The Impossibility Thinking of Robert Schuller* (Richbarry Press, 1983), pp. 11, 14.
20. Schuller, *Self-Esteem*, p. 31.
21. Joseph Alleine, *An Alarm to the Unconverted* (London: Banner of Truth, 1964, reprinted from 1671 edition), pp. 16-17.
22. Letter on file dated Sep. 30, 1986.
23. Dave Wilkerson, "Straight Talk—The Fellowship of His Sufferings," in *The Evangelist*, Oct. 1986, p. 16.
24. Tozer, *Gems*, p. 42, cited from *The Root of the Righteous*.
25. J. I. Packer, *Keep in Step with the Spirit* (Revell, 1984), p. 97.
26. Craig W. Ellison, ed., *Self-Esteem* (Southwestern Press for Christian Association for Psychological Studies, 1976), p. 6.
27. Schuller, *Self-Esteem*, p. 116.
28. Adams, *Self-Esteem*, p. 25.
29. Schuller, *Self-Esteem*, p. 19.
30. Ibid., p. 145.
31. Calvin, *Institutes*, Vol. 1, p. 211.
32. Mantle, *Beyond*, front cover.
33. John Vasconcellos and Mitch Saunders, "Humanistic Politics," in *AHP Perspective* (Association for Humanistic Psychology), July 1985, pp. 12-13.
34. Schuller, *Self-Esteem*, p. 35.
35. Adams, *Self-Esteem*, p. 94.
36. Schuller, *Self-Esteem*, p. 12.
37. Ibid., pp. 12, 36, 64, 123, 150-51.
38. Jimmy Swaggart, "The Message of the Cross," in *The Evangelist*, Oct. 1986, p. 6.
39. Andrew Murray, *The Inner Life* (Zondervan, 1980), p. 50.
40. Schuller, *Self-Esteem*, p. 38.
41. Donald Grey Barnhouse, *Romans, Vol. 1, Man's Ruin* (Van Kampen Press, 1952), p. 261.
42. Lewis, *Mere*, p. 112.
43. "Immanuel's Land" in *Hymns of Worship and Remembrance* (Truth and Praise, Inc., 1950), no. 105.
44. Lewis, *Mere*, p. 105.
45. Dan Denk, "I Love Me!" in *Christian Reader*, Sep./Oct. 1986, pp. 33-34.
46. *The Evangelist*, Oct. 1986, p. 13.
47. *Prisoner Bulletin*, ed. Georgi Vins, P.O. Box 1188, Elkhart, IN 46515, Autumn 1986, pp. 15-16.
48. Ibid., p. 17.
49. Ibid., p. 6.

Chapter 9—Self-Exaltation and Humility
1. Dr. James Dobson, *Hide or Seek* (Revell, 1979, expanded, updated edition), inside front cover.

2. Ibid., p. 152.
3. Ibid., p. 145.
4. Stanton E. Samenow, *Inside the Criminal Mind* (Times Books, 1984), pp. 162-64.
5. Myers, *Inflated*, pp. 20-21.
6. Ibid., pp. 20-32.
7. Bruce Narramore, *You're Someone Special* (Zondervan, 1978), p. 129.
8. Lloyd-Jones, *Cross,* pp. 49-50.
9. Lloyd-Jones, *Banner*, p. 11.
10. Schuller, *Self-Esteem,* p. 104.
11. Anthony A. Hoekema, *The Christian Looks at Himself* (Eerdmans, 1975), p. 22.
12. Schuller, *Self-Esteem*, p. 19.
13. Ibid., p. 174.
14. Ibid., pp. 57, 74.
15. Calvin, *Institutes*, p. 210.
16. *The Best of F. B. Meyer* (Baker, 1984), p. 14.
17. Tozer, *Dwelling*, p. 72.
18. Murray, *Humility*, p. 16.
19. Ibid., pp. 51-57.
20. Lewis, *Mere*, p. 114.
21. Lewis, *The Screwtape Letters*, (MacMillan, 1961), pp. 62-63.
22. Craig W. Ellison, *Self-Esteem* (Southwestern Press, 1976), p. 6.
23. David Stoop, *Self Talk: Key to Personal Growth* (Revell, 1982).
24. Lewis, *Mere*, p. 112.
25. W. H. Mallock, "Faith and Verification," in *Nineteenth Century*, IV (1878), cited in Norman & Jeanne MacKenzie, *The Fabians* (Simon & Schuster, 1977), p. 16.
26. Schuller, *Self-Esteem*, p. 22.
27. Ibid., pp. 113-15.
28. Ibid., p. 74.
29. Ibid., p. 104.
30. Narramore, *Special*, pp. 25-26.
31. Hoekema, *Christian*, p. 22.
32. Schuller, *Self-Esteem*, p. 74.
33. Ibid., p. 102.
34. The Bible Science Newsletter, Oct. 1986, p. 10.
35. Schuller, *Self-Esteem*, p. 101.
36. Ibid., pp. 98, 101.
37. Adams, *Self-Esteem*, pp. 92-93.
38. Schuller, *Self-Esteem*, p. 74.
39. Ibid., p. 98.
40. H. Norman Wright, *Improving Your Self-Image* (Eugene: Harvest House, 1983), p. 68.
41. A. W. Tozer, *The Knowledge of the Holy* (Harper & Row, 1961), p. 7.
42. Oswald J. Smith, *The Consuming Fire* (Marshall, Morgan & Scott, 1957), p. 24.
43. Tozer, *Gems*, p. 86.
44. Spurgeon, *Morning and Evening* (Zondervan, 1972), p. 471.
45. Calvin, *Institutes*, p. 210.
46. Lloyd-Jones, *Banner*, p. 9.
47. Lewis, *Mere*, p. 111.
48. Stafford, *Knowing*, p. 66.
49. Lewis, *Mere*, p. 114.

Chapter 10—Is Seeing Really Believing?
1. James Montgomery Boice, *The Gospel of John, Vol. 5* (Zondervan, 1979), p. 326.
2. Calvin, *Institutes*, p. 91.
3. Fanny J. Crosby, "Give Me Jesus," in *Hymns of Truth and Praise* (Fort Dodge, IA: Gospel Perpetuating Publishers, 1971), no. 330. This book includes 23 Crosby hymns.
4. John MacArthur, *The Ultimate Priority* (Moody Press, 1983), p. 9.
5. *Spirit Speaks: Life In The Spirit World*, Issue 7, pp. 28-29.
6. Waitley, *Seeds*, p. 48.
7. Ibid.
8. Ibid.
9. Zig Ziglar, *See You At The Top* (Pelican, 1983), pp. 294-300.
10. *Free Inquiry*, Fall 1985, pp. 14-15.
11. Charles G. Finney, ed. David L. Young, *Crystal Christianity: A Guide to Personal Revival* (Whitaker House, 1985), pp. 194-96.
12. Waitley, *Seeds*, p. 57.
13. Ibid., p. 48.
14. Mack R. Douglas, *Success Can Be Yours* (Zondervan, 1977), p. 37.
15. Editorial by Robert Schuller, "The me I see is the me I'll be," in *Possibilities*, Summer 1986, p. 2.
16. Peale, *Imaging*, p. 10.
17. Gary Greenwald, Pastor of The Eagle's Nest Ministries, in a letter to members dated Dec. 5, 1985.
18. William Wolff, *Psychic Self-Improvement for the Millions* (Bell Publishing, 1969), pp. 15, 30, 34, 59-61, 63, 80-84.
19. Glen Bland, *Success!* (Tyndale, 1983), p. 18.
20. Ibid.
21. Peale, *Imaging*, p. 20.
22. Ibid., p. 77.
23. Norman Vincent Peale, "No More Stress or Tension," in *Plus: The Magazine of Positive Thinking*, May 1986, pp. 22-23.
24. Jamie Buckingham, "A Small Tribute," in *Charisma*, 1986, p. 114.
25. News release dated Feb. 13, 1986, from the Office of Communications, Golden Gate Baptist Theological Seminary, Mill Valley, CA 94941-3198.
26. Morton T. Kelsey, *The Christian and the Supernatural* (Augsburg, 1976), pp. 93, 109, 113-23, 142.
27. Morton T. Kelsey, *Transcend: A Guide to the Supernatural Quest* (Crossroad, 1985), pp. 23, 31; Kelsey, *Adventure Inward* (Augsburg, 1980), pp. 93-95.
28. Morton T. Kelsey, *Christo-Psychology* (Crossroad, 1982), p. 149; *Transcend*, op. cit., pp. 3, 23, 31.
29. Reid and Virkler, *Seduction?* p. 7.
30. Undated audio cassette by Dr. Bruce Morgan.
31. Wise et al, *Church*, p. 46.
32. Don Turner, "Is Inner Healing A Valid Ministry?" in *Fullness*, Mar.-Apr. 1986, pp. 17-23.
33. Wise et al, *Church*, p. 42.
34. Ibid., p. 47.
35. Ibid., p. 60.
36. Ibid., p. 66.
37. Ibid., pp. 69-71.

38. Ibid., p. 83.
39. *Christian Marriage Enrichment,* brochure for The National Christian Conference on Marriage and Family Counseling and Enrichment, May 14, 15, 16, 1986, Minneapolis, MN, sponsored by H. Norman Wright's Christian Marriage Enrichment, Santa Ana, CA 92701, from description of a seminar by David A. Seamands, p. 2.
40. David A. Seamands, *Healing of Memories* (Victor, 1985), pp. 66-68.
41. Ibid.
42. Wise et al, *Church*, p. 68, quoting from Francis MacNutt, *Healing* (Ave Maria Press, 1974), p. 181.
43. Wise et al, *Church*, p. 84.
44. Ibid., p. 70.
45. Ibid., p. 76.
46. "What Does It Take To Be A Christian? An interview with Norman Vincent Peale" in *Plus: The Magazine of Positive Thinking*, Apr. 1986, p. 10.
47. W. H. Griffith Thomas, *St. Paul's Epistle to the Romans* (Eerdmans, 1946), p. 228.
48. Peale, *Imaging*, p. 79.
49. Wright, *Fears*, p. 53.
50. Ibid., p. 143.
51. Morton Kelsey, *Transcend: A Guide To The Spiritual Quest* (Crossroad, 1985), pp. 23-32, 81.
52. Ibid., p. 136.
53. Copy of letters on file.
54. Letter on file from Don Matzat to John Sandford dated Feb. 10, 1986.
55. Letter on file from Don Matzat to Jamie Buckingham dated Feb. 16, 1986; the "classic of this generation" referred to was *Celebration of Discipline*.
56. Jung, *Memories, Adventures and Reflections* (Pantheon, 1963), pp. 104-06; *Tomorrow* magazine, Spring 1961.
57. Jung, *Memories*, pp. 150-61; Ernest Jones, *The Life and Work of Sigmund Freud*, Vol. I, p. 317; Vol. II, p. 146; Nandor Fodor, "Freud and the Poltergeist," in *Psychoanalysis*, Vol. IV, No. 2, Winter 1955-56; "Jung, Freud, and a Newly-Discovered Letter on the Poltergeist Theme," in *The Psychoanalytic Review*, Summer 1963.
58. Carl Jung, *Memories*, pp. 10-11, 48, 171-72.
59. See, for example, Jung's letter to Prof. Fritz Blanke published in *Neue Wissenschaft*, Vol. VII, 1951, p. 14; *Psychology and the Occult* (Princeton Press, 1977), pp. 143-52; *Memories*, pp. 98, 189-92.
60. Jung, *Memories*, p. 312, etc.
61. Jung, *Memories*, pp. 170-99; see also *Seven Sermons to the Dead* (Neill & Company, Edinburgh, 1925).
62. Nick Carver, "Dreaming with Jung," in *PRRM Renewal News*, Mar.-Apr. 1986, p. 13.
63. Ibid.
64. Ibid.
65. Ibid.
66. John and Paula Sandford, *The Transformation of the Inner Man* (Bridge, 1982), pp. 301-09.
67. Ibid., pp. 313-15.
68. Ibid., p. 315.
69. Ibid.
70. Calvin Miller, *The Table of Inwardness* (InterVarsity, 1984), pp. 94-95.

71. William C. Lantz, Jr., review of *The Seduction of Christianity*, in *Journal of Psychology and Christianity*, Vol. 5, No. 1.
72. J. David Stone, *Spiritual Growth In Youth Ministry* (Group, 1985), p. 70.
73. Raphael, *The Starseed Transmissions, Vol. 1* (Uni Sol Publications, 1982), p. 33.
74. Donna Clark, "Being Still With Your Child," in *Circle Network*, Winter 1985, p. 12.
75. Ibid., Donna Clark, "Divine Healing Ritual," p. 6.
76. A. W. Tozer, from his booklet *Total Commitment to Christ*, cited in *Gems*, p. 24.

Chapter 11—Imagination or Revelation?

1. John Koffend, "The Gospel According to Helen," in *Psychology Today*, Sep. 1980, pp. 74-90; Judith R. Skutch, "The Gifts of God," in *New Realities*, Mar. 1982, pp. 48-53; Robert Skutch, "A Course In Miracles," in *New Realities*, July/Aug. 1984, pp. 17-27; cover story, *New Realities*, Sep./Oct. 1984.
2. Helen Shucman, *A Course In Miracles* (Foundation for Inner Peace, 1975), Vol. 1, pp. 49-55, *New Realities*, July/Aug. 1984, p. 23.
3. Kenneth Wapnick, "A Psychotherapy of Forgiveness," in *Common Boundary*, Mar./Apr. 1986, p. 12.
4. Reid and Virkler, *Seduction?* p. 4.
5. Network News, "Shamans With Ph.D.s and Private Practices," in *Common Boundary*, Sep./Oct. 1986, p. 4.
6. Dennis Bennett, "We Would See Jesus," in *The Morning Watch*, Spring/Summer 1986, p. 11.
7. Wise et al, *Church*, p. 71.
8. Reed Jolley, "Language is the Medium," in *Eternity*, May 1986, p. 43.
9. Owen, *The Glory of Christ* (Moody Press, 1949), p. 191.
10. Mike Murdock, *Dream-Seeds* (Tulsa, 1985), pp. 60-62.
11. Richard Foster, *Celebration of Discipline* (Harper & Row, 1978), pp. 169-70.
12. Ibid., p. 170.
13. Schlossberg, *Idols*, p. 160.
14. Foster, *Celebration*, p. 22.
15. From a brochure explaining the curriculum, obtainable from Full Gospel Tabernacle, P.O. Box 590, Orchard Park, NY 14127.
16. Mark Virkler, *Dialogue With God: Opening the Door to 2-way Prayer* (Bridge Publishing, 1986), p. 173.
17. Ibid., p. 73.
18. Foster, *Celebration*, pp. 22, 36.
19. Joan Connell, "The Spiritual Frontier," in *San Jose Mercury News*, June 14, 1986, p. 1C.
20. Kenneth Copeland Ministries undated newsletter sent out early in 1986.
21. Cho, *Fourth*, p. 23.
22. Ibid., p. 59.
23. Ibid., p. 12.
24. Ibid., p. 17.
25. Ibid., p. 12.
26. A. W. Tozer, *That Incredible Christian* (Christian Publications, 1964), pp. 69-76.
27. C. H. Spurgeon, *The New Spurgeon Library, Vol. 2* (Zondervan, 1962), pp. 11-12.
28. Owen, *Glory*, p. 192.
29. Finney, *Crystal*, pp. 191-92.
30. MacArthur, *Ultimate*, p. 40.
31. Reid and Virkler, *Seduction?* p. 44.

32. Virkler, *Dialogue*, p. 72.
33. Reid and Virkler, *Seduction?* p. 45.
34. Foster, *Celebration*, p. 26.
35. Virkler, *Dialogue*, p. 87.
36. Foster, *Celebration*, p. 26.
37. J. I. Packer, *Knowing God* (InterVarsity, 1973), p. 30.
38. James Bjornstad, "What's Behind The Prosperity Gospel?" in *Moody Monthly*, Nov. 1986, pp. 19-20.
39. Tozer, *Man: The Dwelling Place of God,* pp. 56-57.
40. Sylvia LaFair, Ph.D., "On The Future of Psychotherapy: An Interview With Emmanuel," in *Common Boundary,* Sep./Oct. 1986, p. 12.
41. Ibid; *Los Angeles Times*, Dec. 5, 1986, Part V, p. 33; Terry Clifford, "Shirley MacLaine's Spiritual Dance," in *American Health*, Jan./Feb. 1986, pp. 50-55; etc.
42. *Los Angeles Herald Examiner*, Oct. 6, 1985, Section E, pp. 1, 7 and Sep. 29, 1986, Section B, p. 8; the currently most popular is Ramtha, an alleged 35,000-year-old entity that "channels" through J. Z. Knight and has been on the Merv Griffin, Phil Donahue, and other talk shows.
43. Jane Roberts, *The Seth Material* (Prentice-Hall, 1970) and other books in this series; see also books by Ruth Montgomery and many others.
44. Tim Timmons, *Chains of the Spirit—a Manual for Liberation* (Cannon Press, 1973), p. 30.
45. Edmond C. Gruss, *"God Calling. . . A* Critical Look at a Christian Best-seller," in *Personal Freedom Outreach*, July-Sep. 1986, p. 1.
46. Ibid.
47. Ibid., p. 2.
48. "Intensive Journal" brochure, Dialogue House Assoc., 1985.
49. Robert Blair Kaiser, "The Way of the Journal," in *Psychology Today*, Mar. 1986, p. 67.
50. Ibid.
51. Letter on file dated Aug. 29, 1985.

Chapter 12—The Better Way

1. Earl Paulk, *Held In the Heavens Until. . .* (K Dimension Publishers, 1985), p. 11.
2. Atlanta 86—International Conference, held Oct. 26-29, 1986, at Chapel Hill Harvester Church, Decatur, Georgia. Theme was "Let My Spirit Go," and speakers included Harvester Church Pastor Earl Paulk, Oral Roberts, Jamie Buckingham, Larry Lea, Gary North, Tommy Reid, Luther Blackwell, and John Meares.
3. Earl Paulk, *Satan Unmasked* (K Dimension, 1985), p. 125.
4. Earl Paulk, *The Wounded Body of Christ* (K Dimension, 1985), pp. 44, 46.
5. Earl Paulk, *Ultimate Kingdom* (K Dimension, 1984), p. 317.
6. William W. Menzies, *Anointed to Serve: The Story of The Assemblies of God* (Springfield, MO: Gospel Publishing House), pp. 323-25.
7. Charles Capps, *Authority In Three Worlds* (Harrison House, 1980), p. 205; Capps, *Tongue*, p.131, etc.
8. Kenneth Copeland, "Questions and Answers," in *Believer's Voice of Victory*, June 1986, p. 14.
9. Hagin, *How To Write Your Own Ticket With God* (Tulsa, 1979), pp. 5, 20, 21, 32, etc.
10. Hagin, *Words*, pp. 9-10.
11. Kenyon, *Healer*, pp. 20, 21, 44, 54, 67, 74 and *Two Kinds*, p. 42; see also Hagin,

Healing Belongs To Us (Tulsa, 1977), pp. 16-17, etc.

12. Bob Weiner, *The Preparation of the Bride* (Marantha Campus Ministries), pp. 24, 104, 124, 129, 134, 156-57.
13. David Ebaugh in *Monarch*, Oct.-Nov. 1986, p. 3.
14. George H. Warnock, *The Feast of Tabernacles* (Bill Britton, 1951), p. 104.
15. *Monarch*, op. cit.
16. Undated letter signed by Robert H. Schuller; op. cit., *Self-Esteem*, pp. 172-75.
17. Dominion Press brochure advertising "The Biblical Blueprint Series" of four books, one each by George Grant, Gary North, Dennis T. Peacocke, and Ray Sutton. Released by Thomas Nelson in Fall 1986.
18. *Los Angeles Times*, Mar. 29, 1986, Section 1A, p. 3.
19. Schlossberg, *Idols*, p. 51.
20. David Chilton, *Paradise Restored: a Biblical Theology of Dominion* (Tyler, TX: Reconstruction Press, 1985), pp. 23-25.
21. Richard Baxter, *The Saint's Everlasting Rest*, p. 245.
22. Schlossberg, *Idols*, p. 333.
23. Schlossberg, *Idols*, p. 307.
24. Charles Colson, *The Role of the Church in Society* (Victor, 1986), pp. 37-38.
25. Jimmy Swaggart, "The Pentecostal Way," in *The Evangelist*, Dec. 1986, p. 6.
26. Keith Green, *Unity...At What Price? The Divisiveness of Truth* (Last Days Ministries, 1980), Tract LD #18.
27. Black, *Friendship*, p. 217.

For a catalog of audio and video tapes and other materials by Dave Hunt, or to make comments concerning the subject matter of this book, please write:

Christian Information Bureau
P.O. Box 901335
Dallas, TX 75390

Please enclose a self-addressed stamped envelope.